THE UN SECRETARY-GENERAL FROM THE COLD WAR TO THE NEW ERA

Also by Edward Newman

THE CHANGING NATURE OF DEMOCRACY (*co-editor*)

The UN Secretary-General from the Cold War to the New Era

A Global Peace and Security Mandate?

Edward Newman
Lecturer in International Relations
Shumei University
Japan

First published in Great Britain 1998 by
MACMILLAN PRESS LTD
Houndmills, Basingstoke, Hampshire RG21 6XS and London
Companies and representatives throughout the world

A catalogue record for this book is available from the British Library.

ISBN 0–333–68704–3

First published in the United States of America 1998 by
ST. MARTIN'S PRESS, INC.,
Scholarly and Reference Division,
175 Fifth Avenue, New York, N.Y. 10010

ISBN 0–312–21101–5

Library of Congress Cataloging-in-Publication Data
Newman, Edward, 1970–
The UN Secretary-General from the Cold War to the new era : a
global peace and security mandate? / Edward Newman.
p.   cm.
Includes bibliographical references and index.
ISBN 0–312–21101–5 (cloth)
1. United Nations. Secretary-General.   2. Peace.   3. Security,
International.   I. Title.
JZ5008.N49 1998
352.2'2113—dc21   97–35896
                                                          CIP

This book is printed on paper suitable for recycling and made from fully managed and
sustained forest sources.

10   9   8   7   6   5   4   3   2
07   06   05   04   03   02   01   00

Printed and bound in Great Britain by
Antony Rowe Ltd, Chippenham, Wiltshire

Contents

Acknowledgements

This book is based upon research I conducted at the Graduate School of International Relations of the University of Kent at Canterbury. During my time there I was fortunate to have benefited from the unflagging energy, support and wisdom of my supervisor Professor A.J.R. Groom. The intellectual and practical support of the rest of the International Relations team was also invaluable, in particular Dr Keith Webb, Dr Andrew Williams, and Dr Jarrod Wiener. Dr Wiener has continued to be enormously helpful since I left Canterbury and I thank him for his hard work and sharp ideas. Thanks also to Mr T.M. Farmiloe at Macmillan for assistance during the production of this book. I would also like to express my sincere gratitude to all the people I have met and who have helped me over the last few years around the world. Their insights have been inspiring. Obviously, the shortcomings of this book lie with myself alone.

At the University of Kent I received essential financial support from the Economic and Social Research Council for which I will remain eternally grateful. In the same vein I would like to thank the UK Conflict Research Society for the assistance they were able to provide. In addition, I appreciate the efforts of Shumei University for creating an environment conducive to the completion of this book.

Finally, I would like to thank my parents, Ron and Angela, for their kind support and encouragement. This book is dedicated to them.

Introduction

The pioneers of the international civil service intended to form a 'new human category' whose fortitude and creativity would help make a better world for all.[1] The international civil service would forge the vanguard of an international society based upon rules, justice and institutions. Indeed, it would promote and underpin changes in the nature of international politics itself. The first half of the twentieth century witnessed enormous social and political upheaval and violent conflict. Many hoped that the establishment of the United Nations would end this scourge. In the words of one commentator, 'May the International Civil Service now to be set up prepare the way!'[2]

What has become of this 'great experiment' which envisioned the 'international leadership' of the Office of Secretary-General?[3] Even among the most committed liberal internationalists it would be difficult to find such faith in international organizations or international civil servants towards the end of the twentieth century. Such ideas of international leadership are met by scepticism, suspicion or even hostility. Some even question if the international civil service truly exists. While the pioneering spirit may not be entirely dead, the founding principles of the international civil service are not comfortable in the political, and particularly the peace and security, environment of the post-Cold War era. This crisis of multilateralism has been reflected in the Office of the UN Secretary-General.

This book traces the evolution of the peace and security activities of the Office of Secretary-General in the context of developments and trends in the wider international environment. The premise inherent in this approach is that the development of the Office – its roles, opportunities, and constraints – can be seen as a condition of the political complexion of the international environment. Upon this basis the book examines the extent to which the Secretaryship-General has evolved beyond the classical model of the international civil service. This model was

1

regarded as an adjunct of conference diplomacy and increasing international cooperation during the early years of international organization.

The post-Cold War Secretaryship-General has been at the forefront of practices and issues which have raised fundamental questions concerning the roles of international organizations as the practical and legal bases upon which they were formed has shifted. The Office is a focal point of post-Cold War multilateral turbulence as the UN struggles to adapt to rapidly evolving circumstances. It has reflected the friction which accompanies such change, but the Office also has been elevated by a wider conception of peace and security, the burgeoning level of the UN's activities, and developments in political-military thinking in the Secretariat and the Security Council.

After some fifty years of a particular mode of thinking, security has become disaggregated, now focusing on a regional and domestic plane. The 'new' security agenda goes beyond the traditional state-centric military conception. Moreover, in an era of multipolarity and an absence of a tangible global project, leadership and support for the UN has wavered. In the 'post-hegemonic' and post-imperial world the United Nations, and its Secretary-General, have reflected systemic volatility which has forced the members and the international secretariat to reconsider their roles and limitations. Yet the reference points for reconsidering the roles and capabilities of the UN are intangible, and perhaps non-existent. The condition of the Organization in the peace and security field consequently has been unstable in the 'new era', often reflecting the political and material constraints of multilateral fatigue and widely divergent views of what the UN's role should be. The post-Cold War world is unlikely to resemble anything as spectacular as the 'end of history' or the 'clash of civilizations', or any other grand scheme.[4] In a sense, the twenty-first century has already begun, but it defies definition. Ultimately, the UN is being pulled by forces which are sometimes opposites and sometimes symbiotic. Fragmentation, integration, globalization, the evolution of state sovereignty, sub- and trans-state processes, and the demands of the 'new' security agenda, are all in evidence.

These theoretical and practical trends have been reflected in the multifaceted and sometimes paradoxical trends of the post-Cold War Secretaryship-General. In this environment the Office is commensurately in flux. The Office has found new opportunities in conflict settlement and significant political-military advancement. In its activities in areas which were considered formerly to be Great Power spheres of influence the Secretaryship-General is contributing to UN efforts to condition traditional Great Power backyard politics. Moreover, the Secretaryship-General holds an interesting role in the context of domestic transition throughout the globe. There are undoubtedly fewer 'no-go' areas for the Office than ever before. Simultaneously, however, it has suffered from grave material shortages and the constraints which are inherent in an organization which often reflects the narrow interests of a small group of states. Moreover, the Office is buffeted by the uncertainty of the whole Organization towards the unfolding peace and security agenda which confronts it as a result of historical shifts of attitude and the evolution of international politics. It may also be at a critical juncture as the Organization seeks to address a 'new agenda' with old institutional structures.

The Office of the Secretary-General and the international civil service developed from an 'international society' conception of international relations which emphasizes state sovereignty, 'high politics', and the dichotomies between domestic and international, and public and private. In this view, international organizations reflect and underpin rules and order among stable and autonomous states. The central tenet of the United Nations, and that of the League of Nations before it, was to assure collective security. The international community, through these organizations, would uphold standards of behaviour and interaction, and if necessary deter and deal with conflict between 'sovereign' states. This is an inherently dubious thesis, and the premise of peace and security being primarily a military issue between states is now particularly questionable. The 'new agenda' of peace and security embraces socio-economic, environmental and human rights issues as an integrated matrix which forms the foundations of human security. The United Nations and regional organizations are adopting increasingly this wide definition of peace and security at the international level. This has developed in parallel with pressures to the state from above and below in the form of transnational issues, advancements in information, fragmentation, and the deepening of economic interdependence. Clearly, the 'Global Neighbourhood' model of international politics goes beyond the Westphalian conception of an 'international society'.

International politics and international organizations inevitably are conditioned by the evolution of state sovereignty and changes in attitudes among publics and governments. While some commentators have ascribed to this a 'post-Westphalian' and even a 'postmodern' condition, it almost defies measured analysis. In terms of international organization, academics theorize on the subjects of 'new multilateralism', 'global governance', and 'transnational civil society'. But how have these abstract notions conditioned the Secretary-General? Has the Office engaged and reflected the comprehensive and integrated agenda of peace and human security; that is, the *underlying* causes of insecurity and conflict?

It is in this sense that this book questions whether the Secretary-General has a global peace and security mandate. For much of the UN's history, Secretaries-General have presented themselves in a liberal internationalist vein. In reality, the Office largely has been an adjunct of a realist manoeuvring of Great Powers in peace and security. The Office clearly – and perhaps rightly – has been constrained geographically and in the issues in which it can become involved. However, since the late 1980s the Office has extended its activities to address issues and conflicts in areas previously out-of-bounds, or within the sphere of influence of Great Powers. It has also focused attention upon new actors and forces, drawing the international community's attention to issues outside the mainstream international agenda, and urging the United Nations and its chief sponsors in a direction different to that which their natural *Realpolitik* mindset would steer them. Thus, Secretary-General Boutros-Ghali wrote of the global leadership of the Secretary-General in promoting the UN within this progressive agenda of peace and security. He had a vision of the Office as the zenith of the global ethos, almost detached from the intergovernmental forces which appoint and control it, 'an impartial figure with a global mandate'.[5] To serve human needs, rather than those of states, is the frame of reference for the cosmopolitan Secretary-General, unbounded both thematically and geographically. But is there enough substance to the cosmopolitan movement to revive the spirit of the international civil service into a post-Westphalian force? The structures and attitudes that underpin domestic and international politics would suggest that this is a delusion. A prominent American politician warned against the 'global movement toward greater centralization of political power in the hands of elites at the expense of individuals and their local representatives'.[6] Could the Secretary-General, an international bureaucrat, ever be so significant, either for good or ill?

A further key issue of this book concerns the relationship between the individual and structure or environment, in this case the international configuration of power, institutions and norms. The Secretary-General reflects rather than orchestrates political change and policy. However, in some situations the Office can influence the structure to the extent that it can influence actors, organizations and attitudes. Moreover, at a time of transition in international politics and at the UN there have been opportunities for the Secretary-General to expand the role of the UN and to guide it as it embarks upon new directions. Still, the notion of 'global leadership' in the new era has implications for the relationship between the individual and the environment which are very difficult to sustain: how could an international civil servant presume to have such an impact, and is it possible methodologically to test this notion? The world may be in need of 'imaginative and courageous leadership from the United Nations'.[7] But who will follow?

In the immediate term the Secretary-General must aim to reverse the malaise which afflicts the Organization and in particular work towards convincing the United States to reorientate its foreign policy in support of the UN. In the longer term can the Secretaryship-General lead the UN into the wider conceptions of peace and security as the Organization reflects the shifting values and practicalities of sovereignty and international politics? Or will it remain largely at the bidding of the leading *status quo* actors? The post-Cold War Secretaryship-General represents a delicate navigation between these two poles.

To address these questions and issues, it is necessary to look at the evolution of the Office. Chapter 1 outlines the principles and history of the international civil service from its origins as an outcrop of international cooperation and liberal internationalism following the First World War. Upon this basis, the following chapter lays down the political and legal foundations of the Office of Secretary-General and relates these to the formative organizational settings of the League of Nations and the United Nations. Chapter 3 establishes the framework for analysis of the UN Secretaryship-General. This involves identifying the variables which form the shifting parameters within which the Office works. These variables embrace numerous – and often intangible – organizational, personal, legal and political factors. The methodological issues – and problems – involved in such a task are also presented, and the peace and security functions of the Office are outlined. It is difficult to conceptualize the international 'system' and how this conditions the Secretaryship-General. Nevertheless, it is argued that this political environment is fundamental to understanding the Office's constraints and opportunities.

Under this theme the subsequent chapters illustrate the activities of the UN Secretaries-General in the context of developments in international politics. Particular emphasis is given to the challenging developments of the post-Cold War world and the extent to which this has thrust the Office, particularly under Boutros-Ghali, beyond the classical model of the international civil service.

1 The International Civil Service

If relative cohesion exists in the international structure, if forms of action are better organized, if the international organization is able to resist the assaults of adverse forces from all quarters, this is due to the discreet and persevering work of the international civil servant. He embodies the institutionalization of international cooperation.

G. Langrod[1]

The international secretariat holds an important position in the evolution of international organization, as an institutional manifestation of a certain depth of cooperation. The classical conception of the international civil service is an ideal which must be seen in the context of an institutionalist and progressive approach to international cooperation, which views organization as a reflection of the collective will and the manifestation of an international society. Indeed,

International organization is not so much a contrived deviation from the natural course of international relations as a modern expression of some of the perennial tendencies and requirements of states operating in a multistate system ... a part of the political and administrative apparatus of human society ...[2]

This conception of international organization traces a cumulative and positive development of institutionalized cooperation in tandem with the necessity of increasing interaction, yet always dependent on the predilections of the intergovernmental structure. The fragility of the Congress of Vienna, the prudence of the nineteenth-century concert system, the conference diplomacy of the Hague system, and the early twentieth-century arms control endeavours all reflected the needs and limitations of the system at a particular time. Deeper organizational experiments in subsequent years represented a greater collective will, resulting in the partial acceptance of the principle that the collective whole is greater than the sum of its constituent parts. The dividend of this, according to the progressive approach, is invested and manifest in the international secretariat. For Claude,

> the identity of every organization ... tends to be lodged in its professional staff. Members, stockholders, or citizens may control the organization, but they cannot *be* it; the staff, in a fundamental sense, is the organization ... the invention of the international secretariat may be described as the real beginning of international organization.[3]

Yet the origins of the international civil service were essentially functional. In the formative years, form followed function in the Universal Postal Union, the Pan American Union, and earlier in the Danube Commission. Langrod wrote that: '[i]t is nowhere possible to *administer* without *administrators*. At every level this remains axiomatic. Theories and ideas are added *afterwards* to a practice already established.'[4]

Whether or not the practice of international service was lacking in its theoretical basis, the early supporters welcomed Langrod's 'new human category', which was held to personify and foreshadow 'great change'.[5] One theory, if it is possible to speak in such terms, rests upon the domestic analogy, where the administration not only results from the functional imperative, but embodies community and common interest. Similarly, the cumulative task-spillover of modern life naturally develops towards international administration:

> [in] much of the same way that civil servants in national bureaucracies and hierarchies ... generally exercise increasing power in an age of specialization and technology and are far more influential now and potentially than their 19th century predecessors ... the international civil service, especially in the absence of a sovereign executive power, has gained impressive responsibilities, duties, authority, and power.[6]

So for the early supporters the international secretariat was the international community's hope for the peaceful coexistence of states and functional cooperation. This clearly is complemented by an institutionalist conception of international cooperation that sees organizations as more than instruments of leading states, although perhaps not with as great a status as actor. The formative scholars asserted that '[an] international civil service has been recognized as a global imperative. It has become an established fact'.[7]

The international secretariat of an organization will always have its framework and its limitations; its scope is not static. This has become more pronounced in the post-Cold War era. Some years ago Cox and Jacobson observed that 'organizations take on a life of their own and develop their own inner dynamics'.[8] They further suggested that in terms of intra-organizational power differentials, shifting influence should not only be considered on a chronological basis, but in terms of different and sometimes simultaneous circumstances. Therefore, '[n]o actors are likely to be influential to the same extent in all spheres, and thus the pattern of influence is likely to differ by issue-area.'[9] The potential for influence, apart from constitutional or political power, is interesting.

It is difficult to identify the variables in the international system whose alignment determines the scope for performance of the international secretariat, because of the complexity and definitional problems of the 'international system'. Similarly it requires a certain intimacy with the organization in question. However, it is possible to trace junctures in the evolution of the international civil service with international political trends, and perhaps structural changes, if the impact of decolonization, the Cold War, and the end of the Cold War can be regarded as such.

While nineteenth-century efforts were important functional antecedents, the true international civil service was founded in the League of Nations under Eric Drummond in 1919. This was almost by chance, for Maurice Hankey, the distinguished British cabinet administrator and the man also offered the post of Secretary-General, favoured the continuation of the national system of secondment and patronage. Instead, as Drummond explained,

> [the] old system had not given altogether satisfactory results, and when the members of a committee set up by

the Plenary Peace Conference met to consider the matter of organization, I strongly urged that the second plan be adopted ..., we maintained that the execution of decisions should be entrusted to people who, being servants of all the states members of the League, could be relied upon to carry them out with complete freedom from national bias.[10]

The simplicity of this is quaint. Nevertheless, the classical model was thus 'created' in the service of the League of Nations: a supposedly international staff loyal to the aspirations of the international community and theoretically independent from national influence. Traditional thinking in this area was unhesitatingly supportive of this. For Walters, '[t]he creation of a secretariat international alike in its structure, its spirit, and its personnel, was without doubt one of the most important events in the history of international politics.'[11] Elsewhere it was recorded as 'surely one of the most important and promising developments of the twentieth century',[12] and referred to as the 'revolutionary concept of an international civil service'.[13]

On the basis of administrative support, the pioneering international civil service was a genuine, though unashamedly Anglo-French, attempt to embellish international cooperation with permanence, continuity, and identity. The League Covenant was not specific regarding the roles of the bureaucracy, and the evolution followed unique, though conservative, functional lines of development. After Drummond's initial structure was established, based upon independence, anonymity and integrity, Balfour's famous report of 19 May 1920 affirmed that 'the members of the Secretariat once appointed are no longer the servants of the country of which they are citizens, but become for the time being servants only of the League of Nations. Their duties are not national, but international ... Nothing should be done to weaken the sense of their international allegiance'.[14] The early success of the international model, and the progression from the support of conference administration to an organ which was to represent the collective interest, derived from the necessities of stability and continuity, and the dedication and qualities of the pioneers in Geneva. In addition, it paralleled the increase in general public administration as a manifestation of the modern social condition and a steadily increasing willingness on behalf of states and peoples to recognize an international agenda and the need for its embodiment.

The hope and expectation of those who supported the secretariat were that it would reach the peak of efficiency and competence. In fact, the Weberian bureaucratic ideal has been drawn upon as the objective, although the idea that any international secretariat has ever achieved this has few supporters. Within such a system, division of work, channels of authority and communication are clear, and individuals ignore personal inclinations, applying policy with detachment.[15] The impact of international political currents upon the international civil service – such as the growth of nationalism in the interwar period and the anti-communist pressures in the US during the early Cold War years – and the predilections of human nature soon undermined any hope of a Weberian purity, however.

The International Labour Organization provided an endorsement of the concept of the international civil service in this pioneer period. The presence of Albert Thomas was inseparable not only from the ILO secretariat but the organization itself. However, the triumph of the early ILO secretariat initiative must be seen in the context of the functional-welfare basis of the organization. Comparisons between Drummond and Thomas are tempting, but one cannot detach these individuals from their organizations, and the different environments within which they worked. Indeed, Drummond was sure that '[it] is quite, quite certain that Albert Thomas in my job would have been forced to resign'.[16] Still, the Thomas experience is an important contribution to the discussion on the leadership dimension.

The judgement of the formative secretariat writers was generally that the experience of the ILO and League 'had proved that international administration is feasible, that it can be efficient, and that the concept of international civil service is practical'.[17] The main elements of the international civil service, at least before the deterioration of international politics in the 1930s, had found a testing ground in the League: the continuity of cooperation, the embodiment of organizational identity, international loyalty, and perhaps traces of normative progress. However, there are practical and theoretical problems with the traditional model. From the Cold War to the new era the integrity of Article 101 and the staff regulations have been questioned widely. This deterioration in the traditional model has occurred in the context of post-war superpower politics, the politicization of international organizations, budgetary dependence, and human nature. Jordan's elaboration of the problematique is still useful:

> can a formally Charter-inspired denationalized cadre of international civil servants, formed into an international bureaucracy ... focus on global issues, yet work to achieve them in an international political system constrained by the value of nationalism in order to protect the primacy of the national interest?[18]

In the right circumstances functional impetuses could result in an enhanced, even supranational, international civil service for certain issue-areas. But the paradox is that, while there has been some progress, functional development and global discourse have tended to be in an inhospitable environment at the United Nations. The 'new era' is a superficial shift of power, and the international civil service will continue to be a manifestation – and at the mercy – of the international system.

2 The Office of Secretary-General

The progressive view of international organization holds that international interactions are malleable and susceptible to the development of procedural norms. As the potential embodiment of this liberal internationalism stands the entity of the Secretary-General. Pérez de Cuéllar pictured the Office in the wider context: '[t]o understand correctly the role of the Secretary-General is to appreciate the whole mission of the United Nations. And that, in turn, is central to the way international life is organized.'[1] Years ago Schwebel wrote: '[i]t is apparent that the future, if there is to be one, belongs to international organization; that the primary international organization of the present is the United Nations; and that the chief permanent officer of that organization necessarily occupies a unique and strategic position ...'[2] Cox even suggested that 'the executive head may be the explanatory key to the emergence of a new kind of autonomous actor in the international system'.[3]

However, there is little agreement concerning the Office of Secretary-General – or a specific Secretary-General – as a measurable quantity. One recalls the words of one commentator, bemoaning the absence of a systemic explanation of the behaviour of the Office and calling for 'conceptual tools for empirical analysis'.[4] Yet the extent to which it is possible to devise a thorough-going formula in regard to the role and influence of the executive head of an international organization is doubtful, for it surely alludes to a subjective methodological debate.

It is, however, possible to identify the main factors which determine the role of the United Nation's Secretaryship-General, and to identify changes in this role in relation to major political trends in international relations.

The concept of the Secretary-General is often avoided by scholars of international organization because it is not easy to employ the established organizational theories, and in recent years the individual has not been a popular focus of historians or political scientists. The personality factor is an unknown quantity which, on methodological grounds, complicates any analysis of the Office in relation to international politics. Nevertheless, the main theme here is that one can think in terms of a 'development' of the Secretaryship-General – either during one tenure or from one office-holder to the next – as an entity with expanding and contracting influence or scope for performance.

THE INTERWAR YEARS

The League of Nations was in large measure an exercise in experimentation. It was also fatally embroiled in the miscalculation and lack of will of its sponsors, and undermined by the struggle between revisionist and *status quo* forces which characterized the deterioration of international relations in this period. These traits ran through the experiences of the Secretaries-General, and for a number of historians the whole Organization was a symbolic and insignificant contribution to the 'illusion of peace'.[5]

The internationalist appraisal of the creation of the League held that: 'the time had come to commence the construction of a rational and ethical world order in which relationships among states would be influenced and shaped, if not governed, by cooperative international institutions.'[6] Certainly, the League represented the culmination of a growth and tide of internationalist thought and practice, and latterly a reaction to the tragedy of the Great War. For some, it represented 'international social progress'.[7] The Secretary-General, however, along with the whole Secretariat, was the product of compromise and varying aspirations. The League Covenant provided only the barest of details, so that it was left to the first Secretary-General, Eric Drummond, to impose his impression upon the development of the Office in accordance with what was feasible in the pervading political environment. This impression was one of quiet, behind-the-scenes service. Many observers feel that Drummond did not exploit the opportunities at his disposal. He often has been branded as the epitome of the passive, administrative, bureaucratic model of his Office. This is exacerbated by the existence of the colourful and energetic Albert Thomas at the head of the ILO, establishing a practice of comparison between the two and often emphasising personal factors at the expense of organizational and political realities. In a typical comparison with the ILO, Alexandrowicz suggested that everything depended on the personality of the first Secretary-General and that '... Thomas appeared as an international statesman and as a spokesman of world interests and there is room to suppose that, had he been Secretary-General of the League of Nations, he would have acted in a statesmanlike manner to the dramatic events leading to the outbreak of World War II.'[8]

This approach to leadership and administrative influence is inadequate to analyse the nature of executive behaviour in international organizations. It fails to appreciate that influence is determined largely by organizational-political circumstances and the political circumstances of the wider environment, and that public activity on the part of an administrative head does not necessarily equate with power or influence. The ILO and the League were different organizations and the contrasting images of their administrative heads were commensurate with this, even if Drummond and Thomas also had obviously different personalities. Moreover, Barros rejects the image of the League Secretaries-General as little more that administrators; for him, they were 'as politically active behind the scenes as their United Nations counterparts'.[9]

However, the impression still remains that 'the Covenant granted the Secretary-General too little general power and ... subsequent practice did little to enlarge his powers by precedent or usage'.[10] The question is: was it the dual environment of the organization and the international system, and the political and constitutional limitations imposed therein upon the League Secretaries-General, or was it their personalities that were the dominant factors in determining the role of the Office? How can one attempt to evaluate the relative weight of these factors?

Clearly Drummond's personality and civil service background, together with the downgrading of the Office, furnished a cautious approach. Drummond appeared to fulfil his administrative functions admirably. He never made public political statements, he rarely if at all addressed the Assembly or made substantive interventions in the Council, and he invariably confined himself to 'behind the scenes' activity. Yet the absence of public political activity is deceptive, for '[t]hough he might perhaps rationalize his actions and moves on constitutional or administrative grounds he was nevertheless involved in what were essentially political acts. The very nature of the office was unavoidably political.'[11]

The participation of Drummond in 1920 in the dispute between Sweden and Finland over the Aaland Islands established the Secretaryship-General as a focus for confidential communication between parties and constructive advice. In the disputes between Bolivia and Paraguay of 1928 and 1933, and the dispute between Colombia and Peru in 1933, Drummond likewise made his presence known. The Sino-Japanese conflict between 1931 and 1933 typified the inability of the League to halt the degeneration of international relations into violence. Nevertheless, Drummond took part in negotiations, made recommendations of substance and procedure, and served as an important liaison; all this, of course, privately and tactfully.[12]

Drummond's role should be seen not just in the context of his personality, his constitutional limitations, and the political limitations inherent in an intergovernmental organization. The various political machinations and lack of collective will on the part of League members caused a degeneration in the Office of Secretary-General as well as the Organization itself. Thus, the failure of the chief League sponsors to put effective pressure upon Germany, Italy and Japan in the 1930s ran through every organ of the Organization; Drummond realized this and could do little. Even with regard to the nationalistic infiltration of the Secretariat Drummond was powerless in the face of appeasement.

Did Drummond set a good precedent for the political role of the Secretary-General? Increasingly he attracted the respect and confidence of others, in a cumulative manner. However, it is likewise said that he entrenched a rather cautious model of his Office. Ranshofen-Wertheimer regretted that Drummond and his successor Joseph Avenol 'kept scrupulously, even over-scrupulously, within the constitutional limits and did not even avail themselves as fully as they could have done of the marginal possibilities for action and influence open to them.'[13] Yet ultimately they must be viewed in the shadow of Great-Power machinations or outright aggression; in historical terms, they were fairly insignificant factors in a sea of change.

Albert Thomas embodied the leadership model of international administration. In a classic and endearing work Edward Phelan recorded that Thomas was 'much more to the International Labour Office than its successful manager. He came, in fact, to be identified with it to a degree which made it difficult for many people to distinguish between the institution and its Director ...'.[14] This politician, trade unionist, and social reformer certainly was able to instil a certain amount of dynamism and verve into the ILO, although it must be remembered that the welfare organization was amenable to such a style. The status of Thomas must be evaluated in terms of the organizational parameters constituted by his political environment.

The League Secretaryship-General from 1933 to the Second World War was tied both to the demise of the Organization in a spiral of appeasement and aggression, and the personal predilections of Joseph Avenol. The Office was drowned by the tide of history; Sean Lester, a man of integrity, could fare no better during the war.

THE UNITED NATIONS

Various models for the Secretaryship-General emerged during the war-time United States State Department discussions, the academic research in Britain and America within such bodies as the Carnegie Endowment and the Royal Institute for International Affairs, the Dumbarton Oaks Great Power negotiations, the San Francisco Conference on International Organization, the Preparatory Commission proceedings, and the discussions which established the Rules of Procedure for the UN organs. From the outset,

however, the majority opinion was that a stronger office
than that of the League should exist within the new world
Organization. In fact the State Department discussions –
which produced a draft constitution in 1943 – had earlier
included the idea of having a president or political chief,
alongside an administrative chief.

There was not a great deal of discussion on the Secretary-
General's Office at the various stages. The main issues
concerned the type of person who should occupy the position, the balance between administrative and political
duties, the role of the senior tier of the Secretariat, the
country of origin of the Secretary-General, the term of
office and the method of appointment, the implications of
Article 99, and the various rules of procedure governing the
relationship between the Secretary-General and the organs
of the new Organization.[15] Such debate invariably centred
around compromises between different interests: mostly
between small and large states, and states with divergent
attitudes toward the status of international administration.
Most significantly, there was a debate between the 'min-
imalist' administrative model of the international civil
servant – the so-called 'Drummond model' – and the
creative, political model: the 'promoter, inspirer, living
expression of international cooperation, continuous symbol
of the international outlook …'.[16] The motives of the parties
who espoused such ideas varied, depending on their own
administrative experience and tradition, and their political
outlook. A number of factors encouraged either internationalist or parochial attitudes.

Pragmatic considerations were strongly in evidence in the
fora which established the constitutional framework for the
UN Secretariat, and in the formative years which moulded
the practice. Moreover, the power configuration of the
whole Organization pervaded the Secretaryship-General,
despite the intentions of Article 100. The appointment of
the Secretary-General – by the General Assembly upon the
recommendation of the Security Council, and hence subject
to veto – is one such trait. Several smaller states proposed
reserving to the Assembly the entire task of choosing a
Secretary-General. Conversely, some Great Power interests
suggested that the office-holder be elected for a tenure of

just two years which would have further reduced the independence of the Office and the control of the Assembly.[17] Eventually, the first General Assembly set the precedent for a five-year term of office. Thus, alongside the Permanent Security Council member control of the appointment there was a small and Great Power trade-off, a combination of representation and political reality.[18] Yet in spite of the pragmatism and political realism at work, the vision of leadership made its mark:

> The Secretary-General, more than anyone else, will stand for the United Nations as a whole. In the eyes of the world [he] must embody the principles and ideals of the Charter to which the Organization seeks to give effect.[19]

THE CHARTER

The Articles of the Charter relating directly to the Secretary-General are 7 and 97 to 101 inclusive. The Office may derive specified or unspecified authority from a combination of these and in relation to other Articles, such as Article 33 and 96 relating to peaceful settlement and the International Court respectively. Article 7 states that the Secretariat, and *inter alia* the Secretary-General, is a principal organ of the United Nations. Some commentators have assumed that this implies equality with the other principal organs. Certainly practice has attached authority to the Secretaryship-General from this Article; at the least it implies a responsibility on the part of the Office to uphold the aims and purposes of the Charter. Thus, the Secretaries-General have acquired a certain independence from the deliberative organs when circumstances have required and allowed it. Such a practice in the past has been manifested in the field of the peaceful settlement of disputes when deadlock may have paralysed the mandating organs or when these organs are perceived by a party to a dispute to be partial.[20]

Article 97 relates to the appointment of the Secretary-General and his administrative status. It was politically necessary for a Security Council veto on the appointment process, but what has occurred has been a dubious political and geographic Great Power trade-off where practical qualifications are of secondary concern. Years of experience led Brian Urquhart to lament that 'political differences dictate a search for a candidate who will not exert any troubling degree of leadership, commitment, originality, or independence'.[21] After the Cold War one might hope for improvements in this shady process. There certainly have been recommendations for reform, including the creation of a methodical and open search and screening process which incorporates clear guidelines for qualifications and allows the appointment to reflect a wider constituency than that of the Permanent Five.[22] Yet the appointment of Kofi Annan, however welcome, did nothing to suggest a rationalization of the process.

The substantive elements of Article 98 hold that the Secretary-General must perform functions that are entrusted to him by the General Assembly, Security Council, or other principal organs, and that the Office-holder will make an annual report on the work of the Organization. The former has been a significant instrument for delegating authority and tasks to the Secretaryship-General; either routine requests for reports or the most sensitive delegations of responsibility.[23] The area of international peace and security has indicated how the practice of delegation can transform the Secretary-General from the periphery to the heart of decision-making, in the past sometimes through Council inaction or institutional wrangling. To cite a classic example, the United Nations Emergency Force in Egypt 'was the first UN peace-keeping operation to be directed from the outset by the Secretary-General rather than under the umbrella of a special *ad hoc* political commission composed of UN member states specially designated for the job by a UN political organ'.[24] There are trends in the nature of delegation which may be put into the context of historical developments which are reflected in institutional shifts of activity and power. Changing institutional relationships have had a strong bearing on the status of the Secretaryship-General, in particular regarding the shift away from collective security during the Cold War, and in periods when the UN has been peripheral to major political issues.

The annual report is likewise a fluctuating instrument for the development of the Secretaryship-General's role. The annual reports of the League Secretaries-General were not framed as a major instrument of policy. Under Drummond, the reports were predictably little more than a factual account of the work of the Organization. The opposite was the case of Albert Thomas, who sought to produce a 'living report' which would initiate discussion and provide a platform for progress.[25]

With the United Nations the practice of presenting an expressive and creative Introduction to the annual report was established almost immediately although the incumbent rarely writes the document personally. Some are classic: a number of Hammarskjöld's, and especially the 1960/1 treatise which outlined his conception of the 'choice' which the Organization faced, hold a special place in UN history. Likewise, the first report of Pérez de Cuéllar, outlining the crisis of multilateralism, the need to overhaul various aspects of the Organization, and asserting the need for a greater preventive role for the Secretary-General, should be seen as a watershed for the Office after the caution of the 1970s.[26] The annual report can be regarded as a tool of influence, as Thomas had foreseen, for placing issues on the agenda; it is in itself a form of intervention in the immediate term and a means of legitimizing ideas or forming norms in the longer term. Pérez de Cuéllar wrote that the annual report can be a means of initiating debate. It 'is not meant to be, and should never become, a mere rapporteur's job: "the work of the organization" is a broad term.'

Article 99 states that the Secretary-General 'may bring to the attention of the Security Council any matter which in his opinion may threaten the maintenance of international peace and security'. According to Hammarskjöld this 'was considered by the drafters of the Charter to have transformed the Secretary-General of the United Nations from a purely administrative official to one with an explicit political responsibility'.[27] Article 99 forms the basis for a great deal of the Secretary-General's political status and activities. The Preparatory Commission Report is invariably cited in this context for presenting the now famous opinion that under Article 99 'he has been given a quite special right which goes beyond any power previously accorded to the head of an international organization'.[28]

The drafting of Article 99 involved debates which reflected the different attitudes towards the role and status of the Secretaryship-General. In the early US Department of State drafts, before Dumbarton Oaks, the executive-head represented an entity of real significance and potential power, with the equivalent of Article 99 being correspondingly strong. The more modest ideas at Dumbarton Oaks, and then at San Francisco, debated whether Article 99 should be an obligation or a right, whether the right should also be applied to the Secretary-General's relationship with the General Assembly as well as the Council, and whether it should empower the Office-holder to draw to the attention of the Organization matters which constitute a violation of the Charter.[29] The latter point would have given the Secretary-General so much 'power' as to undermine him: subsequent practice has shown that the Office is at its most influential when employing more discreet or subtle methods. The eventual Article retains a great deal of discretion for the Secretary-General, providing that the Office-holder *may* bring to the Security Council *any matter* which *in his opinion may* threaten the maintenance of international peace and security.

The real influence of this Article has derived not so much from its formal invocation but from the legal implications that derive from it and the political aura that it stamps upon the Secretaryship-General. A number of Secretaries-General have observed that this Article can give, in the words of Hammarskjöld, 'by necessary implication, a broad discretion to conduct inquiries and to engage in informal diplomatic activity in regard to matters which may threaten the maintenance of international peace and security.'[30] In this sense a liberal interpretation of Article 99 can endow the Secretary-General with a wide responsibility for activity and initiative in the field of preventive diplomacy and early warning. Pérez de Cuéllar lost no time in presenting a forthright and progressive interpretation within the field of preventive diplomacy.[31] Boutros-Ghali stated that '[t]he Charter recognizes, through Article 99, that preventive diplomacy is a particular responsibility of the Secretary-

General. Early warning, fact-finding, confidence-building measures, personal contacts, and good offices, all are instruments of this.'[32] Yet overuse or ill-timing of personal interventions can prove counterproductive. High profile interventions are rarely the most effective way of dealing with governments.

One of the most liberal interpretations of Article 99, in the context of the progression in international organization since the late 1980s, appears to be that of Thomas Boudreau, for whom:

> [m]atters such as economic recession, social unrest, or even environmental degradation that creates vast refugee flows – as well as international tensions – can contribute to threats to the peace. Hence, the phrase 'any matter' must have an expansive meaning that includes a wide variety of political, economic, social, humanitarian, and environmental factors.[33]

Article 100, which seeks to ensure the independence and impartiality of the Secretary-General should be seen to underpin the political basis of the Office. As Hammarskjöld observed, 'Article 98, as well as 99, would be unthinkable without the complement of Article 100 strictly observed both in letter and spirit.'[34]

The constitutional basis was merely a platform – in fact a compromise – upon which the development of the Secretaryship-General could occur in practice. The constitutional provisions – the Rules of Procedure, the Charter, and to a lesser degree the Report of the Preparatory Commission – were a framework within which a contraction or cumulative development can occur, depending on a number of personal, political, and indeed intangible, variables. A flexible room for manoeuvre exists. While one might not be entirely happy with the sentiment that '[t]he secretary-general of the United Nations has a constitutional license to be as big a man as he can'[35] it is possible to suggest that a certain alignment of variables or circumstances may allow a considerable expansion of the bounds within which the Office works.

3 The Framework and Functions of the Office

It is possible to regard the Secretaryship-General as an Office which has developed, or evolved, its procedural and political status over a number of years. This development may not always be positive or measurable, but it is perceptible, and it can in some manner be paralleled to developments in its organizational and international environments. The corollary of the idea of development is that there is an element of continuity in the Office's role and prerogatives, either within one term of Office, or over a number of Office-holders. Thus, it is possible to think in terms of procedural development and task expansion, or a contrary trend; the contraction of the role of the Office is also possible. The Secretaryship-General, both personally and institutionally, has a history, and there will be few occasions when an Office-holder addresses a case, or an issue in a case, completely afresh. Whether in a positive or a negative sense, a Secretary-General acts with a personal reputation and an accumulation of procedural norms behind him.

The accumulation of procedural norms and the political stature of the Office involved, formerly, the right of the Secretary-General to communicate with and address the Security Council, and to make prescriptive political statements. Hammarskjöld's tenure laid the bedrock of a number of practices which were inherent in his 'Peking Formula', quiet diplomacy and preventive diplomacy. This development is evident more in certain areas of activity than in others. Clearly the employment of the Secretary-General's good offices is one significant area, especially in the years when the peaceful settlement of disputes was the primary basis of activity in the absence of collective security. In the field of peacekeeping the Secretaryship-General has been tied closely to the evolution of arrangements, terms and status of forces which have become custom.[1] Some observers

24

also see the 'special role' of the Secretary-General extending to the protection of human rights and alleviating humanitarian crises, and Boutros-Ghali highlighted his perceived duty to bring the international community's attention to ignored conflicts.[2]

While it is possible to illustrate that a development of the customary duties and rights of the Secretary-General has occurred, the task of detecting determinants of influence, and their relative weight, is far more elusive. Can one construct a formula? Methodologically there are great problems with such an endeavour, because this involves unquantifiable and indeed intangible variables.

It is, however, possible to present a framework which goes some way towards indicating the variables and contingencies upon which a Secretary-General's influence relies. The personality and style of the Secretary-General, the circumstances of each issue, the parties involved, and a host of other political and organizational factors are of key importance. Underlying these, the historical and long-term environment provides a backdrop which is reflected in institutional political dynamics and patterns in the activities of the UN and the Secretaryship-General. A number of commentators have made tentative attempts to evaluate the determinants of influence in international organization. Gordenker's proposition, for example, is that 'the Secretary-General can act within narrow but undefined and shifting limits, and his independent actions influence the course of international politics but never at a constant level. The configuration of international politics always modulates his actions and his influence. So do his character, energy, intelligence, and style.'[3]

The methodology employed here involves applying a number of questions to the role of the Secretaryship-General in a number of cases over the period covered. It is therefore necessary to have in mind what implications or changes of the Office are being examined, which functions are to be explored, which questions will produce appropriate results, and which cases or issues might be chosen for analysis.

Alexander George wrote: 'it is the task of theory to identify the many conditions and variables that affect historical outcomes and to sort out the causal patterns associated with different historical outcomes. By doing so, theory accounts for the variance in historical outcomes; it clarifies the apparent inconsistencies and contradictions among the "lessons" of different cases by identifying the critical conditions and variables that differed from one case to the other.'[4] In this research the historical outcomes are the activities and status of the Secretaryship-General in particular cases and in the institutional and attitudinal framework of United Nations peace and security practice over a number of years. The nature of the Office's mandate, its material and diplomatic support, the execution of its tasks, the statements of the Office, and attitudes towards the Office are all examined. The conditions and variables which contribute to the Office's activities and help explain quantitative and qualitative variations over time and in different circumstances are the stimuli. The proposition here is that the historical outcomes in the Secretaryship-General between 1945 and 1996 reflect trends and patterns, and that these can be related to the variables and conditions of the wider international political environment. It is necessary to make some strong reservations. Chiefly, it is not possible to identify, let alone evaluate in a comparative sense, all the factors and variables which influence the Secretaryship-General's activities. One is not able, in this type of research, to impose rigorous 'brackets around a temporal and spatial domain of the social world',[5] yet it is possible to identify the key indicators.

It may be useful at this point to turn to the question of personality and the Secretaryship-General. This research presents the Office as a bureaucratic entity with accumulated practices in the context of environmental constraints, but clearly personalities shape political processes and history.[6] Yet, it is difficult to evaluate the impact of personality in relation to other variables. Nevertheless, one must at least appreciate the difference between the personal approach of a Secretary-General and the influence of a multitude of environmental variables over which he has little or no control. The challenge is to evaluate the relative importance of personality in order to present the Office in its environmental context rather than purely as an adjunct of the personalities of the respective Secretaries-General.

This issue alludes strongly to the question of what style is the most appropriate for the Secretary-General, and the extent to which the style really determines outcomes in the issues with which the Office comes into contact. On the liberal internationalist side, there has been the argument that the Office should be high-profile, political and public, in the Wilsonian tradition: the embodiment of liberal internationalism. Ranshofen-Wertheimer presents the epitome of this:

> The head of an international agency should be an international leader. He must be a statesman, a man of public affairs rather than a civil servant.... The international leader should be given a rank unmistakably suggesting equality with the top governmental delegates of the organs that shape the policies of his agency.[7]

For James Barros, who puts forward the 'realist' side of the argument, the progressive model rests on a form of escapism: it is a fiction to believe that any Secretary-General can lead states to a goal of which they are not supportive.[8] The fact that such a debate still continues reflects the idea that personality and style are important determinants upon the status and role of the Office and even the outcome of certain issues. While it may be possible to identify the prominent variables which determine the role of the Secretaryship-General, methodological problems prohibit an accurate *evaluation* of their relative significance in any particular case. The personality of a Secretary-General is an important – and sometimes a decisive – variable but it is difficult to think in terms of direct effect or causality between personality and the issues in which the Office is involved. Thus the importance of the personality factor is largely a matter for intuition, conditioned by evidence; an appreciation of the constraints and opportunities inherent in the changing political environment help to keep this variable in perspective. The personality of the Secretary-General can only take advantage of these opportunities; it cannot create the environmental and constitutional parameters itself. Personality is an interesting – and certainly a popular – explanation for the history of the Office but it is not sufficient. The environmental backdrop is an essential part of the equation.

THE FUNCTIONS OF THE SECRETARY-GENERAL IN CONFLICT PREVENTION, MANAGEMENT AND SETTLEMENT

A central theme of this project is that the Office's development can be presented – with methodological reservations – in relation to junctures and trends in the wider political environment. Consequently, it is necessary not only to identify the functions of the Office *per se* – as is most commonly the case – but also to question whether there have been changes in these functions or changes in their execution within the framework presented above. This brings one closer to the *how* and *why* of the Secretaryship-General's activities, in addition to the *what*.

Resources

Within the political sphere of the Secretaryship-General's roles, it is possible to identify a number of resources which are likely to be involved and are characteristic of the Office's political and constitutional nature. A combination of any number might be in evidence at any time. Primarily, there is the backdrop of the Office's Charter provisions, and upon this the accumulation of routinized procedural practices which are largely thought of as 'normal', as a result of accepted practice. The codification and acceptance of this since the late 1980s is cementing such a development, especially in the areas of preventive diplomacy, early warning, and the peaceful settlement of disputes.

There are also mandates. These can be formal, usually in the case of the deliberative organs; and informal, most commonly from one or a number of states; and assumed, on the initiative of the Secretary-General. The personal attributes of the Office-holder are also a key resource: his reputation – in general and with the relevant parties in a particular issue – diplomatic skill and record, and his manipulation of the organizational political dynamics.

Personality factors also make themselves known during the appointment process in terms of what the individual can offer. Another important resource, whose effectiveness is also conditioned by personality, is the impartiality of the Office.

The Secretaryship-General has automatic access to an elaborate communications network, information, travel, and contact with the diplomatic world: clearly an indispensable basis for many of the Office's functions. Some commentators also have identified the political constituency of a Secretary-General as a resource to be called upon in times of need, or as a part of the general power base. There is certainly evidence that Hammarskjöld and U Thant identified with, and perhaps cultivated, the burgeoning Third World and non-aligned forces in the General Assembly.[9] If pursued judiciously, the Office-holder may glean authority from natural support, and in the organs where numerical leverage can be exerted – mainly the General Assembly – there are opportunities for manipulation through such support. Boutros-Ghali fostered a reasonably close relationship with the Third World bloc in the UN, yet it could not save him from the wrath of the US at the end of his incumbency.

Power in the traditional meaning – where a decision has a direct effect through the application of political or physical resources, irrespective of the wishes of others – has not been an effective resource for the Office. Since 1919, experience has indicated that the executive heads of most international organizations fulfil their responsibility most effectively when employing diplomatic skill and tact, as persuaders, bridge-builders, and conciliators. In the general area of mediation, the resources of the third party have also been presented as: reward, coercion, expertise, legitimacy, and the mutual identity between a mediator and the disputing parties.[10] Most observers would view the Secretaryship-General's resources as falling largely within the categories of expertise, legitimacy, and the provision of information. James Jonah emphasized, with reference to Secretariat staff, 'the persuasiveness of their principles, the strengths of their ideas, their objectivity, impartiality and integrity, and the intellectual nimbleness of representatives. Their only leverage is that of persuasiveness and partnership – partnership with the parties in their quest for agreements based on consensus.'[11] Difficulties have arisen when a Secretary-General has been perceived to have been seeking the path of power, especially in an overt sense.

Functions

The execution of formal or informal mandates, tasks and policy is a role which covers the administrative and political spheres of the Secretaryship-General. The routine and *ad hoc* execution of administrative tasks is a wide and important area of activity, involving internal Secretariat affairs and Secretariat services to the Organization. Within the peaceful settlement of disputes, the provision of good offices has been a central area of activity, and one to which the international civil service has long been recognized as eminently suited. It has also been an area of activity which has developed procedurally and eludes precise definition. This service usually involves an unobtrusive intervention by a third party to a dispute, aimed at encouraging reconciliation and an environment where the cessation of conflict and perhaps its solution might be achieved. A classic study of the good offices of the Secretaryship-General has suggested that 'good offices are designed to keep alive the diplomatic process and fill vacuums in available procedures to serve partly as bridges of communication and partly as a reservoir of compromises and alternative solutions'.[12] The Secretaryship-General and its representatives have fulfilled this function on numerous occasions.[13] It is possible to cite within this area of activity a series of levels of participation on the part of a Secretary-General in the settlement of a dispute. The ability to communicate information is a function delegated to the Office and indeed initiated by it. Slightly more focused, but still as a disinterested third party, the Secretaryship-General has acted as an intermediary between parties to a dispute, especially when direct contact is not possible due to the level of hostility. At times, the other organs of the UN may not be perceived by all protagonists to be impartial. The Iran–Iraq conflict, and the role of Pérez de Cuéllar, is an example of this.

Mediation involves all of the above, but a more substantive

role for the Office is more than a channel of communication: it also offers recommendations concerning the agenda of negotiations and possible grounds for solution. One definition describes this as,

> a process of conflict management, related to but distinct from the parties' own efforts, where the disputing parties or their representatives seek the assistance, or accept an offer of help, from an individual, group, state or organization to change, affect or influence their perceptions or behaviour, without resorting to physical force or invoking the authority of law.[14]

Again, the perception of the interested parties towards this intervention is central, and the role is one to which the Secretariat can best bring impartiality, tact and skill. In general, mediation is most viable in certain circumstances: within a prolonged conflict, or when a pattern has emerged; when the disputants perceive the situation to be relatively balanced; when they believe that unilateral action will prove less advantageous, or cannot reap benefit, or will result in unacceptable losses; or if an external force exerts pressure or offers rewards on one or more of the parties to participate in mediation, and the parties overcome the desire to abstain.[15]

Unlike other forms of mediation – such as the US third-party role in the Arab–Israeli dialogue – the Office of Secretary-General is much less likely to have the aid of positive or negative sanctions. This necessitates more strongly the existence and appearance of impartiality. The Secretaryship-General's means of pressure, and its activities, are the application of reason to indicate how settlements can suit all parties. Morality and legitimacy – with the potential for orchestrating moral pressure, embarrassment, or even ostracism – are also means of leverage. In some cases there may be the implication that a failure by the parties to act positively will precipitate the UN organs to consider more coercive measures.

The Secretaryship-General and its representatives are in a suitable position to fulfil such a role, theoretically representing, as international civil servants, impartial and unobtrusive figures, yet not neutral in an indifferent sense.[16]

In the interwar years, among the weaknesses and failings of international organization, a modest mediatory role was demonstrated by the international civil service. Early UN negotiations sought to build upon League efforts in a substantive sense; the existence of Article 99 is testimony to a more political Office in general, and various parts of the Charter have implications for a role in the peaceful settlement of disputes, notably Chapter VI and Article 33. Significantly, the Report of the Preparatory Commission recorded that '[t]he Secretary-General may have an important role to play as a mediator and as an informal adviser of many governments'.[17]

In the United Nations, mediation efforts of some form have been perhaps the most significant role of the Secretaryship-General in the area of the peaceful settlement of disputes and the maintenance of international peace and security. These may be on the basis of a mandate from the General Assembly or the Security Council – under Article 98 – on the basis of an invitation of one or more of the parties to a dispute – Article 33 – or from the inherent authority of the Office to initiate such mediation which has evolved over many years through Article 7 but is still not legally precise.

An activity which is located within the area of mediation, but perhaps discernible in itself, is the Secretaryship-General's face-saving role; or, more euphemistically, the role of 'accommodation'.[18] On a number of occasions the Secretaryship-General has relieved states of burdensome political tasks, or – intentionally or unintentionally – provided a means or incentive for a state to accept a condition which might otherwise be politically difficult or embarrassing. Thus, a state might be willing, or even eager, to stand down under the guise of a Secretary-General's compromise, when national honour, or the threat of domestic repercussions, would otherwise prevent such a resolution.

A further third-party role is that of arbitration, in cases where disputants have given prior consent to the legally binding nature of the eventual settlement. Clearly states generally are loath to accept such preconditions. However, if a party perceives a case to be relatively unimportant, or if it is willing privately to make a concession or stand-down, then the arbitration of the Secretary-General – as with 'face-saving' – may be the least difficult to 'swallow'.

Another distinguishable area of activity always involving some form of negotiation concerns the operative peacekeeping and peacemaking function of the Office. The Secretaryship-General has had an organic relationship with the evolution of peacekeeping: in the initiation, formulation (in terms of the conditions of deployment, engagement, and the complexion of troop contributions) and field operation.[19] Hammarskjöld's roles in UNEF and ONUC, and the norms established therein, were historic in the development of norms which have come to govern the use of international forces. Initially an improvisation and in some sense a side-effect of the failure of collective security in the Chapter VII sense, peacekeeping has become established as an indispensable activity. As a result of wide mandates and developments in the field which necessitate an immediate executive decision-making capability – in contrast to a deliberative Assembly or Council decision – the Secretaryship-General and its staff have often been in positions of great authority. In fact this authority has involved making decisions involving the employment of significant material and human resources without referring back to the mandating organ. While this has led to problems – most notably during and after the Congo, Bosnia and Somalia operations – it has also, in more successful cases, elevated the Office of Secretary-General in peacekeeping.

It is not only in the operative phase of peacekeeping that this appears to be the case. Indeed, the Office has displayed the function of policy formulation on a number of occasions, although under the authority of the deliberative organs: the formulation of UNEF, the first Lebanon force in 1958, ONUC, and more recently the lead Boutros-Ghali took in formulating, codifying, and innovating peacekeeping and other Chapter VI activities, illustrate this. Could one label the Secretaryship-General in peacekeeping situations, as Jordan did of Hammarskjöld in UNEF in Egypt, as 'a commander-in-chief of his own army'?[20]

The discretion of the Secretaryship-General in earlier years was usually the result of failure on the part of the deliberative organs to formulate detailed mandates or to monitor constantly and revise instructions in the face of developments in the field. The extent of the 'commanding' position of the Secretaryship-General in the past was therefore by default or acquiescence, and a tendency which often engendered a conservative backlash, particularly after the Congo. The immediate environment which afforded a significant operative and formulation role in the past was often one of incoherence, or disagreement, especially among the Great Powers, so that a wide margin of discretion was taken up by the Secretaryship-General. The historical environment could be identified as a paralysis of collective security which made necessary the peaceful settlement of certain disputes, and face-saving. In the post-Cold War world, assuming a relatively high level of Security Council coherence continues, this delegation by default might be replaced by a more measured and deliberate policy on the part of the Council. Therefore, the role of the Secretaryship-General in this area might not be as extensive as some observers anticipate, or fear. Alternatively, the 'new' strain of peacemaking and peacekeeping could suggest the contrary. In the context of post-Cold War trends in peace and security, new techniques have been developed for multifaceted operations in situations which do not conform to the traditional interpositional model of peacekeeping. The discussion and practice of this rapidly developing area have reflected a significant procedural development in the Office's operative status. The ambiguity regarding the Secretaryship-General's role in situations where peacekeeping operations are transformed into more coercive measures – either technically or informally – and the specific role of the Office in explicit Chapter VII activity has instilled foreboding in some observers. On balance the increasing activity of the United Nations in all such areas has, by extension, increased the role of the Secretary-General therein.

Preventive diplomacy and early warning, together or separately, represent central functions of the Secretaryship-General, which have varied qualitatively and quantitatively over the years. Preventive diplomacy has been defined as 'action to prevent disputes from arising between parties, to prevent existing disputes from escalating into conflicts and to limit the spread of the latter when they occur'.[21] Early warning concerns the identification of potential conflicts and the wider causes of problems. The intention is to act on the basis of information in order to minimize threats to life and the maintenance of international peace and security. Based, most notably, upon Article 99, Article 7, and a culmination of practice, preventive diplomacy and early warning have developed procedurally, especially in the authority that successive Secretaries-General have assumed to investigate possible causes of friction through personal investigations or diplomatic missions. Until recent years the role of the Office in this area was rather undefined. Points of contention have concerned the potential intrusiveness of his investigatory capability into sovereign affairs, and the possible embarrassment of placing sensitive issues on the international agenda. Clearly many governments prefer a discreet approach.

A less tangible function of the Secretaryship-General concerns the activities undertaken under the Office's leadership as the embodiment of the 'international community'. By delegation or initiative the Office has been an instrument for tasks in the public interest and for bringing issues to the attention of the UN organs, the world's people, and state decision-makers.[22] In the interwar years the Secretaries-General of the League were not significant in this role, although the League did have a network of emissaries. In 1945 there was a noticeable feeling, especially among the more progressive internationalists, that the international community needed a figurehead, a force for collective internationalism. Epitomizing this, Ranshofen-Wertheimer envisioned that the Secretary-General would be 'a statesman, a man of public affairs rather than a civil servant'.[23]

The Secretaries-General have made use of the various media, personal contacts, speeches and statements to express concerns, support causes, condemn practices, and exert moral influence upon the Organization's organs, member states, and private entities. Boutros-Ghali was not challenged, for example, for lambasting the tardiness of the international community's response to the Rwandan tragedy in May 1994.[24] The Secretaryship-General, in the right hands, is accepted and respected as the voice of collective internationalism and the vanguard of efforts to legitimize

international relations.[25] Yet the extent to which any
Secretary-General can make an impact upon attitudes and
policy processes in this manner depends upon his personal
reputation, the reputation of the Office – which has varied –
and the timing and nature of the interventions. One can see
how the personality dimension can make its presence known
within this role: although the Office has an independent
aura and legitimacy, the office-holder's reputation and skill
have a significant bearing on the application of the embodiment of the international community. The nature of the
general environment has a bearing: an atmosphere
conducive to internationalist ideas where multilateralism is
supported by the Great Powers is amenable to expressions of
advocacy by the international civil service.

The leadership role lies close to, and overlaps, a rather
ambiguous policy-influencing role, involving the proposal,
formulation and execution of policy. The Secretaryship-
General has a direct and indirect input into UN policy
formulation at various phases and levels, through public
and private recommendations, and information gathering.
In a 'leadership' capacity, as an instrument of preventive
diplomacy and early warning, and in an operative capacity
in peacekeeping and the settlement of conflict, the
Secretaryship-General has a role in the formulation and
execution of policy.

Clearly these functions overlap, and they are not in
constant use. The difficulty lies in attempting to judge which
factors determine whether the office-holder is able to exercise a particular function in a certain situation, which factors
have a strong bearing on the 'success' of an attempt, and the
extent to which it is possible to identify patterns in the
historical political environment as a significant backdrop.

4 The Development of the Office, 1945–82

TRYGVE LIE

The literature on Lie's incumbency portrays a man who established a number of important practices and contributed to a positive although precarious development of his Office.[1] The development of the Office might have been greater had his style been less robust, for he left in his wake the desire on the part of the permanent members of the Security Council for a more passive successor. Lie felt that his office should be active in pursuit of the interests of the Organization despite the constraints imposed by the Cold War environment. Debate, however, continues regarding the extent to which his assertive style was positive for the Secretaryship-General.

Lie had been the first choice of the US and the Soviet Union for the first president of the General Assembly before Paul-Henri Spaak took that position.[2] Lester Pearson had in turn been the first choice of Washington for Secretary-General. This was unacceptable to the Soviet Union, and Lie, apparently the first choice of no major party, was appointed as the compromise candidate. This would become a trend in the appointment process. Nevertheless, Lie soon entered the political fray in the Security Council by explicitly asserting the Secretary-General's investigatory and preventive responsibilities. In September 1946, the United States proposed a resolution which would instruct the Secretary-General to appoint a small team to investigate the frontier problems in Greece. Lie said:

> I hope that the Council will understand that the Secretary-General must reserve the right to make such enquiries or interventions as he may think necessary, in order to determine whether or not he should consider bringing any aspect of this matter to the attention of the Council under the provisions of the Charter.[3]

The Iranian issue represented a further development in the political and procedural prerogatives of the Secretaryship-General, establishing as it did the practice of intervention into Security Council affairs. Soviet troops had remained in Iran after the war in violation of treaty obligations to withdraw by March 1946. Gromyko had given assurances that withdrawal would occur, yet the United States still wanted the issue to be retained on the Council agenda, for propaganda reasons, even when Iran had dropped its complaint. At this point Lie intervened by way of the first of a number of legal memoranda.[4] This supported in essence the Soviet position that the issue be dropped from the agenda. Lie's 'bitter fight' to gain rights of communication in the Assembly and Council[5] was gradually establishing prerogatives and norms for the Office. The cost of his activism was the risk of appearing partisan in the Cold War context.

The practice of the Secretary-General expressing forthright political opinions was firmly established in Lie's public and private pronouncements on a number of issues. Lie felt strongly that the United Nations should seek to represent the maximum number of people in the optimistic belief that Cold War intransigency could be overcome, or allayed, through cooperation within this Organization.[6] His vocal support for communist Chinese representation, in the face of United States opposition, subsequently put him in the centre of the East–West diplomatic and political war. His public approach was likewise illustrated in the ten-point peace plan and the peace mission designed to promote it: the 'Twenty-Year Program for Achieving Peace through the United Nations'.[7] For six months Lie attempted to bridge East–West differences in a bold gesture which sought to show that his Office could make an impact upon an environment which was fraught with deep antagonism. Whatever the outcome, the project was an explicit demonstration of Lie's cumulative development of the Office's rights to assert normative and political opinions.[8] The public approach put the Office qualitatively in a different mould to its League counterpart, and completely beyond the bureaucratic model. Under Lie, the Office was used to embody the principles of the United Nations Charter and the international community; he adopted, despite a blundering style, a prescriptive and assertive interpretation of this concept, endowed with inherent political initiative.

Lie's response to political issues, such as Iran and Greece, gave impetus to a twofold process: firstly, a rather precarious development of the political role of his Office; secondly, the accumulation of the ill-will of those parties whom he antagonized. Lie's stance towards the Korean issue won him the hostility of the Soviet Union, without whose support his position became untenable. From the outset Lie was at the vanguard of those who condemned the invasion, later claiming that he had invoked Article 99.[9] He was strongly behind enforcement, encouraging troop contributions and attempting to organize a semblance of UN control in what was clearly a US operation under MacArthur.[10] Clearly, with Lie effectively forced to resign in 1953 through Soviet ostracism and the Security Council's evident wish for a more passive successor, there is an important point to be made. Political activity, initiatives and acceptable procedural innovations are positive for the Secretary-General: however, this development must be founded within the exigencies of the political environment – and this includes the attitudes of the leading states – otherwise the opposite will be the case. Lie's stance on Korea did not represent a procedural innovation and the Secretaryship-General is not served by attracting the hostility of a major power.

In conclusion, Lie established a number of important practices for the Office in the realm of creative administration; the Office had accumulated, in rather shaky fashion, a political tradition. He adopted a liberal interpretation of his constitutional duties, and he sought to put his Office in the forefront of UN efforts to maintain peace and security.

DAG HAMMARSKJÖLD

Hammarskjöld is almost a legend among those who support a progressive and creative international civil service. However, it is necessary to evaluate his undoubtedly positive contribution to the development of the Secretaryship-General in the context of the political environment. This will serve to put into perspective two streams of thought surrounding this man. Some have associated with Hammarskjöld an almost mystical quality, attributing most of his successes to his personality and style. Others hasten to caution against misinterpreting the successes, basing them upon fortuitous circumstances. Yet clearly Hammarskjöld was a pioneer of sorts, and he took his Office to new heights.

Most statesmen – and certainly the Permanent Members of the Security Council – had expected and hoped that Hammarskjöld would pursue a conservative approach to the Office after Lie. Yet Hammarskjöld's demeanour did not obscure his activism for long. He is remembered as a creative, brilliant and spiritual man, although the impression that Hammarskjöld was widely liked and supported, especially in the West, is mistaken. In fact most states, and certainly the Great Powers, became wary of Hammarskjöld's conception of his role; he was 'too high minded for their taste and doggedly ahead of his time'.[11] Yet states were guardedly cooperative or even grateful when Hammarskjöld sought a course of action which would harmlessly take an issue out of the paralysis of the Security Council, provide a face-saving mechanism – such as in Suez – or even benefit them against a rival.

The development of the Office of Secretary-General under Hammarskjöld derived from his skill, his aspirations for the international civil service and the Organization, and the circumstances of the time. Regarding the Organization, he envisaged 'a foundation and framework for arduous and time-consuming attempts to find forms in which an extra-national – or perhaps even supranational – influence may be brought to bear in the prevention of future conflict'.[12] Moreover, he imparted a doctrine to the active model of the Secretariat and Secretaryship-General: 'the Secretariat is a living thing ... It has creative capacity. It can introduce new ideas. It can in proper forms take initiatives.'[13] He would later put this into effect in the practices of his good offices, preventive diplomacy, and the 'Peking Formula'.

The first issue that displayed Hammarskjöld's diplomatic skills and indicated a further procedural development of the Office concerned the American prisoners of war in China. The General Assembly, in December 1954, asked the Secretary-General to make 'continuing and unremitting efforts' to secure the release of the airmen 'by the means most appropriate in his judgement'.[14] Clearly this put Hammarskjöld in a rather shaky position, asking China to recognize the United Nations Secretary-General and a mandate from a UN organ when it was itself barred from membership. Hammarskjöld's approach, which eventually contributed to the release of the Americans, was the 'Peking Formula': discussions were not held on the basis of the Assembly resolution but on the authority the Secretary-General could derive from the Charter, as a representative of the international community, in the knowledge that China sought recognition. He made a distinction between his responsibilities as an agent of the Assembly and Security Council under Article 98, and his status as an officer of the Organization under Article 7. This engendered a margin of independence.

The 'Peking Formula' also involved the Office filling the vacuum left by members' disagreement and the vagueness of some of the deliberative organs' mandates, so that freedom of action could be assumed by the Secretary-General if not explicitly prohibited. Of course, this is only possible if an active approach was desirable – or at least not objectionable – to major interested parties.

In the Middle East, after the 1949 Armistice Agreements had failed to bring peace, the development of this role faced complications which placed Hammarskjöld closer to contention. The delicacy and intransigency of the situation resulted in the unanimous resolution of 4 April 1954, requesting 'the Secretary-General to arrange with the parties for the adoption of any measures which ... he considers would reduce existing tensions along the armistice demarcation line'.[15] Thus, as a consequence of Council deadlock – the failure of collective security – the situation was 'given to Dag'.[16] Hammarskjöld was determined to minimize the dangerous influence of extraneous parties and Cold War implications, especially as Britain and France seemed more eager for an interventionist approach in defence of the status quo in the area *vis-à-vis* Israel, reflected in the Tripartite Declaration of 1950. On accepting his mandate Hammarskjöld also indicated that, in addition to being an agent of the Council with this specific task, as

Secretary-General he had an obligation under the Charter to raise any matter which threatened international peace and security. Following a course of 'quiet diplomacy', Hammarskjöld achieved fragile agreements between the parties involved, upon an 'inherent authority', although the effort was essentially flawed by mistrust, not least that of Israel towards the United Nations. Yet still the 'Peking Formula' was applied.

The Suez war involved most of the elements of the Middle East situation: a chapter in the Arab–Israeli conflict, the struggle between Arab nationalism and post-colonial hegemony, and an episode in the Cold War. Hammarskjöld's scope was seemingly weak as the differences of the parties were particularly entrenched, and the European interests were strong. There were a multitude of complications when Nasser announced the nationalization of the canal company. An important step for Hammarskjöld was his initiative – with the support of US Secretary of State Dulles – to call together the Foreign Ministers of France, Britain and Egypt.[17] Hammarskjöld's efforts were undermined by the infamous collusion between Britain, France and Israel, and subsequently the latter attacked Egypt on 29 October 1956. In response to their machinations he made an ultimatum:

> A Secretary General cannot serve on any other assumption than that ... all Member nations honor their pledge to observe all articles of the Charter.... Were the Members to consider that another view of the duties of the Secretary General than the one here stated would better serve the interests of the Organization, it is their obvious right to act accordingly.[18]

After the issue was lifted from the deadlock of the Security Council to the Assembly through the 'Uniting for Peace' mechanism, a ceasefire draft was adopted.

Hammarskjöld's skill and authority were given greater scope – and the Office developed correspondingly – by a mandate to act. Canadian Lester B. Pearson was the first to suggest a United Nations force, and on 4 November the Emergency Session of the General Assembly requested the Secretary-General to 'submit to it within forty-eight hours a plan for the setting up ... of an emergency international

United Nations Force to secure and supervise the cessation of hostilities'.[19] Hammarskjöld was subsequently invited 'to take such administrative measures as may be necessary for the prompt execution of the actions envisaged in the present resolution' namely, to facilitate the cessation of fighting and the withdrawal of troops.[20] The creation of the United Nations Emergency Force was important for securing and maintaining a cease-fire. Hammarskjöld's report for the establishment of the force – 'a conceptual masterpiece in a completely new field'[21] – and his subsequent administration represented a landmark in UN history and the development of the Secretaryship-General. Again, Hammarskjöld had approached the situation both under a mandate, and under the developing inherent responsibilities of his Office: the organization and employment of peacekeeping would henceforth develop as a special preserve of the Secretary-General. In the wider sense Hammarskjöld's tenure 'underlined the changing institutional relationships and the growing centricity of an independent Secretariat that accompanied the UN's transition from collective security to peacekeeping concerns'.[22]

The Secretaryship-General was ripe for expansion, albeit more from Security Council deadlock at a time of almost impromptu invention subsequent to the failure of collective security, rather than an express intention to endow the Office with such a role. Moreover, Hammarskjöld's freedom for initiative and success derived largely from the fact that the Great Power configuration – although reluctantly on the part of Britain and France – was amenable to his approach. Indeed, a comparison with the case of the Soviet intervention into Hungary in the same year puts the Suez case into perspective: the Soviet Union did not have the pressures on it that Britain, France, and perhaps Israel had, and Hungary was within the Soviet 'sphere of influence'. Subsequently, Hammarskjöld's words and efforts were futile in regard to the latter.

The rest of Hammarskjöld's tenure represented a development and consolidation of the use of creative administration, preventive diplomacy, and the use of the 'Peking Formula'. The Lebanon crisis was not dissimilar to that of Suez in providing a role for the Secretary-General to facilitate the withdrawal of Great Power intervention in a volatile Cold War context. The internal problems of Lebanon escalated to global proportions when its pro-Western president, Chamoun, asked for United States defence against the alleged intervention of the United Arab Republic of Egypt and Syria. The Soviet Union warned against Western involvement. The UN observer group in Lebanon (UNOGIL) was based upon a Security Council mandate which authorized Hammarskjöld to 'dispatch urgently an observation group ... to Lebanon so as to ensure that there is no illegal infiltration of personnel or supply of arms or other material' across the border.[23] UNOGIL sought to investigate the infiltration claims while preventing extraneous, especially Western, involvement; in Hammarskjöld's words, it was 'a classical case of preventive diplomacy'.[24] Hammarskjöld again negotiated with Nasser before having some success in allaying the fears of Chamoun; it was said at the time '... here is the quiet diplomat *par excellence*'.[25]

However, the overthrow of Nuri es Said in Iraq in July 1958 caused the West tremendous anxiety. Fearing a communist-inspired Arab takeover of the region, the United States intervened in Lebanon, provoking threatening signals from the Soviets. Preventive action was thus essential 'to forestall developments which might draw the specific conflict, openly or actively, into the sphere of power bloc differences', as Hammarskjöld explained later.[26] When the reality of the Iraqi coup emerged – that it was not a Nasserite or Soviet takeover – a strengthened UNOGIL was essential to facilitate a face-saving withdrawal by the United States. In the absence of a Council resolution enabling this Hammarskjöld was prominent in the diplomatic manoeuvres in the General Assembly which expanded the observer group.[27] Hammarskjöld had successfully assumed responsibility for preventive diplomacy. While he was sure that he must act on the basis of the Charter or the wishes of the deliberative organs:

> I [also] believe that it is in keeping with the philosophy of the Charter that the Secretary-General should be expected to act also without such guidance, should this appear to him necessary in order to help in filling any

vacuum which may appear in the systems which the Charter and traditional diplomacy provide for the safe-guard of peace and security.[28]

A further case which is important to this subject concerns the troubles in Laos, to which the United Nations turned in 1959. Laos represented another typical Cold War pawn, split internally between allegiances to regional and global guardians. In November 1959 Hammarskjöld announced his acceptance of the Laotian request for the UN to look into a potential problem there, not sanctioned by the Council, but based on the unspecified investigatory rights implicit in Article 99. That is, 'a broad discretion to conduct inquiries and engage in informal diplomatic activity in regard to matters which may threaten the maintenance of internation-al peace and security'.[29]

In the Congo Hammarskjöld and the Secretaryship-General became embroiled in questions regarding the manner in which UN peacekeeping had developed, and the role of the Secretariat in this case and in the wider sense. Hammarskjöld exercised a high degree of responsibility, yet this led to a questioning of his authority which would remain long after his demise. Many commentators view the Congo as Hammarskjöld's ruin, the undoing of the internationalist project of international administration. A popular theme holds that 'he went too far, coming up very rudely against the limitations of his job'.[30]

The Congo operation concerned many issues of great importance to Hammarskjöld: the Cold War, Africa, and preventive diplomacy in particular. The obvious vulnerabil-ity of the Congo, upon hurried independence, presented the greatest challenge to Hammarskjöld's deepest convictions. Almost immediately after independence there were military mutinies, the subsequent entry of Belgian airborne troops, and the announcement by rebels of Katangan secession.[31] This secession was supported materially and diplomatically by Belgian mining interests and various other Western governments and parties. Hammarskjöld took the reins on 13 July 1960 in calling a Council meeting under Article 99, the first time this had been officially and technically invoked. With the pro-Western tendencies of Tshombé, in contrast to the African militancy of Prime Minister Lumumba, and the economic value of Katanga, there were sensitive issues involved. An active approach by the Secretary-General would be ambitious and hazardous.

A Security Council Resolution of 14 June 1960 called upon Belgium to withdraw its troops and requested that the Secretary-General 'take the necessary steps, in consultation with the Republic of the Congo, to provide the Government with such military assistance as may be necessary until ... the national security forces may be able ... to meet fully their tasks'.[32] Thus, along the 1956 model, Hammarskjöld was given the task of forming the UN operation in the Congo (ONUC); the urgency of the situation, the wide mandate, and the fact that peacekeeping was still not governed by a comprehensive institutional framework, gave him greater freedom than might normally have been the case. Regarding the mandate, it is significant that early resolutions did not mention Katanga – clearly most of the West favoured, if not supported, secession – so Hammarskjöld had to judge whether the execution of UN policy implied action which might assist or hamper Tshombé, while maintaining that ONUC was not there to interfere with the internal politics of the area. His position was clarified slightly on 9 August,[33] but the appearance of impartiality was difficult to sustain.

With no detailed brief towards Katanga, Hammarskjöld attempted to stick to what he believed was the most impartial approach towards Congolese politics, and the most decisive against extraneous influence. However, this satisfied none of the outside influences – Hammarskjöld's 'impartiality' involved expelling military support for Katanga, thus quelling secession – and the situation worsened when there was a serious rift between the Prime Minister Lumumba and President Kasavubu. This further complicated the relationship between ONUC and the host nation and contributed to the breakdown of the flimsy consensus which had existed between the superpowers. How could the UN be offering assistance 'in consultation with the government of the Republic of the Congo' when the government was split? ONUC, and Hammarskjöld, were on shaky legal and political ground.

The strongest resolution during Hammarskjöld's tenure,

of 21 February 1961, urged that ONUC 'take immediately all appropriate measures to prevent the occurrence of civil war in the Congo, including arrangements for cease-fires, the halting of all military operations, the prevention of clashes, and the use of force, if necessary, in the last resort'.[34] Hammarskjöld's duties were not clarified, and acrimony continued to surround what many perceived as the Secretary-General overstepping his mark and the UN becoming entrenched in an operation of great cost which had escalated beyond the circumstances which had initially prompted intervention. The situation in the Congo had progressed ahead of the piecemeal institutional authority that was designed to substantiate such policy, and the Secretary-General was forced into positions where almost any decision would attract criticism. The Office had left a constitutional vacuum in its wake. Subsequently, many contemporaries, and certainly those desirous of some form of Troika reorganization, felt that the Secretary-General should therefore not be permitted to 'go out on a limb' to such an extent in future.

It is widely believed that had Hammarskjöld's death not occurred in September 1961, his position would have been untenable, despite his faith in the smaller powers and the fact that his standing offer of resignation before the Assembly was met by substantial intimations of confidence. Was Hammarskjöld's undoing the result of structural developments which inevitably placed him in a precarious position, or the result of personal ambition, or both? Urquhart appears to incline towards a personal explanation, suggesting that, '[i]n the end he carried this implicit challenge to national sovereignty further than some of the more powerful states were prepared to tolerate.'[35] Whatever is the case, it may put previous cases into a more realistic perspective, by suggesting that a large element of Hammarskjöld's success was fortuitous and dependent upon a certain alignment of circumstances. Yet, while it may be the case that Hammarskjöld's reputation has been inflated slightly, this does not detract from the significance of his tenure for the political development of his Office and the thesis that the parameters within which the Secretary-General acts can be paralleled to trends in international politics. The remarkable personality of Hammarskjöld complicates this, but it *is* possible to view his behaviour in the context of the institutional changes of the United Nations. This was a reflection of the need for a mechanism of peaceful settlement and face-saving in the context of the paralysis of collective security and an environment of Cold War and conflicts over decolonization.

The manner in which Hammarskjöld defended the actual concept of the Secretaryship-General epitomizes the political status to which he had taken the Office. The Soviet Union spearheaded a reform of the Secretary-General's Office on the basis of a reorganization of the Secretariat according to a Troika representing East, West, and neutral countries. Only this would ensure impartiality in the Cold War context. The questioning of the Secretaryship-General itself – not only by the Soviet Union – was negative for the political development of the Office. However, his personal difficulties did not result in the majority of members wishing to enfeeble the Office to which Hammarskjöld had contributed so much: the development of the Office as a political and independent organ, although ultimately somewhat stunted, still stood.

Thus, the practices of the Peking Formula, preventive diplomacy, and quiet diplomacy in the cause of peaceful settlement survived as prerogatives of the Office. Likewise, Hammarskjöld had maintained the practice of being spokesperson of the international community in various disputes and on such issues as the peaceful uses of nuclear energy and economic development. A consideration of Hammarskjöld's public statements leaves little doubt of this. A popular feeling is that, overall, 'Hammarskjöld provided the most dynamic leadership that any Secretary-General of the League or the United Nations has ever provided.'[36]

However, the development of the Secretaryship-General was certainly hindered and there were numerous expressions of concern regarding independent initiatives, especially when it was based on a constitutional vacuum and liberal interpretations of the Charter.[37] Other commentators urged greater accountability and even a mechanism for removing the Secretary-General.[38] This was a manifestation of an attitude of conservatism – in both East and West – which was to befall the Secretaryship-General after

Hammarskjöld. The restraints within which U Thant and Waldheim worked, and a certain feeling that the status of the Office was in decline, were partly a result of this. Above all, Hammarskjöld should be seen in the context of institutional shifts which were in turn a reflection of systemic trends.

U THANT

U Thant's style, his placid personality, his handling of certain issues, and an environment which did not allow a great deal of flexibility after Hammarskjöld and Lie, have resulted in a reputation far from positive. The quagmire of paralysis and disillusionment at the United Nations, with powerful states putting UN fora increasingly at the periphery of their foreign policy, was to engulf the Organization intermittently from the early 1960s and more persistently from the early 1970s, until the latter half of the 1980s. In the context, the Secretaries-General could work only within severe restraints, and the result has been, for Brian Urquhart, that 'U Thant has, in the West at any rate, been virtually written out of history.'[39] U Thant certainly headed the Secretariat during numerous international crises over which the UN had little influence – Vietnam, the Six Day War, Rhodesia, Nigeria, Cyprus, and India–Pakistan in 1971 are a few – and during a general deterioration of the Organization. However, it is necessary to evaluate the structural constraints within which U Thant worked, and, according to Urquhart at least, the manner in which he was made a scapegoat for inadequacies elsewhere.

U Thant's incumbency has been described as representing a downturn, or levelling-off, of the political status of the Secretaryship-General.[40] Whilst it is wrong to claim that he was politically lame, for reasons mostly beyond his control he did not expand the procedural prerogatives of his Office in the sense that Lie and Hammarskjöld had done. However, it could be argued that he represented a coherent constituency in the Third World and he *maintained*, as far as possible, the practices of those he succeeded.

Upon taking Office U Thant took an anti-Katangan – and characteristically anti-imperialist – line in the Congo, and although he distanced himself from the situation more than Hammarskjöld, he can be associated with the crackdown which ended the secession. Of greater significance to the Office was U Thant's often underrated role in the Cuban Missile Crisis of 1962. In the Council he called for urgent negotiations between the US and Soviet Union. To prevent escalation, U Thant facilitated the process of reaching an understanding and formula for a stand-down. However, when U Thant was not able to secure a UN inspection of the missiles due to Castro's stubbornness the American public was angry and disappointed.

Criticisms of U Thant's style also exist in cases where people feel that he might have spoken out more than he did, even within the constraints which existed. The withdrawal of the UN Emergency Force between Israel and Egypt in 1967, for example, has been judged to have been too compliant with Nasser's wishes and directly linked to the Six Day war that ensued. Yet the basis of UNEF under international law and the emerging principles of peacekeeping necessitated compliance with the host state. The practical and political realities – the Security Council was unwilling to censure Egypt, and if UNEF had remained in place it would have been overrun – made such compliance essential. Similarly, U Thant is sometimes associated with the international community's inadequate response in 1971 to the conflict between Pakistan, India, and what would become Bangladesh. Why had the Secretary-General not invoked Article 99 during the ominous months prior to full-scale conflict? For Bailey, '[t]he situation in the summer of 1971 was the kind of situation which the drafters of the Charter had had in mind when they decided to include Article 99 ... when all members of the Council are inhibited from taking an initiative because of their relationship to one or other of the parties it is in such situations that Article 99 attains its full importance.'[41]

However, while it is possible that the Secretary-General might have achieved something by forcing issues to the top of the agenda, these complaints rest on the presumption that public political initiatives have the highest chance of success. U Thant took the opposite view: that such manoeuvres, if against the grain of a single key state or the general attitude of the Security Council, can be counterproductive for the case in question and for the usefulness of the Secretaryship-General. A prominent academic advocate of this view was James Barros: his common theme is that 'the United Nations secretaries-general have very often by their public political initiatives undermined their political usefulness' and that '[t]o a certain extent the desire for a Secretary-General who takes public initiatives is an escape from reality'.[42] Moreover, much of U Thant's work was in private, and if he determined that a more robust approach, perhaps including the invocation of Article 99, might have been appropriate, the observer cannot be sure that U Thant would not have employed it.

Moreover U Thant could be said to have taken an assertive, perhaps creative, approach to many of the issues he encountered. His identification with the Third World and development issues went some way to creating a constituency of support, thus developing a tendency started tentatively by Hammarskjöld. It is telling that U Thant once said that '[e]conomic problems, ultimately, if there are not solutions, are more explosive than the political problems'.[43] Surely his promotion of development and social issues – the Development Decade is an example – aligned the Secretary-General to a political movement. It would appear that many statesmen, and academics, were conscious of U Thant's partiality to certain causes. Nevertheless, this was still an expression of the political development of the Office, in the environment of emerging development politics.

U Thant's statements concerning the Vietnam war, even though he was allowed no role in the cessation of hostilities, likewise illustrated a public political role, positioning his Office in opposition to a superpower commitment. Such a stance – of obvious annoyance to the United States – in the context of his anti-imperialist, anti-racist, and some might say anti-Western tendencies, did not put the Secretary-General on the best of terms with a number of Western capitals.

One may be led to the judgement that the Secretaryship-General did not develop notably under U Thant. However, he was significant in maintaining momentum and sustaining the existing and developing prerogatives of his Office. Had it not been for an environment, and a number of cases unconducive to productive intervention by the Secretary-General, U Thant's record might well have been more positive. As it is, his passive personality has often been held responsible for the inability of United Nations activity which would be better associated with Council ill-will and structural sources of conflict.

KURT WALDHEIM

Waldheim's tenure as Secretary-General has been eclipsed by discussion surrounding his wartime activities and the extent to which they were known to various parties during and even before his appointment.[44] In addition, his personal idiosyncrasies, and his approach to a number of issues, have left a particularly negative impression of his incumbency. Whatever one's opinion, however, he must be seen in the context of the general condition of the United Nations, and an environment which did not afford a prominent role to the Organization. Indeed, the UN was essentially on the periphery of Great Power concerns, and the 'crisis in the multilateral approach' that Pérez de Cuéllar wrote of in 1982 was clearly in evidence for much of the 1970s. Thus, any assessment of Waldheim as Secretary-General must be framed in the light of the restrictions imposed upon the Office by the environment. This was one which marginalized the UN as a result of the universalization of membership, the Cold War, the influx of Third World members, and a host of financial and political problems.

Kurt Waldheim's approach to the job was high profile but also low key: he was very visible but avoided confrontation with member states and did not use his visibility as leverage to apply pressure upon states. He recorded that: 'the secretary-general should negotiate only at the request of the parties to the dispute. Nothing is worse, and nothing would be less wise, than for him to force himself upon a situation. Successful mediation stands a chance only if it is wanted and worked for by all involved.'[45] Something of a realist, for Waldheim the job required 'diplomatic subtlety and skill and a sure sense of timing, rather than charismatic or daring leadership'.[46]

Most commentators interpret Waldheim's tenure in negative terms. By attempting to avoid confrontation and win friends, Waldheim attracted a reputation of being vacuous and a sycophant. A common theme is that '[h]e did not offer inspiring leadership, if it could be called leadership at all. He did not have the dedication to ideals, principles, or moral integrity to move governments beyond their narrow, short-term self interest ... Instead, Waldheim was a mere broker among governments on the rare occasions when they chose to enlist his services.'[47] However, could Waldheim have achieved anything more in the context of superpower machinations and cynicism towards the UN?

The General Environment

In various degrees throughout Waldheim's tenure the general environment, and the organizational consequences which were a reflection of it, were those of disillusionment and disaffection. Decolonization had resulted in the enfranchisement of numerous Third World states, eventually finding a voice in the UN organs and agencies which were amenable to numerical leverage through solidarity and bloc voting. The Western states grew increasingly alienated from an organization which no longer resembled that which they created. The mechanisms of *détente* were better maintained outside of the politicization of the UN organs, and the Soviet Union was happy to incite the cleavage between the Third World members of the UN and the West. The Strategic Arms Limitation Agreement was largely a bilateral affair, and, as Waldheim recalled, the UN was not invited to play a meaningful role at the landmark Helsinki summit of the Conference for Security and Cooperation in Europe in 1975: '[i]t became clear to me that my role had been envisaged more as a ceremonial one than anything else'.[48] For a variety of reasons, a number of issues and conflicts were outside the realm of the UN and hence the Secretary-General's jurisdiction. Waldheim was conscious, perhaps envious, of Hammarskjöld's almost legendary reputation. Yet, perhaps Waldheim was justified in reminding us that '[w]e look back to the time of Dag Hammarskjöld's Secretary-Generalship with nostalgia for a simpler world now gone forever'.[49]

As the most significant sponsor of the UN in military, economic and diplomatic terms, the attitude of the United States has been a critical factor in the Organization's roles in conflict settlement and international peace and security. Subsequently, the disenchantment felt towards the UN by elements of American society represented a major part of the marginalization of the Organization in the 1970s, especially before the Carter presidency. An important source of this was the 'new majority', the influence of newly independent countries which 'radically altered the entire character of the United Nations'.[50] Demands for economic redistribution and systemic changes through the New International Economic Order coalesced around an increasingly cohesive and militant bloc, making demands and initiating programmes which were the antithesis of the prevalent free-market thinking of the West. The 'common front' rhetoric of the Non-Aligned Movement, inspired by Tito, Nehru, Sukarno and Nasser, and the Third World bravado encouraged by the hopes of the UN Conference on Trade and Development, reached a crescendo in the General Assembly sessions of 1973 and 1974. Observers recalled that 'at the White House, where Nixon and Kissinger were the architects of American foreign policy, there was little regard for the United Nations'.[51] Nixon saw no significant part for the UN in the grand design of history.[52] Kissinger was similarly concerned with Great Power manoeuvring and power balances. Waldheim was resigned to this. However, while Nixon's memoirs hardly mention the UN, Kissinger's clearly suggest that the UN was an instrument at his disposal for the pursuance of his own agenda.[53]

The Soviet Union was in a similar position to the US until the late 1970s. It was not uncomfortable with the tacit norms and rules of the game reflected in *détente*, through which it could consolidate its position on the world stage in a structure of bipolar stability. Subsequently, in common with the Nixon-Kissinger attitude, the Soviet Union sought to maintain the mechanisms of this system outside the organs of the UN and the complications which they entailed. However, the Soviet Union was equally happy to incite the challenge posed by the militant Third World members of the UN to the norms of the international system, thus further undermining the effectiveness of the Organization.

Waldheim's incumbency was conditioned by historical trends which saw a clash of *status quo* and revisionist Third World forces against the backdrop of Cold War antagonisms. The question is, how did this environment colour the official activities of the Secretary-General?

The October War and UNEF II

During the October War Waldheim was a tool of Kissinger, not the United Nations, in the heat of the battle; Kissinger informed him that the US would support a restoration of the *status quo ante*, and 'Waldheim was likely to get that word around in no time'.[54] However, the Secretary-General should have been seeking an immediate ceasefire, in accordance with the Charter, rather than working with a US agenda which was happy to wait until the military situation was suitable before taking such a step.

In helping to separate the warring parties when the time was right, however, and in preventing the need for direct superpower involvement, the UN and Waldheim performed a service that even Nixon acknowledged. On 22 October, Resolution 338 called for a ceasefire, to no avail. The following day the Soviets demanded that Israel, still closing in on the Egyptian Third Army, comply and there were rumours of Soviet troop movements. President Nixon put US troops on a state of alert on 24 October 1973, and a regional conflict was threatening to escalate. A third party which could have the confidence of the parties and the superpowers was essential to prevent the intervention of either superpower which would precipitate the involvement of the other. Subsequently, on 25 October 1973, a resolution was presented by non-aligned countries in the Council for a second ceasefire and a UN peacekeeping force. Two days earlier Waldheim had spoken with Kissinger about this and some have wondered if Waldheim was behind the proposal.[55] Thus, Resolution 340 was adopted, demanding a complete ceasefire, deciding to set up a United Nations Emergency Force, and requesting the Secretary-General to present a report on the Force within twenty-four hours.[56]

This presented Waldheim with some room to manoeuvre: in the shortest possible time he had to assemble a viable force, appoint a commander, and transfer troops on an interim basis. It was a responsibility comparable to the first Emergency Force in 1956, and Waldheim, with Urquhart's assistance, rose to the occasion: there were the makings of a serious confrontation and the speed with which they inserted peacekeepers was a major factor in the de-escalation of the crisis.[57] The speedy interposition of UN peacekeepers is widely regarded as having been an enormous success, even among those generally sceptical of the UN in Washington. Crucially, Nixon was able to use the presence of a UN force in communicating to Brezhnev that superpower involvement was not necessary and he later acknowledged the importance of the UN at a very tense moment in history.[58]

Military talks were established at Kilometre 101, and the ceasefire was largely observed. The conditions necessary for the Geneva Peace Conference therefore had been established. However, it was at this point that the auspices of the UN and Waldheim's status were brought into question. Israel would not recognize the integrity of an organization whose majority consistently rejected Israel's right to exist as it did. The UN could not bring the material and diplomatic leverage to the negotiations that the US undoubtedly could. Kissinger recalled that in the formal invitations to Geneva '[o]ur draft finessed the issue of UN auspices by language that could be interpreted as confining the United Nations to convening the conference, not running it; the Secretary-General's participation was expressly limited to the opening phase'.[59] Although Kissinger's memoirs did not mention US or personal attitudes in this context, one can be sure that he was likewise determined to exclude any participation of the UN which might hinder US manoeuvring and his own agenda. So, in Urquhart's words, Kissinger was the 'super-star'[60] and Waldheim was confined to a peacekeeping role.

Cyprus

The Cyprus problem has been one of the most intractable legacies of decolonization and ethnic strife. As such,

Waldheim's contribution to the peace process should not in this exercise be measured in terms of success or failure, but in terms of the authority, leadership and possibly power that his Office brought to the situation.

The fundamental problem was that of the rights, security and identities of each community and their relationship with their respective motherlands. Following the coup against Greek Cypriot leader Archbishop Makarios in July 1974 the Turkish community felt under grave threat from the ultra-nationalists in Athens and now in Cyprus; Turkey considered the coup 'a kind of de facto *enosis*', or union with Greece.[61]

Waldheim, with Cypriot UN delegate Rossides, called the Council into session and gave an account of the inflammatory situation. Despite this, Turkey intervened on 20 July on the pretext of invoking the 1960 Treaty of Guarantee, aiming to put 'an end to a take-over of Cyprus by Greece and the inevitable destruction of the Turkish community'.[62] Waldheim took the initiative in attempting to help separate the combatants. Indeed, when a shaky ceasefire could be achieved on 22 July, he 'urgently requested all the countries contributing troops to UNFICYP [UN Force in Cyprus] to reinforce their contingents, and within a fortnight, it had been doubled in size'.[63] Still, UNFICYP's mandate and resources could not keep up with rapid developments. Waldheim required further direction from the Security Council, but the Soviet Union initially vetoed a resolution which would have expanded the peacekeeping mandate and extended the Secretary-General's authority. Nevertheless, Waldheim recalled: 'I took it upon myself, as cautiously as possible, to extend the very narrow mandate of UNFICYP – to act as a buffer between the Greek and Turkish Cypriot communities – in order to mitigate as far as possible the hardships of a conflict it was unable to prevent.'[64] Indeed, while Waldheim could not play a prominent high-level diplomatic role in the crises in 1974 – something better suited to the US and Britain – he *was* exercising significant leadership and authority in an operative peacekeeping role and in communicating and facilitating local agreements between the parties.[65] When the integrity of UNFICYP was challenged at Nicosia airport, Waldheim stood his ground and helped to engineer a de-escalation of the crisis which required him to negotiate with Turkish Prime Minister Ecevit.

The division of the island was becoming a *de facto* reality – in February 1975 the Turkish Federated State of Cyprus was established under Denktash – and once UNFICYP established a semblance of order and communication between the parties, attention was given to a resumption of high-level dialogue. In March 1975 the Council requested that the Secretary-General 'undertake a new mission of good offices'.[66] Waldheim chaired six separate rounds of negotiations and had a direct input into the intercommunal dialogue, illustrating both official and personal authority and leadership. A number of guidelines were presented by Waldheim and the parties accepted a number of framework packages. Of course, all such 'breakthroughs' transpired to be hollow.

Lebanon and UNIFIL

By the late 1970s Lebanon was riven by internal, regional and wider international political conflicts. The indigenous conflict between assorted Christian and Muslim groups had been manipulated and exacerbated by the PLO, the massive involvement of Syria, and by Israel's proxy forces.

Israel sought a military manoeuvre which would push the hostile Muslim forces north and establish a friendly proxy authority as a buffer in the south. The pretext for this occurred on 11 March 1978, with a bloody raid by the PLO into Israeli territory. In an atmosphere of rage in Israel the government ordered an invasion of southern Lebanon, overrunning most of the territory south of the Litani River in what they described as 'a mop-up of terrorist deployment'.[67] This coincided with an extremely important stage of the Israeli–Egyptian dialogue under US auspices: Camp David was in jeopardy. As Urquhart noted, 'Begin himself was expected shortly in Washington, but it was clear that President Sadat could not proceed with the peace process if Israel was seen to have occupied the territory of yet another Arab state.'[68] There was, therefore, the need to establish a ceasefire and verify the withdrawal of the Israeli troops in order to re-establish the semblance of peace and save the Israeli–Egyptian peace process.

Members of the Secretariat had discussed, even before the 1978 incursion, the possibility of a UN force to observe the border areas. Subsequently, Resolution 425 was passed, establishing such a force 'for the purpose of confirming the withdrawal of Israeli forces, restoring international peace and security and assisting the government of Lebanon in ensuring the return of its effective authority in the area'.[69] The Resolution asked the Secretary-General for a report on the details of the interim force within twenty-four hours. In anticipation of this, Waldheim was able to present the report immediately, reacting 'with impressive speed'.[70] The report and the activities of Waldheim's team in implementing the mandate reflected a relatively significant operative peace-keeping authority on the part of the Secretaryship-General, despite the misgivings which reportedly existed with the Secretariat.

Waldheim quickly appointed General Erskine as force commander and, with Urquhart, brought together troops from nine countries. According to Mackinlay, '[t]he Secretariat had ... excelled itself in the swift manner in which it convened the force prior to deployment.'[71] They provided regular reports to the Council on the withdrawal of Israeli troops and the restoration of security in the area, and communicated locally with the parties to help achieve these goals. In these areas the Secretary-General exercised significant authority both locally and in New York with respect to operational peacekeeping matters, albeit this was largely the result of US pressure upon the Council to inter-pose a force and prevent the Camp David process from being upset. Indeed, it was partly this pressure and the speedy deployment which resulted in serious problems on the ground.

The problems were many. The original mandate of Resolution 425 did not address the PLO or recognize that Israel's influence would not disappear with the withdrawal of its regular troops, because of the proxy forces under the command of Haddad. The PLO and Israeli proxy forces had not been asked for consent to the operation, nor had their consent been forthcoming; their cooperation was intermittent and sometimes non-existent. It was thus to Waldheim and Urquhart's credit that they managed to establish agreements on the ground on the basis of this unrealistic mandate.

Africa: Mozambique, Angola, Namibia, The Horn, Western Sahara

After years of wars of liberation and then finally the 1974 coup in Lisbon, centuries of Portuguese colonial rule came to an end. Mozambique and Angola were amongst the newly independent states which endured the birth-pangs of decolonization, riven by indigenous political and ethnic conflict, regional Great Power intervention, and proxy superpower confrontation. Civil war was an entry point for regional and Cold War politics, and physical resources were at stake as much as geopolitical factors. Waldheim's efforts to alleviate conflict in such areas were stymied because these conflicts were a result of historical forces, exploited by external factors which prolonged and exacerbated them.

In this context there was little role for the UN or Waldheim in Angola until the sponsors of that civil war could agree to disengage. The Horn of Africa was another area of prolonged conflict which, in the 1970s, was outside the realm of Waldheim's influence and linked to external processes. The legacy of colonialism resulted in spurious state boundaries and revisionist movements. Territorial disputes and demands for self-determination in the context of unstable political entities created a volatile arena for Cold War rivalry. The 1977 Ogaden War between Somalia and Ethiopia involved these issues and was typical of the imperviousness of the area to efforts by the UN and Waldheim to address the problems. As with Mozambique, Namibia and Angola, it is possible to see the UN and Waldheim's position in the context of environmental constraints. These made a constructive role for the Secretary-General extremely difficult until, in the 1980s, various decision-makers saw a UN role converging with their interests in parallel to developments in the general historical environment. Even when the time came, however, the role of the UN was arguably secondary to other efforts.

In conclusion, Waldheim's tenures reflected the marginalization of the UN as a result of the dynamics of the Cold War and *détente*, the burgeoning North–South polarization, and changing Western attitudes towards international politics and the UN. Disillusionment with multilateralism on the part of much of the West, and in particular the US under Nixon, Ford and Reagan, resulted in much of the 'high politics' of international relations being conducted outside the UN's organs. The Organization was largely peripheral to the foreign policy of major powers. The Vietnam war, superpower *détente*, the Middle East peace process, and many crises of decolonization, are examples. One could hardly apply such concepts as leadership, authority, power, and task expansion/widening, to the Secretaryship-General in these circumstances.

5 Javier Pérez de Cuéllar

Javier Pérez de Cuéllar's tenures embraced the most frustrating but perhaps the most productive experiences of the Office of Secretary-General. Until 1987/8, the United Nations was often marginalized within a general climate of political ill-will, and beset by financial crises. On many issues – especially regional conflicts entangled in the upsurge of superpower hostility – the Secretary-General was either emasculated or excluded. Conversely, the changes in the international political environment commonly associated with the ending of the Cold War resulted in great changes in the activities of the Secretary-General. In conflict management and settlement, in particular, the conflicts which were tied to Cold War dynamics became ripe for settlement. The new atmosphere of cooperation, at least initially, seemed positive to the development of the Office, although the new consensus in the UN and among the Permanent Five transpired not always to result in an enhancement of the Secretaryship-General.

Pérez de Cuéllar's tenures straddled the Cold War post-Cold War cleavage; he 'presided over the transition'.[1] He had just the right reputation and skills to fulfil the opportunities presented by the easing of superpower tension towards the end of the 1980s. The Peruvian helped to keep the UN afloat in a time of great doubt, and then tirelessly exploited the opportunities when able to do so. As with all Secretaries-General, Pérez de Cuéllar was not the first choice of all the Permanent Members of the Security Council and his appointment continued the tradition of finding the most compliant individual for the job. The words most often used to describe Pérez de Cuéllar are quiet, diplomatic, discreet and polite. However, given the opportunity, he could and would be creative, persistent and outspoken. Attitudes towards Pérez de Cuéllar, especially towards the end of his tenure and after, have been exclusively positive.

Although he remained rather colourless in the eyes of the press, he earned the respect of governments and diplomats alike. His colleague described him as 'exactly the kind of Secretary-General that governments like and the media hates', taking care not to jeopardize the personal relationships he had cultivated with the major states in the UN and winning the confidence and respect of those he dealt with.[2] For himself, Pérez de Cuéllar claimed to strike a balance somewhere between the extremes of counter-productive exuberance and self-effacement.[3]

Much of such praise resounded at the point of Pérez de Cuéllar's climactic departure. The drama of his delayed exit, due to the eleventh-hour El Salvador settlement in the early hours of 1 January 1992, was symptomatic of the transformation of the UN in conflict settlement that he had both encouraged and been a beneficiary of. This was in stark contrast to the first year of Pérez de Cuéllar's tenure when he lamented that the Organization was frequently being 'set aside or rebuffed' and the international community was 'perilously near to a new international anarchy'.[4] The upturn of the Office of Secretary-General towards the end of the 1980s was largely a consequence of the rapidly increasing utility of the UN. This, in turn, was a reflection of the changing perceptions of key international actors to a number of issues. In this sense the Secretary-General proved most successful in facilitating the end of the Iran–Iraq war, and in ending the superpower dimension to the conflicts in Cambodia, Central America, and Afghanistan.

To an extent, Pérez de Cuéllar's achievements are explained by the changing political climate, and as such he was at the right place at the right time. However, it is to his credit that he managed, orchestrated, and exploited this changing context. Yet it is also important to consider that Pérez de Cuéllar's experiences were not necessarily to set the tone of the Office in the post-Cold War world, in so far as he was involved in dealing with the residue of the Cold War and contributing to a superpower climb-down from previous commitments.

THE GENERAL ENVIRONMENT: FROM THE 'CRISIS OF MULTILATERALISM' TO THE 'NEW ERA'

Until 1987/8 the poor performance of the Organization – by almost any standard[5] – can be seen in its relationship to the 'second Cold War' and a number of ongoing conflicts.[6] The UN was at its nadir when Pérez de Cuéllar became Secretary-General, and the constraints and frustrations that this entailed clearly pervaded the activities of the Office. The 1980s witnessed the culmination of trends which were in evidence in the previous decade: disillusionment towards and within the United Nations, the 'nefarious influence' of the Cold War,[7] East–West and North–South bloc manoeuvring, a reversion to unilateralism, the seeming inability of the Security Council to address a number of threats to international peace and security, the *de facto* abstention of key UN members from certain programmes and agencies, and severe financial problems. In addition, certain circumstances – not least the rise of the New Right in the West and the lack of direction of the UN's Third World membership – created an environment which, at times, threatened to undermine the Organization. The absence of new peacekeeping operations between 1978 and 1988 was one indicator of this organizational blight.

The United Nations of the early 1980s represented a clash of ideals and the continuation of the struggle between revisionist and *status quo* forces. The Third World continued to exploit its numerical advantage to exert leverage upon the agenda of organs which were conducive to majority influence. The realities of universality of membership and majoritarianism provided opportunities for bloc leverage in the interests of egalitarianism and social 'justice', in harsh dissonance to the pervading neo-liberal ethos in Washington and much of the West. The creation in 1964 of the UN Conference on Trade and Development had been an earlier demonstration of this. The clauses relating to the establishment of an International Seabed Authority in the Law of the Sea Convention clearly reflected the spirit of public ownership of natural resources. Indeed, Krasner suggested that '[d]eveloping countries have rejected liberal regimes'.[8] Again, it was a triumph of collective leverage that the developing countries managed to influence the final form of the Law of the Sea Convention to the extent that they did, in an attempt to challenge the superpowers' monopoly over the sea. This was perhaps a last vestige of the declining centre–periphery or structuralist challenge to the systemic *status quo*. With the grand revisionist schemes of the 1960s and 1970s – such as the New International Economic Order – largely without hope, the 'renaissance' of the Third Word shifted in the 1980s towards rhetoric and posturing. One might say that the cohesion of the 'new majority' was waning.

There was still an institutionalized hostility towards South Africa and Israel in the General Assembly, which clearly undermined the role of the Secretary-General in his efforts to settle the conflict to which these two states were a party. For example, in very common General Assembly termin-ology, a Resolution requested that the Secretary-General work towards the implementation of UN resolutions con-cerning Namibia while condemning South Africa's 'racist regime', its 'illegal occupation of Namibia, its brutal repres-sion of the Namibian people and its ruthless exploitation of the people and resources of Namibia', and '[r]eaffirming its [the General Assembly's] full support for the armed struggle of the Namibian people under the leadership of the South West Africa Peoples' Organization'.[9] On many occasions the West, and particularly the United States, perceived itself also to be the object of attack. The drifting Third World was exploited by the Arab contingent, and the Soviet Union – although since the intervention into Afghanistan somewhat estranged from the majority – was happy either to acquiesce or to encourage this. The politicization of the specialized agencies and the creation of apparently politically orien-tated and sometimes extravagant programmes were also manifestations of the excesses which Ambassador Scali, US Permanent Representative to the UN, had described as the 'tyranny of the majority' a decade earlier.

In addition to tensions associated with the Third World, there was also a deterioration in East–West relations as the years of *détente* gave way to renewed confrontation. This was partly a result of Soviet adventurism in Africa, Afghanistan and Central America, the Sandinista victory in Nicaragua, the

Vietnamese invasion of Cambodia, the Soviet deployment of SS-20 missiles towards the end of the 1970s, and martial law in Poland. In the West, the ascendency of the New Right in the US and Britain, the challenge to Soviet influence in the Third World, the establishment of diplomatic relations between the US and China, the deployment of cruise missiles and the development of Strategic Defence Initiative anti-ballistic missile technology, and the imposition of sanctions on the Soviet Union by the US in December 1981, all contributed to the 'second Cold War'. The comfortable bipolar stability of *détente* was swept away by a resurgence of ideological fervour in the West and by the mismanagement and excesses of the Soviet Union's foreign policy. The United Nations had little impact on this process, but it did suffer as a result of it. The Security Council failed to fulfil its Charter responsibilities until the late 1980s and a climate of ill-will pervaded the whole Organization. The Secretaryship-General was consequently stymied and tainted.

As the primary diplomatic, economic and military sponsor of the United Nations, it is necessary to pay particular attention to US attitudes and practice towards the Organization during the 1980s. During the 1970s the Nixon-Kissinger-Ford attitude had been largely one of sceptical and often scornful circumnavigation of the UN in the sphere of high politics. The Organization had little substantive role to play in their grand agenda, apart from serving as an instrument to aid the balance between East and West, such as in the settlement of the Yom Kippur War, and in the provision of certain functional services. However, the agenda of the New Right, epitomized by Reagan and Representative Jeane Kirkpatrick, was much more combative and largely viewed *détente* as a mistake which had resulted in Soviet gains. At the UN, the Kirkpatrick team – in a manner reminiscent of Representative Patrick Moynihan – made quite clear the Reagan administration's intolerance to the Soviet and Third World 'antics'. Outside the UN the administration was shedding the Vietnam syndrome: it would meet Soviet adventurism. It may be that '[i]n the space of 40 years, the United States had gone from believing that the United Nations should and could do anything, to believing that it should and could do nothing'.[10]

Kirkpatrick's aim was to halt the decline of the West, and especially the US, in international politics and at the UN. Her style was forthright, confrontational, unapologetic, sometimes undiplomatic, and not afraid of isolation. This was not just her personality, but represented the cleavage between the Reagan and Carter attitudes. Deeper still, the Reagan approach reflected declining '[n]orthern commitment to universal multifunctional organizations'.[11] Haas borrowed the concept of regime decay and applied it to the declining-hegemony thesis to find some link to the waning capability of the Organization in conflict management.[12] From the 1970s, indignation grew as the UN reflected the end of American dominance and Western cultural universalism, yet the US was still shouldering the heaviest financial burden.

Kirkpatrick embraced this populist attitude. She was a vociferous critic of the declining US influence at the UN, which she felt was a result of mismanagement rather than an historical process. Therefore, '[m]y mandate was to go forth and represent the policies of the Reagan administration and certainly those involve a restoration of American influence and an end of the period of American retreat and apology'.[13] There was a certain idealism to the project of the New Right in attempting to halt, or turn back, the clock of systemic change and globalization. Similarly, Margaret Thatcher drew a parallel between her and Reagan's ascendancy, putting the 'reassertion of western influence' in a heroic context.[14]

The Kirkpatrick team at the UN felt that the Organization – and especially the General Assembly and the specialized agencies – were 'irretrievably politicized',[15] wasteful, bureaucratic, and actually made conflict worse. The latter argument, also strongly emphasized by the conservative Heritage Foundation, suggested that conflicts were exacerbated by the UN because the number of parties to a conflict became extended as countries felt obliged to take sides, even if they had no direct interest. The Arab group using the Afro-Asian bloc against the US and Israel could be an example. It was in accordance with this that the frustrations of the US resulted in a resurgence of unilateralism. The policies towards Angola, Israel, Namibia, Nicaragua, El

Salvador, the Law of the Sea Convention, the specialized agencies, and the 'liberation' of Grenada, are a few examples.[16] In addition, the US began to monitor the behaviour of countries in the Organization and to hold them accountable. The US – and to a lesser extent the United Kingdom – also imposed a number of economic sanctions and withdrew or restricted their diplomatic support of agencies which manifested the worst excesses.

It was not just the economic sanctions which defined the general environment of disillusionment and UN impotence. The resurgence of Cold War polarization contributed to the prolongation of regional conflicts in Afghanistan, Indo-China, between Iran and Iraq, in Africa, and in Central America. The US and the Soviet Union obstructed efforts by the Council and the Secretary-General to address such issues until the latter half of the 1980s, and there was a general reversion to unilateralism and bilateralism. The ill-fated 'multinational' force in Lebanon was a striking symbol of this, and part of a trend lamented by Pérez de Cuéllar in his historic first annual report.

In this report, of September 1982, the Secretary-General expressed his frustration at the failure of the Security Council to operate effectively and a climate which was 'perilously near to a new international anarchy'. He continued,

> I believe that we are at present embarked on an exceedingly dangerous course, one symptom of which is the crisis in the multilateral approach in international affairs and the concomitant erosion of the authority and status of world and regional inter-governmental institutions ... Such a trend must be reversed before once again we bring upon ourselves a global catastrophe and find ourselves without institutions effective enough to prevent it.

The general environment for the first half of Pérez de Cuéllar's incumbency saw a continuation of the tension between *status quo* and revisionist Third World forces against a backdrop of inflamed Cold War antagonisms. The Office of Secretary-General was either barred from a substantive role or severely constrained, and tainted by the machinations of the deliberative organs which made it difficult to establish credibility or autonomy. At other times, the Secretary-General was able to establish credibility with parties, but the Security Council members were unwilling to apply pressure upon their clients to end conflict and Pérez de Cuéllar was relegated to a secondary role. Many conflicts were tied to external historical trends, so the Office had to wait until there were changes in the external dynamics.

THE COLD WAR'S END

The changes within states and across the international system commonly associated with the winding down of the Cold War brought significant changes to the activities of the Secretary-General. Explanations for the end of the Cold War need not be given here, although Western military superiority, Soviet over-stretch, and Soviet liberalization at home all played an important part. The bilateral rapprochement between East and West was signified by summits in Reykjavik in October 1986 and in Washington in December 1987. The signing of the intermediate nuclear forces treaty, calls by the Warsaw Pact for a large reduction of conventional forces in Europe, and Gorbachev's internal reforms also helped to change the atmosphere at the UN. More importantly, cooperation between the superpowers would encourage the resolution – or at least the cessation – of a number of conflicts. The Soviet 'new thinking' manifested itself in the innovative statements and articles by Gorbachev and Deputy Foreign Minister Petrovsky which called for an enhancement of UN machinery for the settlement of conflict and the maintenance of international peace and security.[17] In encouraging the greater use of peacekeeping, preventive diplomacy and deployments, and a greater role for the Secretary-General in the provision of good offices and mediation, the 'new thinking' marked a reversal of forty, and perhaps sixty-five, years of Soviet practice towards international organization.

President Bush's election to the Presidency brought with it a greater level of sympathy and support for multilateralism, which was to blossom into the New World Order ethos. Following Kirkpatrick's resignation in early 1985, the US approach towards the UN had become less confrontational and more constructive in the hands of Representative Vernon Walters and the likes of Representative Thomas Pickering under George Bush, who was said to symbolize the seriousness with which the new administration took the Organization.

Partly as a result of US economic and political pressure, the excesses of the General Assembly were curtailed in an atmosphere of new realism. Confrontation was increasingly recognized as being counterproductive and the continuing disintegration of the Third World bloc pointed to short-term objectives, rather than grand schemes. Moreover, there was a certain amount of disillusionment among African states towards the Arab states, their former guiding light. The revocation in 1991 of the 1975 General Assembly Resolution which equated Zionism with racism was an important symbol of the majority's desire for moderation. Similarly, Assembly spending was cut in a number of controversial areas and the more radical political antics were curtailed; the US apparently was appeased.

The Soviet Union matched its new thinking with a commitment to pay all outstanding debts, and the US finally began to release money owed and to accept its obligations; some countries even made advance payments. Finally, there was a healthy increase of ideas to improve the effectiveness of the UN and its Secretary-General in the areas of peace-keeping, preventive diplomacy, and the maintenance of international peace and security. Immediately after the Cold War there was a blossoming of UN activity in this area, and commensurately the political role of the Secretary-General also *appeared* to be expanding. The question is, how did the historic developments of the 1980s have a bearing upon this Office? To answer this, a number of cases will be presented to illustrate the historical context of the Secretary-General's peace and security activities.

The Falklands Crisis

In many ways, the Falklands was a traditional type of war, involving pride, principle and territory.[18] There was no strong Cold War dimension to Pérez de Cuéllar's role. The crisis resulted from Argentina's seizure of the British Falkland Islands after a history of dispute between these states. Legally, Britain was the victim of aggression, according to the UN Charter and Resolution 502, for which Britain's Permanent Representative Anthony Parsons mustered support with the utmost urgency. As he recalled, 'we would obviously prefer implementation of the central paragraph of SCR502 – total Argentine withdrawal – but we would not in the meantime allow anything to inhibit us from exercising our inherent right to self defence under Article 51 of the Charter'.[19] Although there were colonial overtones to the British position the balance of opinion at the UN was in Britain's favour due to Argentina's use of force. Britain activated a military response in parallel to the acceptance of diplomacy and mediation, notably through the US Secretary of State and the UN Secretary-General.

The first phase of mediation was under the auspices of US Secretary of State Alexander Haig's shuttle diplomacy. This is generally recognized as being a failure, and some have speculated that the outcome might have been different if Pérez de Cuéllar had taken the role earlier.[20] Pérez de Cuéllar remained courteously on the sidelines until Haig faltered, recognizing the influence of the United States and the possibility that his South American background might jeopardize his credibility with the British.[21] However, he discreetly established a Falklands crisis team on 8 April in the Secretariat to consider contingency plans in the event of Haig's failure.[22] On 1 May, Pérez de Cuéllar subsequently offered to mediate,[23] and the UN mediation phase began, even though the Secretary-General was not mentioned in Resolution 502. We are concerned here as much with process as outcome: what was the authority and status of Pérez de Cuéllar, with whom did he have contact, and what leverage did he exert upon the parties? Could he have averted war, or was he an instrument of the diplomatic manoeuvring of the protagonists?

With regard to the Secretary-General's role as a mediator and intermediary, a certain amount of authority was self-evident. Immediately, he presented to Foreign Secretary Francis Pym and his Argentine counterpart a 'set of ideas' for a negotiated settlement. These involved a mutual withdrawal of military forces, the commencement of diplomatic negotiations for a full settlement, which could involve some form of interim UN administration, the lifting of sanctions and exclusion zones, and the establishment of transitional arrangements in the Falklands in advance of the outcome of the negotiations. Pérez de Cuéllar was seeking to freeze the situation and to encourage the protagonists to commit themselves to a diplomatic solution before the military point of no return was reached, especially by the British. On the basis of these ideas the parties accepted Pérez de Cuéllar's mediation. As Parsons explains:

> The most intensive and vigorous series of negotiations, attended by maximum public interest, continued until 19 May. The Secretary-General saw myself and my Argentine colleague, vice-Minister Enrique Ross, once or more often twice a day throughout the whole period, weekends included, working in an orderly and systematic way towards the elaboration of an agreement which would embrace the points in his original document, and which would put the islands under temporary UN administration for a defined period during which negotiations for a final settlement would be carried out under his auspices.[24]

This indicates a key creative mediatory role of the Secretary-General. By participating on this basis, Argentina had relinquished its former demand that sovereignty be transferred to it as a prerequisite for talks. Britain had agreed to negotiate substantive issues – including the possibility of an interim UN administration – when it would have been within its legal rights to demand an unconditional return to the *status quo ante*, under Article 51 of the UN Charter and customary international law. Both sides had also committed themselves to the process; both had an interest in being seen by UN allies as trying to avoid war, so they listened and responded to the Secretary-General. Pérez de Cuéllar was also the chief channel of communication between the parties. After Parsons was recalled to London 15–16 May, the 'final position' of the British government was communicated to Pérez de Cuéllar immediately upon Parsons' return to New York, and the closing responses by both sides likewise were channelled through the Secretary-General.[25]

If the obstacles to a settlement had been simply practical then war might have been averted. However, President Galtieri had incited a great deal of popular support for his stance, and so had Thatcher for the defence of people, territory, and 'our honour as a nation'.[26] Neither side could be seen to back down without an extremely effective face-saving device, and Pérez de Cuéllar provided the best hope for this.

As military skirmishes increased Britain made clear that it would veto any resolution for a ceasefire that was not tied to an Argentine withdrawal, as it did on 4 June. However, Council Resolution 505 had been passed on 26 May 1982, which asked the Secretary-General to 'enter into contact immediately with the parties with a view to negotiating mutually acceptable terms for a cease-fire, including, if necessary, arrangements for the dispatch of United Nations observers to monitor compliance with the terms of the cease-fire'.[27] This put a tight time-frame upon his efforts and by this stage few people expected a peaceful solution. As Anthony Parsons recalled, given the weather and logistical considerations, the British Task Force in the south Atlantic could not be maintained indefinitely 'while we fought over words in New York'.[28] While Pérez de Cuéllar had been making last minute appeals to Galtieri and Thatcher, he admitted defeat in early June.

On a superficial level, the Secretary-General achieved status and influence in his mediatory role, through the structure of mediation, as a channel of communication, and as an organ of creative diplomacy. However, the wider picture is less positive. A number of observers have suggested that the protagonists' contact with the Secretary-General was largely a disingenuous manoeuvre to cover themselves diplomatically.[29]

If Thatcher's memoirs are to be believed, this opinion appears to be borne out and Pérez de Cuéllar's role was more one of procedure than substance. At key stages of the mediation effort there were clear signs that the British government was 'going through the motions' in order to maintain legitimacy for its own agenda, and American support. Most strikingly:

That Sunday [16 May] at Chequers was mainly spent in

drafting our final proposals, to be put to the Argentinians
by the UN Secretary-General. The vital consideration was
that we bring the negotiating process to an end – ideally,
before the landings – but in such a way as to avoid appearing intransigent. It became clear that we would have to
make a very reasonable offer. I accepted this because I was
convinced that the Argentinians would reject it, and
strictly on a take-it-or-leave-it basis: the Argentinians must
accept the offer as a whole, or not at all, and once rejected,
it would be withdrawn.[30]

The *Rainbow Warrior* dispute

The *Rainbow Warrior* arbitration demonstrated the utility of
face-saving through a public servant. The constitutional
authority and personal reputation of the Secretary-General
were theoretically brought into play in the interests of
justice and international harmony. However, the eventual
outcome of the case casts some doubt on the constitutional
authority of the Secretary-General, especially when sensitive
national interests are perceived to be at stake.

On 10 July 1985 the Greenpeace ship *Rainbow Warrior* was
sunk in Auckland harbour while preparing to demonstrate
against French nuclear testing in the Pacific. One member of
the vessel died. At first the French government dissociated
itself from the two French people arrested and tried for the
crime.[31] However, it eventually became known that the two
agents were members of an official operation to halt the
activities of the *Rainbow Warrior* in a region which opposed
nuclear testing. The French agents attracted a great deal of
sympathy from their compatriots and pressure mounted
upon the government to secure their release. Europe is New
Zealand's largest market and France was capable of tighten-
ing the European Community quota on New Zealand
products. Under the threat of economic sanctions New
Zealand reluctantly realized that the case had to be
reopened. However, Prime Minister David Lange had taken
a strong domestic line against the French attack, earlier
insisting that justice had been served by the imprisonment
of the agents. Public opinion was high; how could Lange

bow to French pressure and compromise on an issue of principle?

The Secretary-General was well placed to provide a face-saving mechanism, and as arbiter performed a role rarely undertaken by the Office; under Article 33(1) of the Charter he was able to accept such a role without a formal request from an organ of the UN. The decision was to be binding, which put significant authority and responsibility in Pérez de Cuéllar. He too had to accept the political realities of the situation, most notably the leverage which France holds within the Organization.

The ruling eventually decided that the French government should pay financial compensation to New Zealand, the two agents were to be confined to a remote island for three years, and the French government had to apologize and agree not to oppose access of New Zealand's products to Europe.[32] To add to New Zealand's chagrin, the agents were allowed by their government to return home in advance of the agreed three years; the arbitration ruling was not fulfilled.

Did the final outcome challenge the authority and the legitimation role of the Secretaryship-General? Some might suggest that the outcome laid bare the Office's dependence on good-will and political realities. In fact, Thakur has questioned the wisdom of the Secretary-General's decision to take the role. The cooperation of France was necessary for his re-election and the effectiveness of the Organization; 'Pérez de Cuéllar could not, therefore, afford to antagonize France.'[33] Despite this, having committed itself to the process France could hardly have rejected it out of hand. The Secretary-General, while balancing political realities with the demand for organizational integrity, performed a useful task.

Afghanistan

The withdrawal of Soviet forces from Afghanistan was the result of diplomatic and military factors at a number of levels, in the context of the decline of Cold War tensions and internal Soviet developments. This case is one of a number where external leverage came to bear upon a client–patron relationship and UN mediation provided a legitimation and facilitation framework for the negotiations and a settlement. Simultaneously, military pressure on the part of the US and Pakistan was critical. This case was also one of a number of examples when the Secretary-General found it necessary to create some independence from the deliberative organs because of the history of the Organization's resolutions and attitude towards the parties.

Since the 1979 Soviet intervention into Afghanistan an East–West proxy-war became entrenched. The Soviets installed a puppet government and *mujahidin* rebels provided an Islamic-oriented military opposition dependent upon Pakistani and American assistance. In the US attitudes were split. Some felt that the situation could be exploited to help bring down the Soviet Union by perpetuating the costly Afghan adventure and harrying the pro-Soviet government at every opportunity. This attitude was dominant during the first half of the 1980s and was a major cause of the UN's failure. Others sought a negotiated withdrawal. The influence of these attitudes indicates how the US was more conciliatory towards the end of the 1980s. The Soviet Union would have been satisfied with a much earlier withdrawal if a suitable face-saving mechanism had existed, and if it had received guarantees that the Americans and the Pakistanis would stop their support for the efforts of the *mujahidin*.

However, for many years the efforts of Pérez de Cuéllar and special representative Diego Cordovez were frustrated – and even obstructed – by the machinations engendered on all sides by the political climate. A General Assembly Resolution of 18 November 1981 instructed the Secretary-General to attempt to negotiate a political settlement and 'proximity talks' began in June 1982. The Assembly Resolution emphasized the importance of the sovereign territorial integrity of the state of Afghanistan and the need for 'foreign' forces to withdraw.[34] Pakistan would not recognize or communicate with the Kabul regime, and as the Resolution called for immediate troop withdrawal, the Afghan and Soviet governments were not comfortable with it as a basis for negotiation. Therefore, Pérez de Cuéllar's approach involved distancing the talks from the Resolution in order to retain an element of manoeuvrability: 'a variation of the "Peking Formula"'.[35] For many years Cordovez worked on the ground with frequent interventions by Pérez de Cuéllar, who was chiefly encouraging progress at the superpower level. It is important to consider that a patron–client conflict involves different levels of negotiations, both formal and informal. The evolving global political climate was critical – the changing attitude of the US and Soviet Union to each other and towards their Third World proxy conflicts – but it could take time to filter down to the warring factions. In addition, for a number of years the hawks in Washington were particularly unsupportive of Cordovez and there was therefore little incentive for Pakistan to curtail its support for the *mujahidin*. As Harrison observed, the divided Reagan administration often insinuated that the UN effort was being exploited for Soviet propaganda purposes, and when a breakthrough seemed possible early in 1983, 'the administration sent negative signals ranging from scepticism to bitter hostility'.[36]

After the first Reagan–Gorbachev summit the US at least publicly supported Cordovez and Washington began to consider the UN framework for a monitored withdrawal of Soviet troops in exchange for US and Pakistani assurances that military assistance to the rebels would cease. So, '[i]t was only after Gorbachev took the diplomatic initiative that the dealers in Washington made their first tentative moves to assist Cordovez.'[37] When the superpowers were willing to disengage – and in the case of the US, allow the Soviets to disengage – the UN was well situated to overcome the stalemate and to facilitate the modalities. The remaining distrust between the superpowers, and the fact that Pakistan did not recognize Kabul, placed the UN in a critical position. However, it would be wrong to believe that the US and the Soviet Union exerted complete control over their clients in this conflict. Satisfying the concerns of the local actors – particularly the Afghan government, Pakistan, and the *mujahidin* – was a difficult aspect of the process.

Throughout the 1980s Pérez de Cuéllar had been in contact with the Soviet Union and the US, both of whom were sensitive to the fate of post-Soviet Afghanistan and distrustful of each other regarding intervention and interference. The Secretary-General held talks with Reagan in

January 1983, in which he pushed the ideas of a timetable of phased Soviet withdrawal and the return of Afghan refugees, in return for assurances of non-interference by the US, and an eventual coalition government.[38] These were the bases of the eventual April 1988 accords, but the UN efforts were stymied until the superpowers were prepared to use their leverage in the region. In March 1983 Pérez de Cuéllar had talks in Moscow with communist party leader Andropov and Foreign Minister Gromyko, while Cordovez held proximity talks in Geneva between the parties directly involved. This was the pattern of UN mediation throughout, until Pérez de Cuéllar announced – after the accords had been signed – that he was taking personal charge of efforts to find a political settlement in the country.

The roles of the Secretary-General, in person or *inter alia* through Diego Cordovez, involved creative mediation – for example through the development of a 'package of understandings' regarding Soviet withdrawal, guarantees against further intervention, and reconstruction – and face saving, in enabling the Soviet Union to make a dignified retreat. One observer stated that Cordovez 'mediated and largely crafted the accords'.[39] The utility of the Secretaryship-General was contingent upon the will of the US to exert leverage where necessary – in particular upon Pakistan – and to desist in its own support for the Afghan rebels. In addition, given that the US clients had the upper hand militarily, especially with the success of the 'stinger' anti-aircraft missiles, the peace process was largely tied to US willingness to allow the Soviet Union to make a negotiated withdrawal. Thus, a hawk might suggest that the 'stinger' was more responsible for the settlement than the UN Secretary-General. For the Soviet Union, internal changes and the wish by Gorbachev to improve relations with the West provided the impetus for a role by the UN. The Secretary-General was a facilitator through which these historical changes could have practical effect. Pérez de Cuéllar later suggested that 'the UN role was essential but not decisive'.[40] In addition, in the midst of the civil war which continued to afflict the country, the UN and its Secretary-General were moving towards the 'new era' of domestic peace-building and reconstruction. In late 1989 the General Assembly adopted a resolution which asked the Secretary-General to 'facilitate ... a comprehensive political settlement'.[41]

Hostages held in Lebanon

The Office of Secretary-General has been involved in efforts to release prisoners or hostages on a number of occasions.[42] As with other UN activities this can involve mediation, facilitation, and face-saving. The humanitarian dimension is thought to make this area of activity particularly suitable for the Secretary-General. The Office is often the channel through which powerful forces are at work, and this was partly the case in Lebanon, through the influence of the US. However, there is also evidence that the hostages had simply outlived their usefulness and that the Secretary-General was a convenient mechanism through which their release could be facilitated.

After other intermediaries – in particular the Swiss foreign minister – failed to achieve the release of the hostages, the Secretary-General began his efforts without any formal authorization from either the Council or Assembly. Special envoy Giandomenico Picco was sent to the area to negotiate with the groups and governments involved. Syria exerted considerable influence in Lebanon and Iran held sway over the fundamentalist groups in the territory which held the prisoners, in particular Hezbollah and Islamic Jihad. Among their objectives was the release of Islamic brothers-in-arms held in Israel or by its client militia, the South Lebanon Army. Israel had its own reasons for exchanging some of the prisoners it held, in particular to secure the return of seven Israeli prisoners held in Lebanon. However, the influence of the US in encouraging Israel to release some of the 375 Shiite 'prisoners' was important to the freedom of many Western 'hostages'. Pérez de Cuéllar and Picco were therefore important in encouraging the various parties to bring their influence to bear upon the situation, and in representing the public face of the releases.

During 1991, while Picco was spending considerable time in the Middle East, Pérez de Cuéllar presented proposals directly to Iran's representative to the UN, Kamal Kharrazi. The Secretary-General was evidently able to help convince

Iran that its post-Gulf War position in the region and its relations with the West would be served by using its influence to hasten the release of the Israelis and Western captives. Similarly, he urged Israel to release the Islamic prisoners, realizing that a reciprocal arrangement would appear the most honourable. Given that the UN Secretary-General did not enjoy a particularly favourable relationship with Israel, this involved urging the US to exert pressure upon Israel. The US clearly took the Secretary-General's plan seriously, for Pérez de Cuéllar had a secret line to President Bush via National Security adviser Brent Scowcroft; apparently the two had meetings which were not even known to the US Ambassador to the UN Thomas Pickering.[43]

When Briton John McCarthy was released by Islamic Jihad in August 1991 he held a confidential message to Pérez de Cuéllar from his captors.[44] McCarthy was certain that 'these people wanted this business concluded, and that they had a huge trust in Pérez de Cuéllar as a man of honour'. Surely Islamic Jihad also savoured the prospect of being taken seriously and raising their profile, both inevitable results of having John McCarthy as their envoy to the UN.

The final chapter was signalled by a meeting between Pérez de Cuéllar and President Hashemi Rafsanjani in Tehran on 11 September 1991. The President promised that Iran would use its influence to end the plight of the hostages, and by the end of the year this was achieved. The hostages had outlived their usefulness, and after the Oliver North controversies their captors and Iran realized they could not be used as bargaining chips on substantive issues with the US. Although all sides denied the existence of deals there were inevitably rumours. The releases were linked by some to the speeding up of compensation to Iran resulting from the US impounding of Iranian assets as a result of the events of 1979–80, and in December 1991 the Secretary-General issued a report which blamed Iraq for starting the Iran–Iraq war. While the full story may never be known, it is clear that the constitutional authority and the personal reputations of Pérez de Cuéllar and Picco encouraged and facilitated the release of the hostages.

Western Sahara

A further instance where the evolving international power complexion held parallels to the fortunes of the Secretary-General was Western Sahara. Since Spain ceded this territory in November 1975, Morocco's occupation of the territory has been a source of tension with Algeria and the secessionist Polisario movement. Polisario proclaimed the independence of the territory as the Sahrawi Arab Democratic Republic, and serious fighting was frequent in its war of national liberation. A number of external actors recognized the need for a referendum on the future of the territory and had sympathy for the group's cause. The US and the West generally desired stability in the area and this was likely to result from a settlement of the conflict and improved relations between Algeria and Morocco.[45] The US had, however, come to accept *de facto* Moroccan adminis-tration and was providing the moderate and secular government with military support. This was later to provide a valuable source of leverage.

In 1975 the General Assembly passed a resolution affirm-ing the right of the people there to self-determination and asked the Secretary-General to 'make the necessary arrange-ments for the supervision of this'.[46] For a decade there was little movement. In 1985 an Assembly resolution called for direct negotiations between the parties, and the Secretary-General and the Organization of African Unity were involved in encouraging the process. However, King Hassan of Morocco would not communicate with Polisario, and although he acknowledged in principle the need for a refer-endum many felt that he looked upon it as a means of confirming Moroccan rule.[47] Furthermore, Polisario would not accept a referendum under the 'occupation' of Morocco. A number of factors came together towards 1988 to make timely the proposal of a plan by Pérez de Cuéllar. Improved relations at the superpower level resulted in a decrease of superpower support to both sides, an increase of pressure by the US upon Morocco to accept a referendum, and a consen-sus within the Security Council to bring the conflict to an end. Relations between Algeria and Morocco were improv-ing, and more than seventy countries and the Organization of African Unity had recognized Polisario as the representative of the territory. In addition, the Secretary-General was a suitable intermediary between Morocco and Polisario. After presenting his findings to the Council the Secretary-General was requested to 'transmit to it as soon as possible a report on the holding of a referendum for self-determination'.[48] Pérez de Cuéllar broke the deadlock on the ground with a plan which envisaged that Morocco withdraw two-thirds of the estimated 150 000 troops from the territory and confine the remainder to barracks during the UN supervised referendum. A further point of importance was the criteria upon which the right to vote would be based.

The proposals were accepted in principle, and once again the Secretary-General managed to cajole the interested parties towards a settlement. However, the referendum did not occur during Pérez de Cuéllar's tenure and fighting flared up. It appeared that – in contrast to certain other conflicts – external actors did not have sufficient weight or will to push the parties to compromise and evidently Morocco was still reluctant to hold the referendum. The Secretary-General's proposals still held and were accepted by the Security Council at the end of Pérez de Cuéllar's tenure.[49] The manner in which the Western Sahara conflict was not overtly driven by Cold War dynamics – and more by the politics of a secular struggle against Islam in a North African context – may help to explain why the end of the Cold War did not enable the Secretary-General to facilitate a solution at that time.

Cyprus

The Cyprus conflict is essentially intercommunal and has not been strongly linked to global political developments. However, changing attitudes at the UN towards Cyprus and towards peace and security in general have been reflected in the Secretary-General's engagement with the conflict. Pérez de Cuéllar inherited a frustrating task in Cyprus. During his tenures the catalogue of disappointments continued. His personal skill and reputation could not overcome the entrenched, and sometimes intransigent, positions of the parties. This was apparently worsened by the Greek efforts to further internationalize the issue, which had the result of hardening the position of the Turkish Cypriots. The Security Council requested, on a regular basis, that the Secretary-General 'continue his mission of good-offices'.[50] In 1983 Pérez de Cuéllar attempted to restart talks by introducing 'three indicators' which sought to establish parameters for negotiation. However, these efforts were overtaken by the Turkish Cypriot unilateral declaration of independence in November. As their leader explained, '[t]he way to make the world face reality was to assert our right of self-determination and declare our Statehood. Only then would the world realize that two nations lived in Cyprus and that the Greek Cypriots had no mandate to speak for the Turkish Cypriots.'[51] This solidified the Turkish-defended northern enclave and was met with wide condemnation. However, it did have the effect of forcing the Greek Cypriots' hand somewhat and the following year Pérez de Cuéllar judged that progress was possible.

The Secretary-General was still working on the basis of a bicommunal federal framework with certain shared central institutions, which was established in principle in the 1970s. On 16 March 1984 Pérez de Cuéllar gave each party a five-point paper involving confidence-building measures, ideas for the development of a governmental structure, and territorial adjustments. On the basis of these, 'proximity talks' began in September 1984 in New York. Progress was made on a number of issues under Pérez de Cuéllar's auspices, and a package arrangement was worked out. His formula involved agreement on a bizonal, bicommunal federation, with the withdrawal of a proportion of Turkish troops, a bicameral legislature and a Greek Cypriot President. On the basis of apparent agreement the Secretary-General scheduled a summit to conclude publicly the new arrangements. The proximity talks were handled by Pérez de Cuéllar – involving creative mediation – and a summit was subsequently planned for January 1985. The role of outside parties was important, but not decisive. The US and Britain, in particular, were keen to prevent serious conflict between two NATO members, and both supported the UN effort. Pérez de Cuéllar reportedly required US pressure upon Turkey to encourage Denktash to make concessions. Indeed, according to one analyst, the January 1985 summit 'resulted in large part from an important reversal of US policy toward the Cyprus problem'.[52] He suggested that the two sides were brought together by Congressional pressure and a letter in November 1984 from President Reagan to Turkish officials, urging Turkey and the Turkish Cypriots to make concessions.

Pérez de Cuéllar played an important part in arranging the first face-to-face meeting between Kyprianou and Denktash in six years. However, the summit was yet another disappointment, through misunderstanding and last-minute policy reversals, apparently on the Greek Cypriot side.

After the summit collapsed Turkish Cypriot leader Denktash realized that he had conceded too much and seemed relieved that he would not be held to what he had offered. Furthermore, he felt that he might not make such concessions again.[53] Such a setback was typical of the history of this issue and the volatility of the parties. Pérez de Cuéllar could bring them together but the will of the communities, and the pressure of external actors, was not sufficient to take advantage of the opportunity for progress. Kyprianou complained – correctly – that the Secretary-General did not have the necessary leverage to bring to bear.[54]

Even with the lessening of East–West tensions and the declining threat to NATO, the increasing climate of the cooperation within the UN and the international community could not induce substantive progress during Pérez de Cuéllar's incumbency. The Secretary-General continued to mediate, although it seemed that a solution was possible only through significant outside pressure; the parties themselves, and in particular the Turkish community, were not particularly uncomfortable with the situation as it stood. Pérez de Cuéllar presented a 'Draft Framework Agreement' in March 1986, and brought Denktash and the new Greek Cypriot leader Vassiliou together in August 1988 in Geneva. This led to talks later that year, and in 1989 and 1990. Pérez de Cuéllar continued to produce 'ideas' to little avail. Furthermore, the relationship between the Secretary-General and Denktash became strained from July 1989; Denktash believed that Pérez de Cuéllar had overstepped his authority through one particular 'set of ideas'.[55] The peacekeeping force meanwhile continued its work in crisis diffusion and truce maintenance, and perhaps helped reduce the urgency of the situation.[56] Greek President Papandreou and Turkish premier Ozal met at the Swiss resort of Davos in January 1988, giving hope for a wider political agreement necessary for settlement. Unfortunately the interests at stake continued to defy settlement. The Secretary-General's involvement here was a reflection more of the nature of intercommunal conflict than evolving international structures and evolving attitudes towards peace and security.

Namibia–Angola

The course of developments in south western Africa was connected strongly to developments outside, and especially the attitude of the US. The role – or lack of a role – for the UN and the Secretary-General reflected this reality. A number of levels of patron–client relationships existed and provided the opportunity for leverage by outside actors. In the early 1980s Reagan and Thatcher's New Right agenda of 'constructive engagement' with South Africa involved alleviating pressure from Pretoria and steering clear of UN mediation. While the US was indeed the decisive influence upon South Africa, South Africa itself had clearly rejected a substantive role for the UN in the region many years before Reagan's election. Frequent attacks upon South Africa's domestic and regional practices and the support of such groups as the South West Africa People's Organization and the African National Congress by the General Assembly had undermined the Secretary-General's mediation efforts. While the Secretary-General had managed to create some independence from the deliberative organs in cases such as Cambodia, Afghanistan and Iran–Iraq, the history of hostility between South Africa and the UN majority was simply too great for the Secretary-General to overcome. This was compounded by the US attitude. Initially, the Reagan administration was wary of UN involvement, and even later when the attitude improved the State Department wished to keep the thrust of the mediation under Chester Crocker and US auspices. Nevertheless, when the December 1988 accords were signed it was with an element of UN facilitation, and the Organization was to play a leading functional role in the reconstruction of Angola and Namibia.

In 1970 the General Assembly declared that the occupation by South Africa of Namibia was illegal and declared support for the South West Africa People's Organization (SWAPO) in 1973. The general framework for the decolonization of Namibia was agreed among the Western Contact Group – Canada, Britain, France, Germany and the US – in its work towards the end of the 1970s, and embodied in Security Council Resolution 435.[57] However, the position of South Africa under P.W. Botha hardened, and with Reagan came a more conciliatory attitude towards South Africa. Indeed, the new administration saw the question of Namibia in the context of Soviet-sponsored aggression throughout southern Africa, and viewed South Africa as a bastion of capitalism. Therefore, the US administration felt that the decolonization of Namibia should be linked to Soviet or communist concessions, especially in Angola. The Security Council continued to condemn South Africa's occupation of Namibia and unrealistically mandated the Secretary-General to 'undertake consultations with a view to securing the speedy implementation of Security Council resolution 435'.[58]

The approach of Chester Crocker and 'constructive engagement' was that of linkage. As Thatcher recalled, 'I knew that the Americans would not press the South Africans to withdraw from Namibia unless the 20,000 or so Cubans also withdraw from neighbouring Angola. What is more, I privately thought they were fully justified in asserting this linkage.'[59]

Pérez de Cuéllar was out of touch with reality in rejecting US efforts to link the withdrawal of Cuba from Angola with that of South Africa from Namibia. This, in addition to the South African and American attitude to the UN, ruled out a substantive role for the Secretary-General. He did make the first visit to Namibia by a Secretary-General in 1983, and visited South Africa in 1988 in preparation for a settlement. However, the latter visit – the first since 1983 – was largely the result of progress made by Crocker, and was primarily to assure South Africa of the impartiality of the UN in the transition of Namibia to independence. On that occasion

Pérez de Cuéllar made clear that it would not be proper for him to speak to Cuba on the subject of its withdrawal from Angola, or to involve himself in the next round of talks between Angola, South Africa, Cuba and the US. The Security Council was still demanding the unilateral with-drawal of South Africa, and the Secretary-General's status was conditioned by this.[60] It was clear that the US, while hardly an impartial mediator, could exert leverage upon all the parties, and help give rise to a settlement which was basically acceptable to all.[61] The Secretary-General's Special Representative, Martti Ahtisaari, played a key role in nego-tiating in the wake of Crocker's momentum and informally building on the work of the US while carefully trying not to appear out of step with UN declarations.[62]

By mid-1988 military stalemate and war weariness on the ground coincided with Soviet 'new thinking' and the general climate of cooperation between the superpowers.[63] The 'superpower midwifery' of the US,[64] and the realization by Angola and the Soviet Union that this was backed-up by superior firepower, provided the momentum which resulted in the 1988 accords. In turn, Soviet diplomatic pressure upon Angola and Cuba to induce flexibility – and to agree to the exit of Cuban troops – was significant. The UN role was then one of implementation: assisting in the transition of Namibia to independence, monitoring the withdrawal of Cuban troops, and legitimizing the guarantees for the settle-ment. This was in itself an achievement. Pérez de Cuéllar had gone some way towards mending relations with South Africa. Furthermore, when violence threatened the accords in 1989 Pérez de Cuéllar was at the forefront – with Under-Secretary-General Marrack Goulding – of efforts to investi-gate the problems and report to the Council.

Iran–Iraq War

In his first tenure Pérez de Cuéllar's involvement in the Iran–Iraq war demonstrated his understanding of the constraints inherent in the international environment and an entrenched conflict. Similarly, when the military circum-stances of the parties and the diplomatic climate were later to change, he urged the Security Council into action. The

Secretary-General's efforts may be divided into four inter-linked areas: his attempts to limit the targets and destructiveness of the war, urging the Council to adopt the ceasefire resolution, mediating the acceptance and imple-mentation of the resolution, and after the ceasefire mediating the modalities of the peacekeeping operation. This was in the context of – and partly responding to – regional and international changes.

The 1979 revolution in Iran had upset the regional balance. Saddam Hussein believed that there existed the opportunity to establish regional hegemony and to deter or pre-empt a future Iranian attack.[65] Years of territorial and religious differences were thrown into crisis by the funda-mentalist upheaval. The reaction of the international community to Iraq's attack upon Iran was somewhat muted and the West perhaps even gave tacit approval. Security Council Resolution 479 lamely referred to 'the situation between Iran and Iraq', called upon the countries to 'refrain immediately from any further use of force' and casually supported the 'efforts of the Secretary-General and the offer of his good offices'.[66] As the victim of aggression, Iran felt that these non-mandatory words were far too even-handed. However, the West feared the prospect of a fundamentalist hegemony in a strategically important area. The US and the Soviet Union appeared to be in tacit agreement that a major change in the region's power balance or direct intervention by either superpower was undesirable.[67] Subsequently, in the context of the general problems and inadequacies of the UN in the first half of the 1980s the Security Council was not disposed to take positive action as long as the flow of oil was not interrupted. There was an air of bias against Iran, from which Pérez de Cuéllar struggled to dissociate himself.

While Iraq had superiority in weaponry and organization, Iran's soldiers were motivated and plentiful. The war settled into an entrenched and bitter struggle, lurching from stale-mate to advantage for one side or the other. The war was characterized by the targeting of civilians and cities, the use of chemical weapons, and the targeting of other Gulf states in the 'tanker war' in 1986.[68] While both Iran and Iraq favoured a military solution and harboured hope of victory, and while the Council remained indifferent, efforts by Pérez de Cuéllar were stymied. He followed a two-track approach which involved seeking to end the conflict, but also managing and limiting the war's effects, especially upon non-combatants. In March 1985 Pérez de Cuéllar met with both sides separately in New York and presented his 'eight-point plan' embracing these objectives. He subsequently presented his proposals to the Security Council and then visited the region in April. In ten days he visited Iran, Iraq and Saudi Arabia, Iraq's largest financial backer for the war. Apparently, the Secretary-General made his visits conditional upon their consent to discuss all aspects of the conflict, and he reportedly received such assurances.[69] Pérez de Cuéllar was essentially the only channel of communication between the two countries and he had won the confidence of both the protagonists. Indeed, Iran had rejected the resolutions of the Council, perhaps correctly perceiving them to be politicized, yet was prepared to receive the Secretary-General.

In April 1985 Pérez de Cuéllar made no progress on a ceasefire so continued efforts to limit fighting. He had sent observers to both countries in 1984 and 1985 to investigate the use of chemical weapons, brokered a moratorium on attacks against cities which held for six months, and in early 1985 he sent a team of experts to both countries to investigate the treatment of prisoners of war. These efforts to alleviate suffering and to manage the conflict were of the greatest significance in a context where substantive progress towards a ceasefire was not possible. Boudreau suggested that '[t]hrough these initiatives, the Secretary-General created, in effect, a humanitarian regime in the midst of a savage and bloody war.'[70]

By January 1987 the political climate of the Security Council was improving and Pérez de Cuéllar urged the Permanent Members to coordinate their influence with him informally to find a settlement. He called publicly for the Permanent Five to act and also 'arranged' for them to meet informally.[71] For the next six months representatives of the Permanent Members discussed issues for the most part suggested by Pérez de Cuéllar. These included responsibility for the war, the protection of merchant shipping, chemical weapons, the supply of weapons, a ceasefire and withdrawal of troops, and reparations.[72] The Permanent Members finally worked out a mandatory ceasefire resolution which represented a juncture in the Council approach to this conflict and in a wider sense.[73] Resolution 598, acting under Articles 39 and 40 of the Charter, demanded that Iran and Iraq immediately observe a ceasefire and withdraw forces to recognized boundaries. It also authorized an inquiry into responsibility for the war, and gave the Secretary-General a clear mandate to negotiate the implementation of the resolution. His role thereafter theoretically had the backing of Chapter VII Security Council action.

In September 1987 Pérez de Cuéllar made a four-day visit to the Gulf in an effort to gain compliance with the ceasefire resolution, which Iran was resisting.[74] Iran placed great emphasis on the inquiry into responsibility for the conflict, wishing this judgement – against Iraq – to be reached before ceasefire and withdrawal. Iraq maintained that the resolution should be implemented according to the order of its paragraphs, beginning with the ceasefire. Pérez de Cuéllar's efforts in the Gulf and in trying to push the Security Council into action to back up Resolution 598 did not have much impact. Serious fighting continued, including the use of chemical weapons and the bombing of cities. Iraq had taken the military advantage, and it was now Iran which sought a way out of the conflict. With a loss of morale and a number of serious battlefield blows, Rafsanjani needed to settle. The accidental loss on 3 July 1988 of an Iranian civilian airliner to US forces provided the opportunity to announce compliance with the ceasefire.[75] It should be noted that Iran expressed its intention to Pérez de Cuéllar.[76]

Following the ceasefire, Iran and Iraq met officially under Pérez de Cuéllar, in proximity, in Geneva. In effect, the Secretary-General 'renegotiated' the Security Council ceasefire resolution with the parties, perhaps to remove the political taint.[77] He told Iranian Foreign Minister Akbar Valayeti and Iraqi Foreign Minister Tariq Aziz of his proposals for a timetable for negotiations on the exchange of prisoners, the withdrawal of troops, and an investigation into responsibility. Pérez de Cuéllar shortly appointed Jan Eliasson as his personal representative and the Secretary-General continued to enjoy the confidence of the parties.

On 9 August the Security Council adopted Resolution 619, setting up the UN Iran/Iraq Military Observer Group. Although progress was slow, the two foreign ministers met in person under Pérez de Cuéllar. However, it was Iraq's invasion of Kuwait which appeared finally to result in a full withdrawal from Iran. Nevertheless, in his relationship with the parties, and his nudging of the Security Council, the Secretary-General helped to hasten the settlement.

Central America: El Salvador and Nicaragua

During the Reagan administration the UN was almost as marginalized from the Central American conflicts as it had been from the Vietnam war. Yet the El Salvadoran settlement at the end of Pérez de Cuéllar's tenure was a victorious parting achievement. It had been another client–patron proxy conflict with indigenous causes and superpower support. During the early 1980s US unilateralism and confrontationalism was most evident towards this region. The US has a long history of hegemony and protectiveness over the southern Americas, based on material and security interests. The upsurge of Cold War proxy confrontation in the Third World from the 1970s and the ascendency of the New Right in Washington provided the pretext for a rigorous defence of US interests around the world. Pro-Western or capitalist regimes and insurgencies – even those of a totalitarian nature – were deemed worthy of support against the forces of communism, and Central America was a stark example of this. Indeed, Nicaragua was a test case for the 'Reagan doctrine'.[78] So confrontational and unapologetic was US policy in this case that it was found by the International Court of Justice, for its support of right-wing contra rebels, to have acted 'in breach of its obligation under customary international law not to intervene in the affairs of another state'.[79]

During at least the Reagan period there was little incentive for the rightist government of El Salvador to compromise with the rebel Farabundo Márti National Liberation Front (FMLN) because of the steady flow of US aid. Similarly, the rebels were the beneficiaries of Soviet aid via the Sandinista government in Nicaragua. Neither side, but especially the El

Salvador government, was interested in serious negotiations while a military solution appeared to be possible, and while their external sponsors continued to support their efforts. Negotiations subsequently failed during much of the 1980s, until international political changes came to bear.

The government of El Salvador wanted the FMLN to disarm and to accept the constitution, an amnesty, and elections. The rebels, however, would not accept the constitution or elections in a climate of oppression. They wanted power-sharing, land reform, a reform of the army and the brutal police, and an investigation of abuses of human rights. By the end of the 1980s certain internal and extraneous developments pushed the parties towards an acceptance of mediation on a more serious basis. The decline of Cold War hostility was decreasing external aid, and in particular the US was increasingly doubtful of the nature of the El Salvadoran practices. The hard-line approach of the Reagan administration had given way to a more flexible policy that could no longer justify supporting a regime associated with atrocities; the murder of six Jesuit priests brought this home. In El Salvador a military stalemate and the realization that external aid was drying up convinced the parties, and most importantly the government, that a negotiated settlement was unavoidable. The new President, Alfredo Cristiani, was also more pragmatic. The military officers under him remained reluctant to give away their power, however.

In November 1989 FMLN leaders contacted the UN and met Pérez de Cuéllar's mediator, Alvaro de Soto, in December. Concerned Central American presidents also invited the UN to take a greater role and in April 1990 Pérez de Cuéllar announced that he would oversee a political settlement. Subsequently, Mexico, Colombia, Venezuela, and Spain formed the 'Group of Friends' to assist the Secretary-General's efforts. The two broad strands of the mediation concerned political issues and a ceasefire. The central obstacles appeared to concern the reform of the armed forces, a purge of human rights abusers, and the integration into the army of the FMLN, before genuine reconstruction could be achieved. However, while deadlock existed here Alvaro de Soto managed to maintain momentum by the achievement of smaller agreements on human rights and a consensus to place greater emphasis on the role of the Secretary-General and his representative.

It was no coincidence that the flexibility on the part of the El Salvadoran government correlated with pressure and a reduction of aid from the US, its chief external sponsor. The US public, Congress, the European Community, the Group of Friends, and Central American presidents had been urging the US to press Cristiani. It is interesting to observe how a Cold War patron–client relationship could be modified to exert leverage. Similarly, Soviet pressure and an agreement between the superpowers to push the 'endgame' and Pérez de Cuéllar's role therein were crucial. In the Summer of 1991 Bush and Gorbachev expressed their desire for the Secretary-General to become directly involved, and on 1 August Secretary of State Baker and Soviet Foreign Minister Aleksandr Bessmertnykh wrote a letter to Pérez de Cuéllar asking him to take personal charge.[80] In accepting, Pérez de Cuéllar made it clear that he expected external actors to exert as much leverage as possible and he made specific suggestions to the US and Soviet Union, asking that the superpowers help him 'to cut the Gordian knot' facing the peace talks.[81]

With the genuine backing of the Security Council – both formally and informally – the key issues could be addressed. Council Resolution 693 was fully supportive of the Secretary-General's efforts and established a UN Observer Mission in El Salvador to monitor all agreements made. After eighteen months of inconclusive and fractured talks Pérez de Cuéllar invited Cristiani and five rebel commanders to New York in mid-September. It was here that the Secretary-General tackled the central problem: instead of the FMLN occupying positions throughout the army, which the government rejected, it would be allowed representation in the new civilian police force. In addition, the National Commission for the Consolidation of Peace, agrarian reforms, and a committee to evaluate the armed forces were agreed. This was in the context of superpower support and pressure. For example, the US pledged a multi-million dollar assistance plan to help Salvadoran soldiers return to civilian life, in return for the government's acceptance of reductions in the army. Pérez de Cuéllar had 'revitalized' the negotiations.[82]

In December 1991 the international community – the European Community, the Group of Friends, and the Central American Presidents – and the US channelled their influence into the peace process under the auspices of the Secretary-General. The parties were persuaded to return to New York in the middle of the month for an all-out effort before Pérez de Cuéllar's tenure expired at the end of the year, which would risk upsetting the momentum.

The El Salvadoran government agreed to purge the officer corps, to incorporate former rebels into the police, and to embark upon a more reformist agrarian policy. The FMLN dropped its demands for broader socio-economic reform and participation in the army, and accepted the National Commission for the Consolidation of Peace, the Truth Commission, and the UN as the guarantor of security. Together with the constitutional, electoral and political reforms accepted earlier, an accord was reached. Pérez de Cuéllar delayed his departure from the UN to see the agreement signed, late at night on 31 December 1991: 'a dramatic farewell gift'.[83] The historical context – the reversal from a supportive patron–client scenario into superpower leverage through the decline of Cold War hostility – was central to the successful outcome. In addition, the realization of military stalemate among the parties coincided with this external pressure.[84] The conflict was clearly ripe for settlement. However, this should not detract from the creative mediation and momentum provided by Alvaro de Soto and Pérez de Cuéllar in providing an impartial framework for agreement and helping both parties to feel that they had won.

The Nicaraguan conflict and the various mediation efforts therein resembled the dynamics at work in El Salvador. During much of the 1980s US policy sought to dislodge the Sandinistas militarily through the support of contra rebels and to circumvent regional efforts at a political settlement formed around the Contadora peace process. Simultaneously, the Nicaraguan government received support from the Soviet Union. Thus, mediation efforts were frustrated until a decline in Cold War hostility, a reduction of external support for the parties, and momentum for a negotiated settlement engendered flexibility in the positions of the protagonists. The regional Contadora process – and the framework of the Esquipulas Agreement – comprised Panama, Mexico, Venezuela and Colombia and sought to separate Central American conflicts from the Cold War and thus hasten their settlement.

In late 1986 when the Contadora framework was losing steam, the Secretaries-General of the UN and the Organization of American States became informally involved.[85] The role of the UN Secretary-General primarily involved providing impartial assistance to the agreements which were brokered from 1989, and also in helping to diffuse the hostility which existed on the border between Nicaragua and Honduras, the location of many of the contra bases. Efforts by the UN, the Organization of American States and the Contadora Group resulted in a ceasefire in Nicaragua by 1988, an agreement on elections and contra demobilization in 1989, and in 1990 a national reconciliation commission.[86] Eventually, internationally supervised elections resulted in a relatively peaceful transition of power to an opposition coalition. The Esquipulas framework, and in particular the leadership of Oscar Arias, provided the main impetus to these accomplishments. However, when the timetable for elections became disrupted Pérez de Cuéllar mediated talks in New York, with the OAS Secretary-General, between Nicaraguan President Daniel Ortega and the rebels.[87] Subsequently, talks on the demobilization and the ceasefire were re-established.

In addition, the implementation and verification of many aspects of the peace process were performed and guaranteed by the UN and its Secretary-General. The establishment of the UN Observer Mission to verify the electoral process in Nicaragua, and the UN Observer Group in Central America (ONUCA) were central to post-conflict reconstruction, and its creation and implementation were under the operational auspices of the Secretary-General.[88] Furthermore, the following year the Council mandated, upon the Secretary-General's suggestion, an expansion of the tasks of ONUCA to undertake the 'complete demobilization of the Nicaraguan resistance'.[89] In common with other cases, Central America was interesting in the depth of international involvement and the extent to which the Secretary-General had interaction with non-state actors.

Lebanon

For much of the 1980s Lebanon's travails continued whilst the UN remained on the sidelines. As was the case in the 1970s, the country suffered from a number of indigenous conflicts exacerbated by regional and international struggles. The President of Lebanon wrote, 'we are a nation of minorities.'[90] The conflict within this environment was exploited by the PLO in its war against Israel. Attacks and reprisals continued, until PLO provocation became unacceptable. Again, Israel invaded Lebanon, seeking to rout the PLO bases and re-establish a buffer between Israeli settlements and hostile forces north of the border. The 'multinational force' of US, French, Italian, and later British contingents, designed to facilitate the withdrawal of Israeli troops, seemingly epitomized the 'crisis of multilateralism' and US illusions of global unilateralism. There was little support by the Reagan administration for UN mediation efforts in this area, and sometimes actual competition.[91] The outright hostility of the Israeli government towards the Organization continued to rule out a substantive UN role, and continued to help undermine the UN Interim Force in Lebanon, despite the Council's ruling that the Secretary-General 'undertake all possible efforts' to encourage the cessation of the conflict.[92]

At a press conference in September 1982 Pérez de Cuéllar suggested that the UN Interim Force in Lebanon could reach Beirut in a short time,[93] and in early 1984 there were calls for a replacement of the multinational force by UN peacekeepers. Again, Pérez de Cuéllar noted that the UN was 'available and ready'.[94] The invasion of Lebanon, brushing aside as it did UNIFIL, was a blow to the UN at a difficult time. As the Secretary-General noted, 'the credibility both of the United Nations and of peace-keeping operations as such is severely shaken.'[95] The multinational force was, firstly, a challenge to the UN, and after massive American losses, a humiliation to the West. Pérez de Cuéllar could only express frustration, although he undertook measures to coordinate the activities of humanitarian agencies to help alleviate suffering.[96]

In UNIFIL the Secretary-General was saddled with the

problems which resulted from its flawed terms of reference of 1978, and the Israeli invasion of 1982. The mandate remained as unrealistic as ever, because of the presence of PLO, Syrian and Israeli forces or client forces. UNIFIL did not represent an uninterrupted cordon along the Lebanese border. It appears that the initial rush and political pressure upon Waldheim to deploy left a legacy of political and organizational problems to his successor. The Secretary-General's efforts in the 1980s – personally and through Brian Urquhart and then Marrack Goulding – to bring peace to southern Lebanon and 'restore' Lebanese authority were largely frustrated.

However, at a more local level opportunities to quell small-scale fighting, facilitate communication, and protect the local population were fulfilled to an impressive extent.[97] The UN continued to communicate with senior representatives of the principal parties, achieving minor agreements in an exercise of conflict management. The Secretary-General continued the interaction with the troop-contributing countries.[98] This involved the precarious management of finances and the difficulties inherent in maintaining a viable force with an operation which had a particularly hazardous reputation. The Secretary-General's Office continued to issue frank and sometimes outspoken public reports on the status and frustrations of UNIFIL, thereby exerting at least some leverage upon the parties. In addition, Pérez de Cuéllar frequently suggested methods of improving the UN's performance and extending its mandate, most notably in 1982 and 1984 when he suggested that UNIFIL extend north to Beirut to assist in the withdrawal of Israeli and multinational force troops. While this was politically unrealistic, it demonstrated the Secretary-General's wish to involve the UN substantively in an area where it was formerly something of a badly supported pawn.

At the operational peacekeeping level the Secretary-General was able to maintain some authority in trying circumstances and within a difficult mandate. This at least helped to keep UNIFIL operational, when troop-contributing countries might otherwise have withdrawn their support.

Cambodia

The October 1991 Agreements on the Comprehensive Political Settlement of the Cambodian Conflict were the result of a convergence of interests of the Security Council and the diplomatic support of actors who had previously prolonged the conflict through the sponsorship of the warring factions. Superpower, regional and Cambodian actors had become war weary – for humanitarian, financial or military reasons – and more pragmatic, accepting the UN to facilitate the transition of the country.

There were a number of layers of patron–client support for the factions in Cambodia; it was indeed a kind of 'Southeast Asian Lebanon'.[99] Anti-Vietnamese opposition groups were sponsored by Thailand, China, and a number of Western states. The Vietnamese-supported government, since 1979, was dependent upon Vietnam which was in turn supported by the Soviet Union. The peace process, of which Pérez de Cuéllar played a significant part, therefore had to satisfy the Cambodian factions but also their external patrons if it was to be lasting. For the Office of Secretary-General, 'his role as a neutral good officer was affected by a history of resolutions passed by the political organs.'[100] Indeed, the General Assembly continued to seat opposition factions, including the Khmer Rouge, and frequently demanded Vietnamese withdrawal. Subsequently, the Secretary-General had to assert some independence from the deliberative organs – *à la* 'Peking Formula' – in order to gain the confidence of the parties. His efforts were clearly in conjunction with the weight of international pressure behind the peace process, and perhaps the image that the UN had in some ways cleansed itself from the overtly politicized and biased stances of the past.

In early 1985 Pérez de Cuéllar visited the region, conferring with the influential Association of South East Asian Nations and Vietnam.[101] Although they received his overtures seriously, they still had faith in the military option and there was external support to encourage this thinking. Nevertheless, the Secretary-General outlined a number of elements which seemed to be generally acceptable as a basis for a settlement. Vietnam would not consider any settlement in which the Khmer Rouge would have a role, and China refused to negotiate. Crucially, the external parties which could encourage a more cooperative attitude through diplomatic and material pressure – primarily the Permanent Five – were still entrenched in a geopolitical and ideological struggle in that and other areas. The Secretaryship-General was stymied.

By 1988 regional and international developments engendered flexibility among the parties external to Cambodia, and this forced the warring parties to adopt a more cooperative attitude. Vietnam was looking for an end to its expensive occupation of Cambodia, and the Soviet Union was seeking to reduce its commitment to Vietnam.

In 1990 the major UN states began to put their weight behind the peace process and an enhanced UN peacemaking role. Moreover, the Permanent Five were particularly supportive of an initiative by the Australian Foreign Minister designed to overcome the power-sharing stalemate. The UN would assume responsibility for the administration of Cambodia – with the parties' consent – between the ceasefire and election, and the Council asked the Secretary-General to continue 'preparatory studies' regarding the form this would take.[102] In Paris on 23 October 1991 the accord was signed, and the Security Council endorsed it on 31 October. This involved a verified withdrawal of foreign forces, mine clearance, the disarmament and cantonment of factions, a UN administration to organize elections, ensure law and order, the repatriation of refugees, and the introduction of a rehabilitation and reconstruction programme.[103]

The peacekeeping mission was, as Pérez de Cuéllar observed, 'probably the most important and most complex in the history of the United Nations'.[104] Indeed, this was an example of what Boutros-Ghali would later describe as post-conflict peacebuilding: a wide involvement of international agencies to build a lasting peace.[105]

Moreover, within the context of this internal peace operation the Security Council had authorized the Secretary-General to prepare a plan for the UN mandate, and then to deploy UNTAC 'as rapidly as ... possible' in accordance with 'his plan'.[106] The UN was involved in a seemingly unprecedented situation at the implementation stage, exercising authority and undertaking tasks normally the responsibility of sovereign states. By extension, the Secretary-General, as executive head of such an operation, was on new ground. In combination with cases such as Central America, Namibia and Mozambique, this idea is given more support. The Secretary-General exercised his operative peacekeeping role to a qualitative and quantitative extent not experienced before 1988.

Iraq–Kuwait

The Iraqi invasion of Kuwait, an attack by one state upon another, was characteristic of the type of conflict that the United Nations was established to deter and deal with. It is likely that such interstate war will continue to be a rarity compared to the trend of increasing civil war, state failure, and fragmentation. Therefore, it may be inappropriate to place too much emphasis on one case.

However, this case is significant in indicating possible trends in the Office of Secretary-General when the Security Council is in consent or under the will of activist states. Under such conditions, although the quantitative burden of the Office may flourish, the room for manoeuvre and quasi-independence of the Secretaryship-General may decrease in critical situations. This can be seen as a corollary of the Cold War context, when the Office often gleaned room for manoeuvre – with the informal support or acquiescence of major states – as a result of the inactivity of the deliberative organs.

In the case of the Iraq–Kuwait crisis it was the agenda of the US, and to a lesser extent Britain, rather than the collectivity of the Council, which lay at the heart of Pérez de Cuéllar's marginalized status and the dominance of the activist states over the UN. This was indicated early on by the manner in which the US and Britain had maintained the right to act independently under Article 51 of the Charter and customary international law.[107] In addition, the galvanized Security Council – under the coaxing of the United States – was resolute that the UN live up to this post-Cold War test case. The Security Council was in consensus when the key resolutions were adopted and these were explicit in their demand for Iraqi withdrawal. No independent room for manoeuvre existed for the Secretary-General. In fact, the activist states avoided any commitment to mediation which might be implied by the involvement of the Secretary-General.

Nevertheless, in late August 1990 Pérez de Cuéllar claimed to be acting on his own initiative when he met Iraqi Foreign Minister Tariq Aziz in Jordan.[108] The Secretary-General was attempting to persuade Iraq to release the remaining Western hostages and to convince Aziz that the Council was serious. The experience of a decade earlier, when the West essentially had acquiesced in the face of Iraqi aggression, could not have helped. Pérez de Cuéllar's personal relationship with Aziz was reasonably good. However, the Secretary-General notably announced that his mission was defined by the parameters of the Council resolutions.[109] The resolution of 29 October asked him 'to make available his good offices and, as he considers appropriate, to pursue and undertake diplomatic efforts in order to reach a peaceful solution to the crisis'.[110] Pérez de Cuéllar was actually only able to communicate the Council's demand for unconditional withdrawal. There was no room for manoeuvre, no independence from the Council in the tradition of the Peking formula. This was without doubt a source of frustration to Pérez de Cuéllar,[111] who might have had greater success in providing some form of face-saving mechanism for Iraqi withdrawal if given more authority.

Pérez de Cuéllar's second trip was even less productive for the settlement of the dispute and for the development of the Office of Secretary-General. After a number of mediation efforts by the Arab group, France, Russia and the US, there had been a 'pause of goodwill' leading to the 15 January deadline for final diplomatic efforts, but the US was not particularly comfortable with independent efforts which threatened to split the consensus. It was a sign of Saddam Hussein's lack of judgement that he remained defiant, for any meaningful concession might have postponed the use of allied force. Despite the 'pause of goodwill' in January, the Bush administration determined to remain dominant. Secretary of State James Baker failed to budge Aziz in Geneva, and the latter appeared not to have any authority to make concessions.[112] It was only after this failure and a telephone call by Baker that Pérez de Cuéllar was prompted to 'go through the motions' again. He spoke with Bush by telephone and at Camp David, and there was a strong feeling that he represented the last chance for peace. Theoretically, he still represented the hope that Iraq might accept some form of face-saving capitulation. In reality he was caught between the stalling tactics of Iraq and the desire of the activist states to be seen to have exhausted all peaceful channels. Pérez de Cuéllar stated: '[i]t is my moral duty as Secretary-General of the United Nations to do everything in order to avoid war. My only strength is a moral strength.'[113] However, he clearly could not do much. Pérez de Cuéllar might have supported a tenuous linkage to a Middle East conference *after* Iraqi withdrawal to attempt to create a possible face-saving scenario, but he did not have the authority to negotiate on this basis.[114] His mission failed and had given support to the activist argument that the international community had given Iraq every opportunity to withdraw and restore the rule of law. The restrictions were overwhelming in the context of US and Council faith in a policy of coercion rather than 'stick and carrot'.[115] Richard Falk lamented that the last-ditch visit by Pérez de Cuéllar was 'belated and half-hearted and was explicitly restricted to the Bush guidelines that deliberately provided no room whatsoever for diplomatic manoeuvre'.[116]

During the fighting the UN played even less of a role. The UN had no preparatory framework for any such military campaign, and dependence upon US forces and command and control was unavoidable. The Security Council can act quickly in certain circumstances, but cannot conduct command and control. The Secretary-General is even less disposed to be involved.

After the war, however, the wide and unprecedented involvement of UN agencies in Iraq *did* constitute a significant array of activities that the Secretary-General was involved in, albeit again under the influence of the activist states. The 'mother of all resolutions', 687, and those thereafter, established an unprecedented width and depth of activities for humanitarian, arms control, compensation, peacekeeping and boundary demarcation under Chapter VII of the Charter. At the ground level the Secretary-General's Office, by extension, was on new ground, working under mandatory Council authority. This chiefly involved organizing the modalities of the Gulf War settlement and monitoring, verifying and assessing the implementation of the terms. The Commission on weapons of mass destruction – seemingly a post-war precedent in arms control enforcement – under Rolf Ekeus involved a multitude of innovative powers and investigative methods. The humanitarian agenda in the north and south – albeit with its political dimensions[117] – was of great significance. It gave rise to a number of organizational changes at the UN, such as the creation of the Department of Humanitarian Affairs, which saw an enhancement of the Secretary-General's organizational apparatus. The peacekeeping operation likewise broke new ground in including military observers from the Permanent Five and having the threat of enforcement action behind it. This tripwire with teeth invested a significant level of operational authority in the Secretaryship-General.

With the implementation of the settlement of the Gulf War the Secretary-General's authority and quantitative functions were enhanced, largely by extension of the Security Council's appearance of consensus and activism. However, before Desert Storm the Office was marginalized by the activism of the Council and the concern of the leading powers to maintain control over the situation.

INSTITUTIONAL FRAMEWORK FOR THE MAINTENANCE OF PEACE AND SECURITY

The Secretaryship-General, since its inception, has developed roles in early warning, preventive diplomacy and international responses to conflict. The Office-holders constantly struggled against the constraints inherent in the organizational and political environments. These constraints had resulted in a reactive, *ad hoc*, and politicized institutional framework, which had lapsed into cynicism and almost disuse in the 1980s. Pérez de Cuéllar made an admirable attempt to fight this condition, an effort which transpired to be before its time. His celebrated first annual report urged:

> In order to avoid the Security Council becoming involved too late in critical situations, it may well be that the Secretary-General should play a more forthright role in bringing potentially dangerous situations to the attention of the Council within the general framework of Article 99 of the Charter ... I wonder if the time has not come for a more systematic approach.[118]

Although this report created a great deal of discussion, the condition of the UN at that time stifled any genuine progress in early warning and preventive action in the attitude of members. In institutional terms the creation of the Office for Research and the Collection of Information (ORCI) in March 1987 did represent an important development, although evidently superficially. Its functions were to assess global trends; to prepare country, regional and issue-related profiles; to provide early warning of developing situations requiring the Secretary-General's attention; to monitor factors related to refugee flows and comparable emergencies; and to carry out *ad hoc* research and assessments for the Secretary-General.[119] The office was practically important because it provided a support network for the Secretary-General's everyday tasks and sought to enhance his institutional early warning capability by way of information gathering and 'perceptive analysis'.[120] Given that the Secretaryship-General is endowed with an early warning function under Article 99 of the Charter, such a body was overdue. ORCI was also symbolically significant: a quasi-independent office of international civil servants performing fact-finding and analysis under the auspices of the Executive Office of the Secretary-General.

The immediate attitude of many UN members was that ORCI represented an intrusive intelligence gathering operation which was not befitting of the international bureaucracy.[121] This was in spite of the fact that ORCI worked largely upon the basis of public information and the sources from Secretariat officials around the world. Nevertheless, political support for the new office was weak. In addition, there were bureaucratic and administrative problems: 'it was not managed well, [and] it faced enormous internal opposition from people within the Secretariat who, for one reason or another, thought it was going to be an invasion of their camp.'[122] Subsequently, ORCI became a rather disheartened collection of individuals who spent their time reading the newspapers and writing the Secretary-General's speeches.[123] The fate of ORCI cannot be attributed wholly to a hostile external political environment, although ultimately one could locate the frustrations of early warning and preventive diplomacy in the context of a statist system. The systemic context is such that anything which appears remotely intrusive, especially under the auspices of the Secretary-General, is regarded with suspicion by member states.

Although the easing of Cold War tensions did encourage discussion of early warning and preventive diplomacy, it is still too early to judge if this can overcome the systemic obstacles that exist. In the case of Iraq–Kuwait the Office of Secretary-General should have had access to information which would have enabled preventive action. For practical and political reasons this was an organizational failure.[124] Evidence has indicated that Pérez de Cuéllar was aware of the movement of Iraqi troops toward the Kuwaiti border prior to the invasion, yet discreet approaches to Arab representatives did not shed much light on the situation. However, at that point the US and Russia held satellite photographs which indicated massive forces. Pérez de Cuéllar believes that if he had known this he would have brought the threatening situation to the Council, possibly through the formal use of Article 99, and that might well have dissuaded Iraq from a dangerous course of action. A Council challenge to Iraq *before* it had actually invaded Kuwait would have given Saddam Hussein cause for pause. Thus, if the Secretary-General had access to an effective early warning and analysis office, he might have helped prevent the Gulf War. Yet, as one veteran UN employee suggested after working under five Secretaries-General, 'anything that makes the Secretary-General either more influential or more independent, governments will resent'.[125]

CONCLUSION

The first half of Pérez de Cuéllar's tenure reflected the frustrations and constraints which were a result of the condition of the Organization. In turn, this 'crisis of multilateralism' was a reflection of historic trends which coalesced around an upsurge of Cold War hostility and Third World discontent and militancy. Major actors – and most notably the US – circumvented the UN at critical stages, and proxy Cold War confrontations were impervious to constructive intervention by the UN. Financial crises and disillusionment within and outside the UN compounded the Organization's despair. Subsequently, the Office of Secretary-General was stymied both as a result of the ill-will and lack of support invested by the major members towards the UN in general, and the involvement of Security Council members in many of the regional conflicts and hence their obstruction to a substantive UN involvement. The institutional improvements urged by Pérez de Cuéllar for maintaining peace and security and early warning went largely unheeded; the innovative Office for Research and the Collection of Information foundered under member states' suspicions and lack of support. Nevertheless, the intervention of the Secretary-General in cases such as the *Rainbow Warrior* arbitration and the Falklands crisis illustrated the inherent utility of the Secretaryship-General in spite of a difficult political climate in Pérez de Cuéllar's first tenure. Similarly, the attempts by the Office at conflict management during the Iran–Iraq war indicated the opportunities possible with a skilled Secretary-General.

From 1987 the international political tide changed and the Organization's activities flourished, especially in the settlement of conflict. The Permanent Members of the Security Council had rediscovered the utility of the UN and appeared to support the Organization in the areas of international peace and security. Former Cold War patron–client relationships between warring parties and their superpower sponsors underwent an important transformation with the decline of Cold War hostility. In areas such as Central America, Afghanistan, Iran-Iraq, Western Sahara and Cambodia, this global change coincided with a local movement towards political settlement on the part of the combatants. The new climate of cooperation was manifested in the Security Council with a consensus among the Permanent Five and the application of collective leverage upon these conflicts in tandem with, and often under the auspices of, the Secretary-General. Thus, from a position of frustration and in some cases even irrelevance until 1986–7, the Secretaryship-General came to represent an organ of authority and facilitation in the roles of creative mediation, face-saving, and facilitation. In the context of the historical and external factors which came to bear upon the Secretaryship-General, one must also note the personality factor. Throughout his tenures Pérez de Cuéllar had always been very careful never to sour his relationship with the Permanent Members of the Council.[126] This was an acceptance of political realities – in contrast perhaps to Trygve Lie – which some may have regarded as over-compliance until 1987. However, when the time came Pérez de Cuéllar was reprieved by the involvement he played in conflict settlement, and this undoubtedly derived in large part from the confidence and trust built up over the years.[127]

In cases such as Iran–Iraq and Central America the Secretary-General informally urged the Council to work in unison with him and on an informal basis in a manner rare before 1987. Clearly the activism of the Security Council, and the determination of the Secretary-General to be involved as a vanguard of the new climate of consensus, was resulting in a quantitative and possibly qualitative expansion of the Secretaryship-General's roles. In the window of opportunity between 1987 and 1992, the Secretary-General was a useful instrument through which a superficially united Security Council could bring to an end some of the residual conflicts of the Cold War. It is interesting therefore that the source of Pérez de Cuéllar's earlier marginalization – superpower involvement – was later to pave the way to his activism. As he recalled, '[t]he necessary objective was, as it will continue to be, to mobilize the constructive efforts of the major powers toward an identified goal and to make known to them the particular contribution the United Nations could offer in bringing a solution. The contribution in each case was indispensable.'[128]

During this process another important feature was the extent to which the Secretary-General communicated and interacted with non-state actors with the support of the Security Council. Moreover, in a number of peacemaking efforts – such as El Salvador and Afghanistan – the superpowers explicitly called upon the Secretary-General to increase his involvement, and put their weight behind him. For the Soviet Union, this was a departure from more than forty years of attitude and practice towards the international Secretariat. Another notable characteristic of the Council's support of the Secretary-General in the 1987–92 period was that it was positive and cooperative, in tandem with Pérez de Cuéllar and in the context of an apparent resurgence of internationalism. In the past, numerous examples saw the Secretary-General acting in the face of Council paralysis and ill-will, or fulfilling a need for a cynical trade-off between Council members, whose support of the Office was negative or acquiescent. In contrast, it has been suggested that Central America was the first time in history that the US allowed the UN to take the lead through the Secretaryship-General.[129] Pérez de Cuéllar's tenures have been a case study of how activism need not mean confrontation.

Many of the cases presented here demonstrate what could be achieved when the Secretary-General and a superficially united Security Council work together. However, this period saw the Office of Secretary-General blossom in clearing the residue of the Cold War. This mode of operation was not to continue in the patterns of conflict which emerged in the 1990s in the context of state failure, civil war, fragmentation and ethnic strife, especially when the leading Council members did not perceive that they had an interest. In spite of a plethora of Council resolutions under – or alluding to – Chapter VII, earlier optimism has been undermined and the Secretaryship-General often thrown into disarray by lack of political will and support, financial constraints, isolationist tendencies, and splits within the Council. To a large degree the celebrated latter years of Pérez de Cuéllar represented the post-Cold War honeymoon and not the multilateral issues and problems of the international civil service in the post-Cold War world. Nevertheless, Pérez de Cuéllar's final achievements indicated the utility of his

Office when the Security Council works on the basis of coherence in issues it has an interest in.

6   Boutros Boutros-Ghali

The post-Cold War Secretaryship-General has reflected a number of constraints and opportunities. There is an air of transition at the UN as the Organization adjusts to the systemic changes and challenges of international relations, and especially the wider concept of peace and security. The complexion of global economic and political-military power likewise remains in transition. In addition, the UN continues to be buffeted by uncertainty both in terms of its role and the support of its chief sponsors. In the context of this, a post-Cold War 'model' of the Office of Secretary-General may be illusory as it continues to reflect a tumultuous international environment. In fact, there has been a multifaceted and, perhaps, paradoxical evolution of the Secretaryship-General. Thus, while there have been opportunities for the Office as an extension of the blossoming of UN activity, the Secretaryship-General has encountered constraints, frustration and precariousness. These trends will be examined in the next two chapters. The following are the themes which were reflected in the Secretaryship-General under Boutros-Ghali's tenure:

- The UN as an instrument of activist states and a directorate within the Security Council. The predominance, although not necessarily leadership, of the US.
- The absence of direction of the international community and an element of transition.
- The quantitative increase of the Secretaryship-General's roles.
- The redefinition and expansion of UN roles, especially into the domestic context. Experimentation in UN peace operations followed by caution from 1993, especially in the face of state failure, civil war, and fragmentation. The qualitative expansion of the Secretaryship-General as a result of the expansion of new areas of activity, especially within the domestic context.

110

- The Secretaryship-General in the context of UN over-load and financial crisis.
- The Secretaryship-General in relation to the explosion of resolutions alluding to, or under, Chapter VII, and resolutions sometimes not supported in practice.
- The movement of peace operations and multilateralism towards the use of force or coercion.
- UN support for, or legitimization of, regional peace-keeping.
- Volatility of members' support for UN operations, fatigue in multilateralism, and political prioritization in Security Council's decision-making and resource allocation.
- The lack of Great Power interest from many UN involvements, in contrast to the successes of 1988–92.
- The Secretary-General expressing frustration toward missed/lost opportunities and dashed expectations; attempting to wield declaratory leverage to lead the Organization into a wider conception of governance and wider responsibilities, and the implications of this upon the classical roles.

Boutros-Ghali was in many ways suited to an environment which offered the UN and the Secretaryship-General opportunities to increase their activity in international peace and security. The post-Cold War period, at least initially, was such that the personality of the incumbent could help to shape the post-Cold War model of the Secretaryship-General. The forthright, outspoken, and perhaps confrontational style of Boutros-Ghali certainly helped to stamp an activist demeanour upon the Office, and some within the Secretariat applaud this effort and think it was necessary and unavoidable.[1] Others felt that Boutros-Ghali was something of a loose cannon, high-handed, distant, aristocratic and arrogant toward his staff.[2] Despite the overbearing methods employed by the US – and spearheaded by Ambassador Albright – to undermine Boutros-Ghali's reappointment campaign, countless Secretariat staff welcomed his replacement by Kofi Annan, a thirty-year veteran of the UN and considered to be much more accessible. In fact, many of Boutros-Ghali's colleagues were sceptical of his vision of 'global leadership after the Cold War', so it is unsurprising that the US was not won over. At a practical level, Boutros-Ghali was known to have grated on the sensibilities of powerful UN members by disregarding certain procedural courtesies and asserting unreserved opinions.

Boutros-Ghali was particularly outspoken in the area of peace and security, employing public declaratory leverage and the Office's inherent 'charismatic capacity'[3] to push political leaders and the Security Council. Given an almost free hand in 1992 to publish innovative recommendations on preventive diplomacy, peacemaking and peacekeeping, the Secretary-General since then continued to make proposals in the light of developments. Perhaps Boutros-Ghali's most thoughtful linkage of the UN with international political trends was reflected in his January 1996 Oxford University speech. There he presented the seemingly opposing forces of globalization and fragmentation as a dialectic which the Organization must seek to help reconcile and in which the Secretary-General is a critical actor.[4] The second dialectic he identified relates to the disparity between increasing demands and resources. Yet it is indicative of the vulnerability of the post-Cold War Secretaryship-General that while some UN commentators believed that Boutros-Ghali had been too outspoken in the field of peace and security, others have argued that he had become morally bankrupt through his avoidance of justice and indifference towards human suffering.[5]

Boutros-Ghali's style contributed to the activist stances of his Office, although the environment has allowed and encouraged this. One must judge his performance in the context of the constraints and opportunities which exist within the political framework. One commentator suggested that Boutros-Ghali has been the 'most stubbornly independent' Secretary-General and that he has made the Office 'an international player in a way that has not been seen since the days of the Congo crisis'.[6] The other side of this is the argument that he overstepped his authority, forcing the hand of governments in support of unrealistic UN operations.[7] Whether Boutros-Ghali could have had such an impact is open to question.

THE GENERAL POLITICAL ENVIRONMENT: FROM THE NEW ERA TO UNCERTAINTY

In the international and organizational climate of optimism and expectation in 1992, there had been reason to believe that an historical juncture had occurred in the evolution of multilateralism. Cooperation had breathed new life into the UN, and the leadership of the Security Council had underscored conflict settlement between 1988 and 1992. This process culminated in the historic Security Council Summit meeting of January 1992. This symbolized the New World Order ethos which was to give way to disillusionment and uncertainty in the following years.

After major upheavals in international relations, and particularly those which involve conflict followed by systemic change, there is a tendency for the leading actors to agree to certain norms and structures through which to maintain stability and standards of conduct. The Treaty of Westphalia of 1648, the Congress of 1815, the Versailles Treaty of 1919, and the territorial agreements together with the UN Charter of 1944–5, reflected this concept. Although the Cold War was not directly comparable to these earlier times, it did represent a prolonged conflict followed by systemic upheaval against the backdrop of normative values. The values which underpinned the New World Order were economic and political liberalism, democracy, state territorial integrity, commitment to the peaceful settlement of disputes and international organization, and respect for human rights. In light of the 'End of History' thesis and the liberal basis, the New World Order was an attempt to transpose and reassert Western enlightenment themes on to the rest of the world in the belief, or hope, that the post-Cold War Order was universal. The structure of the new order was believed to be that of US leadership in cooperation with like-minded middle powers through the legitimization and functional framework of the United Nations.

The credibility of UN diplomacy was reborn in the late 1980s as the superpowers sought to facilitate the settlement of conflicts which they had directly or indirectly supported. The reversal of Iraqi aggression against Kuwait, although dominated by the US and to a lesser extent Britain, also

bolstered the UN because the operation, in theory, represented collective security. The theme pushed by the activist
states was that Desert Shield and Desert Storm represented
mobilization on the part of the international community to
uphold shared values and accepted norms of behaviour:
exactly the process of collective security that the UN and the
League of Nations before it were established to uphold. The
directorate of the Permanent Members continued its cohesion into the 1990s, at least superficially. In fact, as a
consequence of this, the wider UN membership requested
greater transparency and representation from the Council.

Debate existed regarding the nature of the New World
Order, around the poles of the cautious neo-realists and the
liberal internationalists. While the former more pessimistic
school of thought had its eminent advocates,[8] in the immediate post-Cold War honeymoon the popular feeling was of
a new era of cooperation in international relations and at
the UN. Moreover, when it became clear that the new era
was likely to be one of great instability the early hopes were
that the UN would adapt to the new challenges. These
included the evolving theoretical basis of security in its
broadest meaning. Boutros-Ghali wrote of 'the start of a new
phase in the history of the Organization', and of a 'new
chapter in history'.[9]

The Secretary-General was certainly given reason for optimism in the Security Council Summit Meeting of 31 January
1992, a symbol of liberal internationalist rhetoric which was
subsequently not fully borne out by the behaviour of the
leading UN members. Security Council President John
Major echoed the other participants' sentiments in observing the 'common purpose' of the Council and its
commitment 'to reinforce collective security and to maintain
international peace and security'.[10] He pledged to the new
Secretary-General the Council's 'full backing' in his 'vital
role'. The Declaration of the Security Council invited
Boutros-Ghali to prepare recommendations on ways to
strengthen and make more efficient preventive diplomacy,
peacekeeping and peacemaking. Thus, the process of
redefining and evaluating the machinery of peace and security was set in motion in what, in hindsight, was an
over-optimistic climate. The Summit submerged itself in the

New World Order ideas of universalism, democratization, justice and international society ideals of collective security without a full realization of the cost or practical problems involved. It was in this context that Boutros-Ghali began his tenure, in many respects on false premises. The Council's unequivocal statements of support to the UN and for an expanded role of the Secretary-General puts Boutros-Ghali's later outbursts of frustration into perspective.

Throughout 1992 there was a great deal of verbal support for the improvement of instruments of preventive diplomacy and the settlement of conflict, coalescing around the *Agenda for Peace* process. Simultaneously, the Security Council was adopting a number of resolutions committing the international community to deeper and wider peace operations in 'domestic' conflicts or peace settlements. Thus, the Organization was attempting to reassess its roles at the same time as experimenting in ever more ambitious activities. The misunderstanding was prevalent in 1992 that the deficiencies of the Organization during the Cold War emanated primarily from the Council vetoes – 279 of them – and so as a corollary the absence of vetoes in the post-Cold War era would enable the UN to address the ills of the world. This impression was bolstered by the successful UN involvement in the settlement of conflict in Iran–Iraq, Namibia–Angola, and Central America and in facilitating the Soviet withdrawal from Afghanistan, in the 1988–92 period. However, the buoyancy of 1992 was mistakenly based on the successful 1988–92 period, when the UN facilitated the settlement of a number of regional conflicts in which the superpowers had been involved; the US and Soviet Union had an interest in supporting the UN in its activities then. It was a mistake to believe this level of support would continue. Again, Boutros-Ghali began his tenure on false premises.

At the beginning of Boutros-Ghali's tenure, the Organization was involved in unprecedented levels of activity quantitatively and, perhaps, qualitatively. The clearest indication was the burgeoning agenda of domestic peace-keeping, peacemaking and peacebuilding, involving humanitarian assistance, civil administration, mediation and security. This contrasted pointedly with the classical inter-state military observation of the past. There was almost an unconscious acceptance on the part of many governments and the UN Secretariat that the UN could address any manner of security issue, and that the methods and guidelines of previous UN operations were sufficient. In 1992 a choice confronted the international community regarding the future of the UN. It concerned the question of the UN adapting to the wider agenda of peace and security which embraces the domestic realm. While many believed that a united Security Council had made the choice to embrace this wider definition of collective security, the members in fact continued to have their own perceptions of the UN.

As the chief sponsor of the United Nations and the country which sets the tone of multilateralism in the post-Cold War world, it is necessary to give particular attention to the United States. In 1991–2 the US, under the triumphalist influence of Bush, projected an image of leadership through the UN. As the remaining superpower, many believed that US support of public services and international security structures would be renewed after something of a lapse over the preceding fifteen years. Joseph Nye, observing the need to encourage democracy, market liberalism and effective organization, suggested that the position of the US in world politics might have changed but it was still 'bound to lead'.[11] However, this internationalism was not to last long, if it really ever existed at all; according to Nye, the Bush administration 'thought and acted like Nixon, but borrowed the rhetoric of Wilson and Carter'.[12] The internationalist rhetoric was made before the realization of the burdens of leadership in the post-Cold War world.

Initially, the Clinton administration upheld the internationalist theme through its Representative to the UN, Ambassador Madeleine Albright, under the banner of 'assertive multilateralism'. This took even further the idea of US leadership in support of the UN and peace and security. It was in this context that much was expected of the United Nations and its Secretary-General in peace and security, where there was thought to be a commitment to the idea that peace and security was a collective interest and responsibility. The dubious logic within the Security Council was that '[o]ur triumph in the Gulf is testament to the United Nations mission: that security is a shared responsibility'.[13] Amidst this optimism the Security Council passed an unprecedented quantity of Resolutions in the years 1990–3, many under or alluding to Chapter VII. While an historic debate addressed the issues of the UN's roles and structures the Organization was already entering the fray of the new era.

As a result of experimentation, overreach and even crisis in certain peace operations, and an evidently endless list of cases which warranted UN attention, the fortunes of the UN and Boutros-Ghali began to turn in 1993. Earlier pledges of support by many members were forgotten, as the cost – in human and material terms – of the 'new' agenda was realized. The limitations of the UN were learned the hard way, most pointedly in Bosnia and Somalia. Ideas of nation-building were abandoned and an environment of cautious realism and multilateral fatigue subsequently pervaded the Organization. From October 1993 the US Congress began to cut back its support to the UN. A wave of public opinion and Republican attacks were directed against the UN, and when the Republicans took Congress, they immediately embarked upon further legislation. A mixture of unilateralism and, to a lesser degree, neo-isolationism underpinned the 'America First' and 'Contract with America' policy guidelines. Republican Bob Dole, although a believer in US leadership and not an isolationist, promised that 'when we recapture the White House, no American boys are going to be serving under the command of Field-Marshal Boutros Boutros-Ghali'.[14] The Republican majority in Congress backed their words with various financial sanctions and by the beginning of 1996 the Secretary-General announced that the Organization was on 'the edge of insolvency'.[15] In response to Boutros-Ghali's proposal of modest levies on certain transactions to help address the financial crisis and his desire for the UN to operate on a 'secure and steady independent financial foundation',[16] all the political parties in the US vied to challenge the idea; presidential candidate Bob Dole immediately introduced the 'Prohibition of United Nations Taxation Act' in January.[17]

Not so long after Bush had proclaimed the New World

Order and commitment to the UN 'mission', many politicians in the US and the West had become acutely wary of
collective internationalism as the 'slippery slope'.[18] The
manner in which many US politicians blamed the UN falsely
for the US casualties in Somalia in October 1993 was typical
of this attitude, put into context as 'irresponsible internationalism', in the words of Dole.[19] Perhaps unsurprisingly,
the Heritage Foundation called for 'no more Somalias' and
Kissinger warned of a 'recipe for chaos' in US involvement
in hazardous situations on the basis of vague ideas of
humanitarianism and collective internationalism.[20] The
Clinton administration also reflected the trend. The starkest
example of this was Presidential Policy Directive 25 of 1994,
which imposed severe constraints on the use of US soldiers
in UN operations.[21] It stated that such a use must be tied to
the national interest, risks must be acceptable, an end-point
for US participation must be identified, and public and
Congressional support must exist. The waning of political
and material support and commitment for UN peace operations has also manifested itself in the atmosphere of the
Security Council. In the context of this new realism,
Boutros-Ghali's statements became less optimistic. In a
speech in Vienna in March 1995 Boutros-Ghali spoke of
'hard decisions': after Somalia, 'we have learned a lesson:
how and when to withdraw.'[22]

A common theme is that the US has washed its hands of
the responsibility of leadership.[23] This is unlikely as long as
the US perceives that it has an interest in maintaining stability and free markets and the need for an organization to
help facilitate these. However, it is natural that the concept
of interests, among all leading states, should become diffuse
and ambiguous in the absence of a simple external threat.
Despite the blurring of the distinction between domestic and
international politics and the increasing recognition of the
need to manage interdependence many states retain the
traditional 'national interest' mind-set and seemingly fail to
see the need for commitment to deeper structures of international governance. Moreover, the extent to which the
United Nations requires leadership in the post-Cold War
world is uncertain.

In his farewell address to the Assembly Boutros-Ghali

defined the phases of enthusiasm, disillusionment, and finally realism which had characterized the Organization during his tenure.[24] In the context of these twists and turns the Secretaryship-General was often in tumult. The elements of transition and experimentation have manifested themselves in a quantitative and qualitative new status for the Office, but also in paradoxical trends of activity.

INSTITUTIONAL AND ATTITUDINAL FRAMEWORK FOR CONFLICT PREVENTION, MANAGEMENT AND SETTLEMENT

In 1992 Boutros-Ghali was the beneficiary of a wave of enthusiasm for collective internationalism and also an apparent consensus that the peace and security mechanisms of the UN could and should be improved under him. The increased activity of the Organization in election monitoring, human rights observance, the repatriation of refugees and displaced persons, non-military and domestic sources of instability, and an evolving conception of state sovereignty, were all manifestations of a 'new era' of multilateralism. The Security Council observed changes in state structures and non-military threats to peace in the economic, social, humanitarian and ecological fields and that '[t]he absence of war and military conflicts amongst States does not in itself ensure international peace and security'.[25] The involvement of the Organization in post-conflict peacebuilding in Nicaragua, El Salvador and Cambodia was already supporting these sentiments. The Council Summit pledged its commitment to the Secretary-General and invited him to recommend ways of strengthening the UN's capacity for preventive diplomacy, peacekeeping and peacemaking. This represented a seemingly historic juncture for the Secretaryship-General after years of struggle to win prerogatives in pursuance of peace and security: Boutros-Ghali was shown the green light to codify and expand the Secretariat's duties, which culminated in the publication of *An Agenda for Peace*.

The Secretary-General established a 'task force' of senior academics and Secretariat staff for this task. He had to balance a number of interests. Firstly, the Western desire for more effective multilateral instruments through which to maintain their perception of order. As a counter to this, there were practical, legal, financial and political constraints which are inherent in an intergovernmental organizational structure. Finally, there was wariness within the non-Western world towards a Western or Permanent Five directorate and a trend of intrusiveness in new attitudes to international peace and security. In light of the competing interests – and the nature of bureaucracy – it is not surprising that the final product was a compromise which reflected both old and new thinking, and a hint of contradiction.

The main recommendations of *An Agenda for Peace*, with particular reference to the Secretary-General, are worth recalling. The document urges 'an increased resort to fact finding ... either by the Secretary-General, to enable him to meet his responsibilities under the Charter, including Article 99' or by the Security Council or General Assembly (paragraph 25(a)). The deliberative organs should send a fact-finding mission under their immediate authority 'or may invite the Secretary-General to take the necessary steps' (paragraph 25(c)). With respect to early warning he suggested that there is a need to 'strengthen arrangements in such a manner that information ... can be synthesized with political indicators to assess whether a threat to peace exists and to analyze what action might be taken by the United Nations to alleviate it. The analysis and recommendations for preventive action that emerge will be made available by me, as appropriate, to the Security Council and other United Nations organs' (paragraph 26). He also recommended that a 'reinvigorated and restructured' Economic and Social Council provide reports on developments which might threaten international security (paragraphs 26–27), and a greater role for regional organizations in maintaining peace (paragraph 64).

An interesting and contentious recommendation was that of preventive deployment. He suggested that a UN presence could be deployed to remove the likelihood of hostilities between two consenting countries (paragraph 31) and that in cases where one country fears attack, the Security Council should consider preventive deployment on one side of the border with the consent of only the requesting country (paragraph 32). This idea had an early endorsement with the preventive deployment in Macedonia, dispatched without the consent of Serbia.[26] As another form of prevention, the Secretary-General recommended the policy of a UN demilitarized zone on both sides of a border with the consent of both parties (paragraph 33), which also points to an increasingly interventionist attitude.

In the area of peacemaking the Secretary-General highlighted a point of legal interest and recommended that his Office be authorized, under Article 96(2) of the Charter, to take advantage of the advisory competence of the World Court and that all UN organs make use of this more frequently (paragraph 38). In addition, he recommended that all members accept the general jurisdiction of the International Court of Justice, without reservation, by the end of the year 2000 (paragraph 39). The Secretary-General recommended an improvement in the inter-agency mechanism through which the Security Council, General Assembly or Secretary-General can mobilize the resources necessary for 'positive leverage' upon disputes (paragraph 40). When sanctions are required to exert pressure, the Secretary-General recommended that countries with special economic difficulties should have these taken into consideration (paragraph 41).

The Secretary-General sought to affirm the tenets of collective security by recommending that the Council 'initiate negotiations in accordance with Article 43 ... which may be augmented if necessary by others in accordance with Article 47, paragraph 2 of the Charter' (paragraph 43).[27] Equally contentious was the recommendation concerning the use of 'peace-enforcement units in clearly defined circumstances ... under the authorization of the Security Council and ... under the command of the Secretary-General' (paragraph 44).

In the area of peacekeeping the Secretary-General recommended that clear standby arrangements be confirmed for the provision by UN members of personnel and equipment in advance of new operations (paragraphs 51 and 53). Similarly, the report requested the immediate establishment of a peacekeeping fund of $50 million, and more flexibility for the Secretary-General in the placing of contracts (paragraph 73). The Secretary-General also urged a review of training for peacekeeping and police contingents and improvements in Secretariat field support for peacekeeping (paragraph 52).

In the area of post-conflict peacebuilding the Secretary-General urged that concrete cooperative projects and economic, social and rehabilitation programmes be promoted (paragraphs 56, 58, 59). Other recommendations concerned the safety of personnel, the streamlining of the Secretariat and future Security Council minister-level meetings.[28]

The most contentious ideas of the *Agenda for Peace* are the recommendations to fulfil Article 43, peace-enforcement units, standby peacekeeping arrangements, and preventive deployment. However, some commentators have expressed disappointment that the *Agenda* is based on conventional thinking: it fails to embrace non-state actors as far as it might have, and it is too entrenched in statist thinking.

Meanwhile, the feeling amongst many governments was that *An Agenda for Peace* was too ambitious financially and practically, and philosophically unrealistic.[29] When the Security Council met in July 1992 to consider the document it was 'generally cautious'.[30] The developing world, embodied in the Jakarta Non-Aligned Conference, was conditioned by fears of Western hegemony and the UN being used as an instrument of interference under the guise of principles relating to human rights and democracy. They feared a dilution of sovereignty and ever-more intrusive peacekeeping techniques, while the West still failed to acknowledge its obligation to development. In addition, states committed to the classical model of peacekeeping feared its contamination by 'new techniques' such as pre-emptive deployment and peace-enforcement.

Nevertheless, Security Council statement S/24728 of 29 October 1992 encouraged members to inform the Secretary-General of their willingness to provide forces and equipment, and favoured an enhanced peacekeeping staff and operations centre. Security Council statement S/24872 of 30 November 1992 supported a wider use of fact finding as a tool of preventive diplomacy: members should provide the Secretary-General with detailed information 'on issues of concern'. In addition, the statement encouraged methods to improve information gathering and analysis in the Secretariat and the Council welcomed the Secretary-General's readiness to make use of his powers under Article 99. The General Assembly, after an extensive debate on *An Agenda for Peace*, adopted without vote an eight-point Resolution 47/120, of 18 December 1992. This also invited the Secretary-General to strengthen the UN's capacity for early warning, the collection and analysis of information, and confidence-building measures. The General Assembly established the Informal Open-Ended Working Group of the General Assembly to look at each chapter of the document. The discussions, which were noted and summarized by the Secretariat, illustrate that the vocal developing states were impressed with the emphasis on post-conflict peace-building and a wider integrated approach to peace and security, as long as it is based on economic and practical development and not on ideas of 'good governance'.[31]

The Security Council guardedly enunciated a set of guidelines for peacekeeping which appeared to reflect the evolution from the classical interpositional model. In May 1993 a statement directed that: a clear and precise mandate must exist; the consent of the government or parties still stands except in 'exceptional circumstances'; emphasis must be on impartial peaceful settlement of conflicts and political solutions so that peacekeeping is not prolonged. It also declared an inherent right of peacekeepers to use force in self defence and a right of the Council to authorize 'all means necessary' to carry out the mandate; and the readiness of the Council to take 'appropriate measures' against parties failing to comply with its decisions.[32]

As a result of the momentum of *An Agenda for Peace*, and the response to developments on the ground, there have been concrete institutional advancements. The establishment of the Department of Peace-keeping, after years of informality, affirmed the Secretary-General's authority over coordination. The establishment of the Department of Political Affairs further rationalized and codified political-military matters in the Secretariat. The existence of the Department of Humanitarian Affairs acknowledges the centrality of the human dimension in contemporary conflict and seeks to improve the Secretary-General's overview of the whole network of Specialized Agencies and NGOs in this area, long an issue of contention.[33] The Secretary-General has a military adviser, and since 1993 a twenty-four-hour operations situation room.[34] Stand-by arrangements were later defined by the Secretary-General as 'a precise understanding of the forces and other capabilities a Member State will have available at an agreed state of readiness, should it agree to contribute to a peace-keeping operation'.[35] The logic of this has yielded some pre-planning. Indeed, the Secretary-General has gone some way towards identifying the 'building blocks' necessary to set an operation in motion.[36] Similarly, General Assembly Resolution 47/217 authorized a reserve peacekeeping fund of $150 million, which exceeded the sum requested by the Secretary-General in *An Agenda for Peace*.

The rationalization of Secretariat procedures through the creation of the Departments of Political Affairs, Peacekeeping and Humanitarian Affairs, and the coordinating role of the Secretary-General, suggests an elevation of the Office. There does appear to be progress in making peace operations less *ad hoc* and in rationalizing lines of command and control. However, the case-by-case approach of most states is likely to continue; it increases their control and reduces commitment to situations which are not foreseeable. Given the hazards of contemporary UN peace operations and the domestic political repercussions of entanglements in 'messy' foreign conflicts, this is not surprising.

The institutional improvements and codification of activities in the area of peace and security have acknowledged and improved upon activities already performed by the Office of Secretary-General, and as such may finally give a framework to many of its vague roles. The coordination of fact-finding missions, for example, is now recognized as being within the Secretary-General's realm. In effect, this codification contributes significantly to the accumulation of 'normal' and accepted practice. Yet, in many situations, as one veteran employee of the Executive Office of the Secretary-General observed, 'the beauty of that Office is its flexibility; it is not systematic'.[37] Indeed, the Office has derived important functions from tacit political agreements and trade-offs, and it may not be possible to codify such discreet roles. Members may quietly accept or acquiesce in certain roles but are not comfortable with anything which resembles supranationalism in an institutional form.

Two and a half years after *An Agenda for Peace* was published the supplement of the Secretary-General highlighted, albeit diplomatically, the frustrations and constraints which existed. One can detect an element of defensiveness in his comments about command and control and the need for peace operations to function as 'an integrated whole' after the 'experience in Somalia'.[38] Regarding the availability of troops and equipment, 'problems have become steadily more serious'.[39] Similarly, equipment and adequate training are of increasing concern. From this he concluded that the UN should give serious thought to the idea of a rapid reaction force. Brian Urquhart also gave weight to the concept in his call for a third category of activity in between peacekeeping and enforcement: an 'initial rapid deployment operation', to quell random and uncontrolled violence before the situation deteriorates irreparably beyond the stage where the Security Council will wish to intervene.[40]

The Secretary-General also warned – in moderate terms – of the danger of pulling out of a post-conflict peacebuilding situation too early, a reflection of a growing tendency of impatience in the Security Council. In addition, the Secretary-General reported having difficulties in finding representatives and envoys for his burgeoning preventive and peacemaking activities. Moreover, the Secretary-General suggested that in the long term the UN should develop a capacity to deploy, direct, command and control enforcement operations itself. It seems more likely in future that the tendency will continue to involve the UN authorizing states and coalitions to undertake such activities.[41]

The *Agenda for Peace* process generated much discussion, and some institutional developments, which have had a bearing upon the status and the role of the Secretaryship-General in peace and security.[42] The more contentious proposals were not taken up, for practical and political reasons. Developments on the ground – and most conspicuously in Bosnia and Somalia – contributed to a climate which was simply not receptive to substantial commitments to standing military-political arrangements or further entanglements in large-scale costly domestic operations. It is also at the heart of the reluctance to improve the Secretary-General's coordination and control of UN political-military structures. In fact, a reaction against the Secretaryship-General's high profile status was perceptible in Boutros-Ghali's replacement by Annan. The classical case-by-case intergovernmental attitude towards peace and security issues is likely to remain. The structural constraints upon the Office will be commensurate with this.

7 The Post-Cold War Secretaryship-General

THE SECRETARY-GENERAL AND MULTIFUNCTIONAL PEACE OPERATIONS

Typically, post-Cold War UN peace operations have involved peacekeeping, peacemaking and peacebuilding. In accordance with wider conceptions of peace and human security these activities are also considered increasingly within an integrated and comprehensive approach. As the Secretary-General proclaimed, '[t]he second generation of peace-keeping is certain to involve not only military but also political, economic, social, humanitarian and environmental dimensions, all in need of a unified and integrated approach.'[1] The internationalization of human rights appears to be irreversible and pervasive. It was interesting for example that the United States warned that 'the tension and instability within Nigeria could have an effect on the peace and security of the entire region'.[2] Moreover, the International Law Commission's draft code of crimes against the peace and security of mankind reflects a much broader approach to the subject than that of traditional thinking.[3] It is also worth noting that the Permanent Five members of the Security Council declared that 'sustainable development is indispensable to the achievement and maintenance of peace and security among and between nations'.[4]

After the relative success of UN operations in facilitating the end of Cold War conflicts, the UN progressed to involvement – perhaps too hastily – in situations of domestic conflict. Certainly the language of the Secretary-General appeared to represent a departure from the classical model of the international civil service. A year after *An Agenda for Peace* was published, he wrote of 'expanded peace-keeping': '[p]rotecting the flow of relief supplies, preventive deployment, and sanctions on commerce and communications are only part of what may be involved in the future. Beyond these measures, when established rules of engagement are no longer sufficient, United Nations forces may need authorization to use force.'[5]

UN domestic involvement has its political and practical hazards, especially if fighting is still occurring. The commitment and consent of the parties may not be stable. The parties are factions rather than states, and may still be involved in a struggle: their attitude towards the UN will be a result of what they believe they can achieve from the operation, and that may change from week to week. Their cooperation will vary, their consent may be withdrawn, such as in Cambodia, the former Yugoslavia, Angola and Somalia. Factions are not subject to the international instruments of leverage and sanction that states are, so their accountability and respect for the 'blue helmet' will be less. The UN is not dealing with regular armies, as was often the case with the classical interpositional model of peacekeeping, but with irregulars and militias, and sometimes renegade and independent forces. Discipline may be weak, especially when passions are running high. The legal regime of a Status of Force Agreement may be worthless, and traditional Rules of Engagement – based on self-defence in the last resort – may not be suitable.[6] The domestic political situation is invariably less stable then that of peacekeeping at the border. Moreover, the impartiality of the UN is put under severe threat as multifaceted intervention invariably contributes something to the local power balance.[7] These factors clearly have increased the political and practical hazards of involvement in domestic conflict. Subsequently, the reassessment of UN peace operations has been reflected in a climate of caution in the Security Council which succeeded the immediate post-Cold War experimentation. In addition, there has been a shift to the idea of UN-authorized multinational forces rather than UN coordinated blue helmet forces.[8] The role of the media and improving techniques of communication in influencing the priorities of governments and the Council contribute to the air of volatility in contemporary peace operations.

After some painful experiences we can expect to see fewer, and more realistic, UN peace operations in the future. At a luncheon hosted by the Secretary-General in September

1994 the Permanent Five reflected the atmosphere of caution in proclaiming that '[a]ny new peace-keeping operation should only be established after careful study, and new commitments should not be entered into before such questions as mandate objectives, availability of forces and resources, security of United Nations personnel and duration of mission are satisfactorily answered'.[9]

The Former Yugoslavia

The UN involvement in the former Yugoslavia epitomized the complexities and the political and practical hazards of multifaceted internal peace operations. The position of the Secretary-General was commensurate with this. The Balkan situation was typical, albeit at its most volatile, of the ethno-nationalist and irredentist conflicts that the end of the Cold War has encouraged.

The response of the international community to the fragmentation of Yugoslavia was inconsistent and fragmented.[10] The involvement of the United Nations began with an attempt to support the Serb-Croat ceasefire in Croatia, and following that it widened and deepened to other areas. Efforts involved preventive activities in Macedonia, peace-making in support of a search for a negotiated settlement, an extensive range of peacekeeping tasks, efforts to bring to trial those guilty of war crimes, a major humanitarian operation, and the first steps towards reconstruction and rehabilitation.

In terms of mediation the European Community and the Secretary-General's Office initiated the London Conference on a comprehensive settlement in August 1992 and established a Steering Committee under Cyrus Vance and Lord David Owen, which became the International Conference on the former Yugoslavia in August 1994 under Owen and Thorvald Stoltenberg. The Vance-Owen peace plan for Bosnia envisaged a canton Swiss-style arrangement, but was not acceptable to the parties or the US. Thereafter the partition of Bosnia was felt likely, and the boundaries of this were to be decided on the battlefield. New impetus was provided in early 1994 by the establishment of the Contact Group of France, Germany, Russia, the US and Britain. While these countries had their own ideas and interests at stake, there was also a common interest in stability and some form of settlement. However, the divisions amongst external actors confused the peacemaking and peacekeeping activities, especially the cleavage between Russia and the West.[11]

The Contact Group reflected the need for Great Power leverage on the parties and agreement among themselves. The Secretary-General's Office was chiefly involved in communicating and facilitating this process, such as his decision for Stoltenberg to go to Belgrade and Pale in August 1994 to seek to persuade the Bosnian Serbs to accept the Contact Group's map. In addition, in July 1994 the Secretary-General gave a letter to the Security Council recommending possible options if the parties continued to reject the peace proposals. In the Autumn of 1995 the UN role in mediation was finally overtaken by the US efforts under Assistant Secretary of State Richard Holbrooke.

The Secretary-General's involvement in peacekeeping was more significant. His Office played a key role in proposing and then implementing the first ever preventive deployment under Security Council Resolution 795 in Macedonia on the borders with Albania and Serbia. Boutros-Ghali's report to the Council proposed 'monitoring and reporting any developments in the border areas which could undermine confidence and stability'.[12] The success of the force – which became the UN Preventive Deployment – in preventing a widening of the conflict in a sensitive area was a boost to the preventive emphasis of *An Agenda for Peace*.

In Bosnia the mandate of the Organization was 'to help alleviate the consequences of the conflict, particularly by providing humanitarian relief to suffering civilians, and to facilitate in various forms the efforts of all parties to reach a negotiated solution.'[13] Beginning with an effort to assist the distribution of humanitarian relief, the mandate of the UN Protection Force snowballed with the passing of endless Resolutions – many under or alluding to Chapter VII – which had little practical or political effect in the field. This credibility gap between the resolutions and the will to support them frustrated and imperilled the efforts of peacekeepers and the position of the Secretary-General. The ill-fated safe haven concept, designed to protect six chiefly

Muslim areas, was perhaps the starkest manifestation of this. The UN Protection Force in Bosnia (UNPROFOR) never had the political or military support to respond effectively to the continuous violations of the areas. As the ultimate field director, this reflected upon the Secretary-General and was an example of the Office burdened with an unrealistic mandate as a result of exaggerated expectations and short-sightedness.

The Secretary-General showed determination to be involved in policy making, and not only in its execution. For example, when the Council accepted in July 1992 a ceasefire negotiated by Lord Carrington involving the location and collection of heavy weaponry and an increase in peacekeepers, Boutros-Ghali objected on the grounds that this would be at the expense of peace operations in Africa, arguing that European regional efforts had a greater responsibility.[14] On a number of occasions developments to the UN's mandate were made on the basis of the Secretaryship-General's assessments and reports. One example was the decision to split the three main strands of the field operation into the UN Protection Force, the UN Confidence Restoration Operation, and the UN Preventive Deployment. In terms of the execution of policy the Secretary-General sought to be as closely involved as possible; in May 1994 he convened a meeting in Paris to discuss the problems and the sense of crisis faced by the peace-keeping operation.[15] As David Owen recalled, the Secretary-General 'prodded' the Security Council when he felt that it could be constructive.

In May 1995 the operation reached a turning-point and its flaws were blatant. Unable to protect civilians yet mandated to protect safe areas, the presence of lightly armed peacekeepers on the theoretical basis of impartial intervention prevented the possibility of more forceful measures because of their vulnerability to attack.[16] Some have bluntly questioned the concept of an impartial involvement, claiming that the UN made the situation worse and a long-term solution more elusive, damaging the reputation and legitimacy of the Organization.[17] The peacekeepers on the ground suffered all manner of attacks, hijacking, hostage taking, and theft. They were not respected because they were not perceived to be impartial by the parties. The safe havens, for example, were seen by the Bosnian Serbs as harbouring Bosnian government forces.

To many people the experiences of UNPROFOR have borne out Rosalyn Higgins' observation that the provision of ancillary relief and peacekeeping without a ceasefire was a 'totally unrealistic mandate' and 'doomed to failure'.[18] To the extent that this has been the case, the reputation of the Secretary-General was tainted along with that of the UN. His position certainly reflected the uncertainties and tensions of the external actors and the volatility of the combatants. On a personal level Boutros-Ghali's unpopularity with the population of Sarajevo when he visited there was symbolic of the position of the UN in not satisfying the parties and providing a scapegoat for the lack of political resolution amongst the Security Council members. Yet suggesting that Yugoslavia was a 'rich man's war' which should not absorb all the efforts of the UN displayed a cold detachment from the suffering which was quite astonishing, considering that Bosnia was the scene of the worst massacres in Europe since the Second World War. Some commentators subsequently argued that Boutros-Ghali had lost patience with Bosnia and had simply become indifferent.[19]

In May 1995 Boutros-Ghali reported that the current role of UNPROFOR was untenable and had to be changed. It was based upon the principles of peacekeeping but had come to include elements of peace-enforcement and '[n]othing is more dangerous for a peace-keeping operation than to ask it to use force when its existing composition, armament, logistic support and deployment deny it the capacity to do so.'[20] The Bosnian Serb taking of UN hostages and the overrunning of the eastern Muslim enclaves in July 1995 underlined the crisis.

Boutros-Ghali suggested that the Organization faced a defining moment in its reaction to Bosnia and set out four options: withdrawal, greater use of force, continuation as before, and a revision of the mandate to include only realistic tasks.[21] Although he presented the report as a proposal of options, Boutros-Ghali clearly advocated the fourth course of action – unless a multinational force was prepared to take over – and therefore placed his Office in a policy influencing role, not merely in an administrative peacekeeping role.

Since then, the Secretary-General advocated in essence a transition of the military command of the operation to NATO, arguing that peacekeeping should only be pursued where possible. The NATO Implementation Force under the authorization of the Security Council, subsequent to the Dayton peace accord, contrasted markedly with the UN operation it replaced, and the Secretary-General readily admitted that the UN was not suited to certain situations.

Indeed, it was interesting to observe how the UN had learnt the lessons of the immediate post-Cold War peace-keeping extravagances. At the outset of the Bosnian operation certain members of the Secretariat were quietly reluctant to become involved.[22] Three years later the Secretary-General was openly reluctant for the UN to super-vise the agreement for the return of Eastern Slavonia to Croatia and its demilitarization in accordance with the Basic Agreement between Croatia and local Serbs, arguing instead that the task would be better suited to a coalition such as NATO. He was overruled and subsequently Security Council Resolution 1043 of 31 January 1996 authorized the deploy-ment of the United Nations Transitional Administration for Eastern Slavonia, Baranja and Western Sirium. He very clearly had reservations based on painful experience.

A further development was the association of the Secretary-General with the use of NATO close air support of UN operations. In January 1994 a NATO summit gave the go-ahead for NATO support for Tuzla and Srebrenica if peacekeepers were attacked, calling upon Boutros-Ghali to draw up plans for the operation and confirming that it would act if asked by the UN.[23] Officially the decision to use force would be a result of an assessment by the UN force commander in consultation with the UN civilian chief, Yasushi Akashi, who would make a request to the Secretary-General, who in turn would request action of NATO. Both Boutros-Ghali and Akashi were cautious of air strikes – some would say too much so – and given the large French and British forces on the ground and the danger of repercus-sions against them, it is probable that the two countries had a veto on strikes. After the tragedy of the Sarajevo market-place bombardment in early 1994 air strikes were possible in defence not just of peacekeepers but also of civilian safe areas. Initially there was something of a turf-war between the UN and NATO regarding the question of the 'final say' on air strikes, and also in some senses between the Security Council and the Secretary-General. Boutros-Ghali felt that his Office could be the catalyst for air strikes under the authority of the Security Council, and apparently wrote to US Secretary of State regarding the use of air power in Bosnia.[24] However, it was not the case that Boutros-Ghali was keen to use this option; his insistence also implied that he be able to *block* airstrikes if he felt they might jeopardize other parts of the operation. This in fact occurred on a number of occasions, in opposition to the US. However, following the February 1994 market place attack the Secretary-General was proactive in asking NATO to prepare urgently for air strikes. He requested, and received, a decision by the North Atlantic Council to authorize the Commander-in-Chief of NATO's Southern Command to launch strikes at the request of the United Nations in a form of dual-key approach.[25]

NATO planes were called in to Bihac by UNPROFOR to protect UN troops in November 1994 on the same basis. However, with the escalation of air strikes in September 1995 the dual-key was overridden and NATO – in effect the US – was at the helm, in parallel with the US-dominated peace settlement process.

The reinforcement of UNPROFOR with the Rapid Reaction Force also had implications for the Secretaryship-General in the context of the use of force. In the summer of 1995, France, Britain and the Netherlands proposed to the Secretary-General the deployment of well-armed mobile units to respond to threats to UN personnel. The force of around 4500 had Council authorization and was under the existing command of the UN and the direction of the Secretary-General and his Special Representative. However, although the troops were under the UN flag, they wore national uniforms instead of blue helmets.[26]

There are a number of problems attached to the use of force in connection with a humanitarian peacekeeping mission and the Office of Secretary-General. Firstly, it is very dangerous to combine the use of force – even by theoretically separate NATO forces – with the presence of lightly armed blue helmets; it risks retribution against the latter and the humanitarian operation. This itself made air strikes few and largely symbolic until September 1995, even in the face of blatant violations of agreements and Council resolutions, thus strengthening the image of the UN as indecisive and toothless. The air strikes therefore appeared in some ways to have been an ill-thought-out response to a need to be seen to be doing 'something' and they put the Secretary-General in a difficult position. The appearance of the Secretary-General having the final decision on air support was a burden, and one which enabled the Security Council to use the Secretary-General as a scapegoat to cover their own divisions regarding the use of force.

The proximity of the Secretaryship-General to the use of force may have endowed the Office with unprecedented powers in blurring the distinction between classical peace-keeping and more coercive techniques. It may also represent a departure from the classical model of the international civil service. However, it is also possible that this trend threatens the Office's traditional roles as an impartial and innocuous third party with the potential for quasi-independent status from the Council. A former senior member of the Executive Office of the Secretary-General agreed that 'giving orders as to whether or not people should be killed' has serious implications: 'this *has* enhanced the role of the Secretary-General, but in my opinion it also threatens the role of the Secretary-General.'[27] Moreover, the Secretary-General's Office is not endowed with the tools of executing force. For the Security Council to acquiesce or allow the Secretary-General to take decisions of a military nature can often mask the Council's own indecision and thus be hazardous to the Secretaryship-General itself. Thus, it may not just be the use of force *per se* that has potentially adverse effects upon the Secretaryship-General but the use of force when poorly executed.

To counter this, one can argue that this trend does not necessarily damage the Secretary-General's traditional roles in *other* cases where an impartial third party is appropriate. While it may taint the incumbent, it does not necessarily taint the Office, although there is some continuity in the Office even if the incumbents change. Thus, to an unmeasurable degree, the Office began afresh under Kofi Annan;

he could disassociate himself from some of Boutros-Ghali's
activism. In addition, as the Organization evolves in accordance with the demands imposed upon it then so must the
Secretaryship-General if it is to retain a role. This was
argued by one officer of the UN Department of Political
Affairs: 'if the UN is to grow and change and adapt, it's part
of the process', although he accepted that the 'closer to real
power, the more dangerous it becomes, because your
actions will have consequences that are much more wide-
ranging and significant than if you were a marginal player
playing an innocuous role'.[28] A former UK Permanent
Representative to the United Nations likewise observed that
although the apparent blurring of the distinction between
classical peacekeeping and coercive techniques might
complicate the role of the Office, this is part of the job in the
modern world and the use of force should not be exaggerated.[29]

Somalia

In Somalia the Secretary-General was again in proximity to
the use of force. The Office was pushing experimental ideas
of nation-building in the belief that the Security Council –
and particularly the US – would continue to support New
World Order ideas of multilateralism and democratization,
and taking advantage of a somewhat impressionable US
foreign policy at a transitional stage. Nevertheless, this
episode displayed a policy-influencing, almost a policy-
making, role for the Secretary-General in the widening and
deepening of the UN involvement, and a qualitatively
unprecedented status for the Office in proposing and implementing precarious peace enforcement techniques. Such
was the key position of Boutros-Ghali in the widening of
involvement that when the US and UN policy unravelled in
October 1993, he became an automatic target of disillusionment and criticism.

With the fall of Mohamed Siad Barre in January 1991
vying clans and drought wrought chaos and suffering upon
Somalia. A ceasefire of sorts was established in March 1992
and the UN Operation in Somalia was formed under
Council Resolution 751 to monitor it and provide security

for UN personnel and humanitarian supplies. The operation was also to 'support' the Secretary-General in 'his continuing mission in Somalia to facilitate an immediate and effective cessation of hostilities and the maintenance of a cease-fire throughout the country in order to promote the process of reconciliation...'.[30] Boutros-Ghali reported in the summer that banditry and looting were undermining efforts and '[h]umanitarian assistance must be provided regardless of whether or not there is an immediate political solution'; he was already thinking in terms of 'nothing less than the reconstruction of an entire society and nation'.[31] Resolution 767 and 775 authorized more personnel and widened the mandate but by the end of the year the situation was 'intolerable', with as many as 3000 dying per day as a result of starvation and lawlessness.[32] Boutros-Ghali reported to the Council on 24 November 1992 that traditional peacekeeping techniques were not working and that it might be necessary to upgrade to peace-enforcement, although he couched his proposal in the context of a set of five options.[33] A former US Assistant Secretary of State for International Organization has revealed that President Bush had already presented a plan to Boutros-Ghali for US forces to provide limited security for the distribution of humanitarian assistance. It is significant that the US administration appeared to put the decision in Boutros-Ghali's hands: '[Acting Secretary of State] Eagleburger stressed that the United States would not proceed if the Secretary-General opposed the plan.'[34] Despite the possibility that Bush's actions may have had an element of domestic politics behind them, they were, in collaboration with Boutros-Ghali, a response to a deteriorating humanitarian situation based partly on proposals made by the Secretary-General.

Security Council Resolution 794 of 3 December 1992, under Chapter VII of the UN Charter, seemingly set a precedent in mandating 'all necessary means' to secure the distribution of humanitarian assistance, to 'proceed at the discretion of the Secretary-General in the light of his assessment of conditions on the ground'.[35] Under this authorization, the Unified Task Force embarked upon Operation Restore Hope on 9 December, under the US, with the intention of handing over to the UN when security had been established. Resolution 794 clearly put the Secretary-General in a key administrative position and explicitly tied the Office to the use of force. It is important to note that the Bush administration had a fairly limited conception of Operation Restore Hope: limited security for the distribution of humanitarian assistance.[36] However, Boutros-Ghali envisaged that the operation would contribute to a 'comprehensive and multifaceted ... reconstruction of an entire society and nation'.[37] According to Bolton, the day after the task force arrived, Bush wrote to Boutros-Ghali to re-emphasize the limited and specific nature of the mission while the Secretary-General was already talking about disarming the factions, setting up a civil administration and training the police.[38] As Bush's Presidency came to a close it appeared that the immediate security concerns were eased, aid was getting through, and a low-key political process was under way involving most political groups.[39] Indeed, US ties with the prominent faction leader General Aidid had been reasonably cordial under the United Task Force because US envoy Robert Oakley refrained from pursuing disarmament in return for a pledge that the warlords would not target US troops, although this broke down when Clinton came in.[40] Boutros-Ghali made no effort to dissociate his Office from the use of force; in fact he appeared to imply that the Secretaryship-General should have a greater role: '[i]f forceful action is taken, it should preferably be under United Nations command and control. If this is not feasible, an alternative would be an operation undertaken by Member States acting with the authorization of the Security Council.'[41]

It appears that the UN Operation in Somalia (II) took over prematurely in May 1993, and as violence continued Boutros-Ghali 'concluded that UNOSOM II should be endowed with enforcement powers to enable it to establish a secure environment throughout Somalia'.[42] The Clinton administration, without the experience in foreign policy of Bush but revelling in New World Order concepts of US leadership and humanitarianism, melded with Boutros-Ghali's determination to widen and deepen the operation. Boutros-Ghali was unhappy with the idea of dealing with the factions and sought disarmament. Thus, with US backing, Resolution 814 brought the mandate into an experimental and perhaps precarious realm. Under Chapter VII, and explicitly tied to the Secretary-General, the UN undertook rigorous policing and disarmament objectives, albeit based theoretically on the Addis Ababa reconciliation process and agreements established therein. Ambassador Albright said that the objective was 'nothing less than the restoration of an entire country'.[43] Resolution 865 further embraced this 'nation-building'. Moreover, Resolution 837, in response to the death of a number of Pakistani peacekeepers in June 1993 and further attacks, '[r]eaffirms that the Secretary-General is authorized ... to take all necessary measures against all those responsible for the armed attacks.'[44] According to one account, '[f]or the first time, the secretary-general directly commanded a military force deployed under Chapter VII.'[45]

The June 1993 attack was the first of a number of bitter clashes involving serious losses on all sides. In late September a US helicopter was brought down with the loss of three lives and in October around 17 US soldiers were killed in Mogadishu. A number of journalists, aid workers and thousands of Somalis had also died between June and October 1993 in the violence which arose from the bungled campaign to arrest Aidid.[46] Much blame has been levelled at Boutros-Ghali and Admiral Howe for rejecting the conciliatory approach of Oakley, attempting to disarm all the factions, and placing key emphasis on the arrest of Aidid. In fact, at root, there was a 'drastically different' perception between the original US objectives and those of Boutros-Ghali.[47] Boutros-Ghali's record in the Egyptian foreign ministry indicated some association with Ali Mahdi Mohamed, Aidid's main rival, so by targeting Aidid's clan the UN and the US had entered the fray of Somali internecine conflict. With the loss of the appearance of impartiality and without even the tools or the will to do the job properly the operation was undermined by its casualties and the hostility it aroused.

Aidid stated that 'UN bureaucrats, from the Secretary-General downwards, have failed time and again to demonstrate an understanding of the intricate political problems in Somalia.'[48] It would seem that some personal animosity had developed between Aidid and Boutros-Ghali which surely exacerbated a volatile situation and probably contributed to the warlord's recalcitrance. Many inside and outside Somalia felt that the realistic US approach under Bush and Oakley,[49] which envisaged a limited humanitarian-security operation with some level of dialogue and cooperation with the strong men on the ground, was upset by the arrogant and unrealistic nation-building ideas of Boutros-Ghali and Howe. For example, it was reported that in late September 1993, shortly before the US losses in October, Secretary of State Warren Christopher told Boutros-Ghali that the US was uncomfortable with disarmament and the search for Aidid and wanted to get back to the conciliatory approach.[50] Perhaps Boutros-Ghali did not want the UN, or himself, humbled, for he apparently resisted Christopher's appeal. Similarly, there were reports that Howe and UN commanders actually rejected a secret deal offered by Aidid to end hostilities and begin a dialogue.[51] A record of the informal consultations of the Security Council indicated that in March 1993 members were already expressing worries about finance, the safety of UN personnel in general and the issue of sovereignty.[52]

Boutros-Ghali later proclaimed that '[n]othing is more precious to the United Nations than its reputation', and that rests upon impartiality, equity, efficiency and independence.[53] Yet in this and other cases the reputation of Boutros-Ghali was severely tainted. To an extent, the reputation of the Organization and Office of Secretary-General was similarly damaged. By September 1993 the US was beginning to have serious doubts about UNOSOM II as a result of the bungled raids and casualties on all sides since June. The October disaster, involving a number of US casualties, finally swung Congress, the public and the administration against the operation and Clinton identified March 1994 as the date for US withdrawal. In the heat of the moment a number of US politicians implied that the US losses had been a result of UN command and control, although in fact the raid was under US command and the UN was only informed of it as it was launched.[54] Nevertheless, it appeared that the United States had turned away from the operation, and indeed the whole concept of supporting hazardous UN operations in distant countries which were not tied to the 'national interest'.

The administration backed away from earlier resolutions and rhetoric. Clinton proclaimed: 'it is not our job to rebuild Somalia's society.'[55] To cement its disillusionment with the UN Clinton sent Oakley back to Somalia to talk with all the factions – including Aidid – and his arrest was abandoned.[56] This was an admission that the UNOSOM II had been undermined and Aidid had effectively triumphed; the UN, and its chief, would be scapegoated. Boutros-Ghali remarked: '[t]he United Nations exists to help countries solve their problems. If it helps the Americans solve theirs by blaming me, I'll be a scapegoat.'[57]

One can defend Boutros-Ghali. The Secretary-General was acting on the basis of resolutions sponsored by the US, and disarmament appeared to be the best way to establish long-term peace; eleven Somali political organizations apparently had expressed full support for the disarmament objectives of UNOSOM in June 1993. Indeed, a former senior US diplomat in Somalia later wrote that the initial US decision to allow the warlords to keep their weapons was a 'tragic mistake'.[58] Moreover, Boutros-Ghali was supportive of all-party talks: he convened the Conference on National Reconciliation in accordance with agreements in Addis Ababa in January 1993 and his Special Representative was in contact with all factions, including General Aidid, in 1994. Indeed, the Secretary-General continued efforts to set up a political presence in Somalia after the withdrawal of the UN by maintaining a small office in Nairobi, on his initiative, to assist reconciliation efforts.[59] This is significant in the face of dwindling media attention and disillusionment among the donor community. The Secretary-General reported that he intended to maintain the UN Political Office in Somalia, perhaps with the implication that he, if not the international community, would not abandon Somalia.[60] What were the implications of UN involvement for the Secretaryship-General?

In taking advantage of an environment of experimentation and optimism in the UN and transition in the US, Boutros-Ghali was able to play a key role in the escalation of UNOSOM firstly to UNITAF and then UNOSOM II. In

UNOSOM II he held significant powers under Chapter VII at an operational and coordination level with the use of peace enforcement techniques. The Secretary-General was directing the use of force in a stark departure from the classical model of the international civil service. However, this position of authority – perhaps even power – transpired to be precarious as the support of the Council, and most importantly the US, was fragile. In addition, the use of force and the abandonment of impartiality undoubtedly affected the utility of the Secretary-General in mediating in this conflict and possibly tainted the reputation of the Office in a wider sense. The use of force in any instance is incompatible with the role of an innocuous and impartial third party. At the same time, history has shown that the international civil service can and must adapt, and must embrace the new demands thrust upon the Organization, including the use of force or coercion in low-level conflict situations. However, the reluctance of member states and the Secretariat to consider peace-enforcement since Somalia casts doubt upon this. The Secretary-General observed, as the operation was withdrawn three weeks ahead of the deadline, that there were 'important lessons to be learned about the theory and practice of multifunctional peace-keeping operations in conditions of civil war and chaos and especially about the clear line that needs to be drawn between peace-keeping and enforcement action.'[61] A blurring of that line puts the international civil service into an uncomfortable, perhaps untenable, position.

Angola

In Angola the Secretary-General and his representatives were encumbered by an overburdened and complex UN peacekeeping workload and an emergent climate of multilateral fatigue. Chester Crocker, who represented the US at the negotiations which established the 1991 Angola accords, observed that 'faced with mounting worldwide peace-keeping costs and peace accords that limited the UN's implementing role, the Security Council decided to bring peace to Angola on the cheap.'[62] Similarly, the Special Representative of the Secretary-General for Angola, Margaret

Anstee, described the constraints under which the UN worked in this 'forgotten tragedy'.[63]

The September 1992 election should have brought some seventeen years of conflict to an end. It was the culmination of a number of processes which yielded the May 1991 Bicesse Accord. The end of the Cold War had facilitated the transition of Namibia and the withdrawal of Cuban troops from the area, and the end of South African efforts to gain regional domination. Soviet and US support to the Angolan government and the UNITA rebels theoretically ceased and there were grounds for national reconciliation. The role of the UN was to monitor the elections and the other elements of the accord.

However, the number of personnel assigned to the country – compared to the high-profile settlement in Cambodia, for example – was widely felt to be inadequate to help to organize the elections in time and promote confidence in the whole process. The second UN verification mission – the first being that which monitored Cuban withdrawal following the 1988 Namibia settlement – comprised 350 military and 126 police observers, with an additional 400 at the time of the elections, to monitor the ceasefire and demobilization and witness the ballot.

Another problem was the nature of the election, which was largely 'winner takes all' – not an appropriate framework for national reconciliation after so many years of conflict and no experience of democracy. In addition, the UN had not insisted on thorough demobilization and disarmament so either side had the means to take up arms if the outcome of the election did not suit it. The UN Secretariat had to work within the confines of an increasingly wary Security Council, especially as Angola did not have much political importance or media attention. As long as oil continued to flow and Western commercial interests were not threatened it did not warrant a substantial allocation of resources. Another factor working against the UN and contributing to the failure of UN Angola Verification Mission II was the private relations of external actors to Angolan factions and former Cold War acquaintances. The US did not recognize the government even after the 1992 election and no pressure was put on Zaire to end its support for UNITA rebel leader Savimbi.

Some subsequently have suggested that UNITA had tacit approval from the West to fight it out after the 1992 elections and that the West's appeasement of UNITA prolonged the conflict.[64]

The governing MPLA won a majority in the National Assembly and dos Santos won the first round of the Presidential ballot. Savimbi claimed there had been vote rigging and quickly mobilized his forces. The troika of the US, Russia and Portugal led international efforts and South Africa joined the fray, although without the leverage it once had. According to Boutros-Ghali, with the renewal of hostilities – which saw the most bitter fighting of the whole civil war – UNAVEM II 'actively engaged in efforts to reach a peace settlement between the Government and UNITA'.[65] Special Representative Margaret Anstee and Marrack Goulding reportedly sought to do this in October and November 1992 while Savimbi accepted one of many cease-fires. However, Pycroft has suggested that, by acting as a neutral arbiter, the UN had strengthened Savimbi's claim to equal status and therefore 'inadvertently legitimized UNITA's decision to return to war'.[66]

This seems unfair. The UN effort, presumably along with those of the 'troika' and South Africa, was directed towards the cessation of violence and UNITA's acceptance of the 1992 election. It is a reflection of the 'new era' of UN activities that the Secretary-General – in fact both Boutros-Ghali and Kofi Annan – had to shake hands with the warlord Jonas Savimbi, and give legitimacy to UNITA, before he had irreversibly committed himself to the peace process. Few peace and security situations in the post-Cold War world – and particularly those of a domestic nature – are 'black and white' and the Secretaryship-General must be seen in this light, even though it may lay itself open to the criticism of flirting with warlords. Unfortunately, the international civil service has to address the local strongmen, however risky or distasteful this may at times appear.

The talks in Lusaka were essentially under UN auspices and sought initially a ceasefire, acceptance of the elections, a withdrawal by UNITA from territory taken since the renewal of hostilities, and thereafter the completion of the electoral process, the new mandate of the UN, and reconciliation.

Under the threat of Council sanctions and the offer of concessions UNITA announced a suspension of hostilities and, with the government, agreed to a ceasefire in August 1994. There was still some doubt – due to Savimbi's absence from the process – and Boutros-Ghali wisely stated that peacekeepers would not be sent until an 'effective cease-fire' took hold.[67] Even on the eve of deployment the Secretary-General reaffirmed that he would 'not hesitate to recommend' the postponement or cancellation of deployment if the parties failed to fulfil their commitment to the peace process.[68]

Boutros-Ghali was responding to the widely felt alarm that the Organization had committed resources and personnel prematurely in some areas which had become embroiled in continuing conflicts, thereby wasting resources and suffering financial and human losses. As this trend clearly was affecting the Organization's willingness to become involved in domestic situations, the Secretary-General had to exercise restraint along with the Council. In Lusaka Special Representative Beye had been orchestrating negotiations on the Secretary-General's behalf and Paul Hare's presence on behalf of President Clinton made clear to UNITA that it no longer had international friends. Negotiations came down to the distribution of ministries and governorships between UNITA and the MPLA, the nature of the peacekeeping force, and disarmament. With the fighting continuing and Savimbi's absence from the signing of the August agreements, doubts remained. Boutros-Ghali refused to commit peacekeepers until Savimbi and dos Santos finally met. In March 1995 the Secretary-General sent a Special Adviser to assess the situation and deliver letters to the leaders of the two principal parties. On this basis he recommended that although there were risks involved the Organization should proceed with preparations for the deployment of some UNAVEM III units.[69]

Dos Santos and Savimbi finally met in Lusaka in May 1995. After a personal visit by the Secretary-General in mid-July 1995 to speed up and consolidate the momentum, UNAVEM III began to deploy in the summer under Resolution 976. In addition, the Secretary-General met the President at the fiftieth anniversary commemorations in

New York.[70] In parallel, a Joint Commission, including the
observer states – Portugal, Russia and the US – and under
the Secretary-General's Special Representative, assisted the
implementation of the Lusaka Protocol for peace and reconciliation. This involved the allocation of cabinet posts, the
ceasefire, humanitarian and social assistance and rehabilitation. However, the fact that only half of the authorized
troops had been dispatched by mid-August and less than one
per cent of the voluntary funds for demobilization and rehabilitation under the 1995 humanitarian appeal had been
contributed by July indicates the caution and conservatism
still prevalent among member states. Whether this had a
bearing on the flare-up of fighting in the end of 1995 is
unclear. The Angolan army initiated an offensive against
UNITA troops and Savimbi responded by withdrawing
cooperation with UNAVEM III.[71] The Secretary-General
made a further personal intervention and his representative
worked hard to get the Lusaka Protocol back on track,
undoubtedly assisted by the visit of US Ambassador Albright.
Her presence and message from the Permanent Members of
the Security Council underscored the 'growing impatience
of the international community' with the parties.[72] When the
Security Council extended UNAVEM III until 8 May 1996 it
was with the proviso that the Secretary-General report regu-
larly on concrete progress.

Mozambique

In the context of an overburdened UN, Mozambique, along
with Angola, was not a priority. Again, the Secretary-
General was in a difficult position with his resources spread
thinly. Many looked towards the UN Secretariat to avoid the
mistakes of Angola, where weapons were allowed to stay on
the ground after the 1991 peace accord. In Mozambique the
October 1992 Rome accords, under Italian mediation,
ended the civil war. Immediately after the summit the
Secretary-General sent a representative to the country to
begin the monitoring/implementation process and step up
the humanitarian mechanism. Government and rebel
RENAMO troops were to be cantoned or demobilized, a new
national army was to be formed and elections were to be

held in 1993. Learning the lessons of Angola, both Boutros-Ghali and his Special Representative Aldo Ajello vowed 'no elections without demobilization'.[73] In having this control over the peace process, Anthony Parsons wrote that, while they were under the authority of the Security Council, Boutros-Ghali and his staff 'were put in the driving seat rather than being helpless passengers, as in Angola'.[74]

However, the whole process soon fell behind the schedule of elections for October 1993 and there was still a lack of confidence and trust. Given the resources committed there was some pressure – as in Western Sahara – to keep the process on track. In an extremely significant personal intervention, Boutros-Ghali managed in October 1993 to help secure a new schedule of October 1994 and maintain momentum for the whole operation. Again, however, problems threatened a delay in 1994. In January a non-governmental organization exposed a child prostitution scandal in which some peace-keepers had been involved and problems appeared regarding the demobilization of parties. In May, after Italy reduced its force contribution, Bangladesh, India and Portugal indicated that they might follow suit.[75] The climate of multilateral fatigue was threatening the peace process, especially as insufficient confidence existed among the people of Mozambique and the two main political groupings, both of which still had access to weapons and could boycott the elections. For this opportunity – and the efforts of the Organization – not to be squandered Boutros-Ghali appealed against further cuts in the operation and, alongside the Council, urged the parties to uphold their commitments. Subsequently, Aldo Ajello was able to declare that the UN monitored elections of 27–29 October 1994 were 'free and fair' after a high turn-out and few problems. The Secretary-General subsequently attributed the 'remarkable success' to the commitment of the people, the pragmatism of the parties and the 'clarity of the ONUMOZ [UN Operation in Mozambique] mandate and the consistent support provided by the Security Council.'[76]

Rwanda

It has been said that Rwanda was the first victim of US Presidential Policy Directive 25, a key tenet of the Security

Council's wariness about becoming involved in messy domestic peace operations.[77] Under the constraints of the post-Somalia multilateral fatigue, Boutros-Ghali symbolized the frustration of the international community in attempting to exert moral leverage in the face of political constraints.

After a century of conflict, the peace process between the Hutu government and the Tutsi rebel opposition achieved an accord in August 1993 at Arusha. It laid down arrangements for power sharing and integration of the rebel Tutsi Rwandan Patriotic Front into the army. The process was to be monitored by the UN Assistance Mission to Rwanda. When President Habyarimana finally gave up his resistance to the process on 6 April 1994 and agreed to speed up the transition to democracy, Hutu extremists assassinated him and Burundi's president. It is fairly clear that the enormous loss of life – mostly Tutsi and moderate Hutu – was deliberate and planned by the new extremist Hutu government. Ten Belgian peacekeepers died trying to protect the Prime Minister, and the Security Council was struck by paralysis. Plant wrote that '[i]n the face of the government-inspired massacres, the UN displayed a degree of indecision seldom seen even in that body's chequered history of decision-making.'[78] More specifically, the leading Council *members* were reluctant to commit troops or resources to another chaotic Third World implosion. It might be close to the truth to suggest that certain states had decided that the UN could not and should not launch an intervention on humanitarian grounds. In accordance with this, US officials were reportedly instructed to avoid describing the killings as genocide and sought initially to avoid that terminology in the Security Council.[79]

Boutros-Ghali tried to muster authority for an interventionary operation. He gave options for the presence of the UN in Rwanda – again indicating his own recommendations – in a manner akin to the spirit of Article 99.[80] These options involved massive reinforcement, withdrawal, or the maintenance of a reduced force. However, the UN Assistance Mission in Rwanda was reduced from 2500 to 270 on 21 April 1994, and modified to act as an intermediary, to monitor and to give humanitarian assistance. President

Clinton stated in a speech, 'our interests are not sufficiently at stake ... to justify a commitment of our folks'.[81]

Boutros-Ghali was at the height of his frustration, telling the Security Council: 'we have failed in our response to the agony of Rwanda, and thus have acquiesced in the continued loss of lives.'[82] The International Committee of the Red Cross reported that 'tens of thousands' had died, while on 29 April the Security Council reportedly turned down a request by the Secretary-General for more troops to be sent. He later lamented, 'I begged them to send troops.'[83] His appeals had little impact in a climate which could barely have been less conducive to mandating coercive humanitarian intervention. The feeling at the UN during the initial atrocities was that the US was not supportive of UN intervention and therefore it could not have been comfortable with Boutros-Ghali's appeals to the world's conscience from his 'bully pulpit'.[84] He later identified this as the 'moral responsibility' he felt burdened with, to draw the world's attention to issues and conflicts which might otherwise be neglected.[85] His efforts to encourage an African peace-keeping force were equally unsuccessful. However, it is interesting that while Boutros-Ghali's admonitions of the Security Council's initial inactivity were not sufficient to prompt action he certainly helped draw media attention to the issue, which must have had a role in prompting the US airlift of humanitarian supplies. Yet despite his apparent efforts, the president of the new Tutsi government would later hold him *personally* accountable for the failure of the UN to stem the tide of violence in a speech at a summit of the Organization of African Unity in July 1996. This was indicative of the predicament of the Secretary-General's position in many post-Cold War domestic conflicts.

The Secretary-General submitted a report on 13 May recommending an expansion of UNAMIR to 5500. Eventually the Council gave a provisional authorization for an increase in the UN presence through Resolution 918 of 17 May. Boutros-Ghali was able to report that the parties had agreed to begin talks on a ceasefire under the auspices of UNAMIR, so he recommended that the additional troops be deployed. Council Resolution 925 endorsed Boutros-Ghali's recommendations, yet his appeals for troops were not answered; apparently 'not one of the 19 Governments that at that time had undertaken to have troops on stand-by agreed to contribute.'[86] Evidently the caution felt among the Security Council members towards volatile domestic operations was shared by the wider international community. Kofi Annan, then Under-Secretary-General for Peace-keeping Operations, spoke of the 'post-Somalia syndrome' among states reluctant to be involved.[87] Another indication of the hands-off approach of the Council was its authorization on 22 June of the French 'Operation Turquoise', despite France's widely reported promotion of the former government and of francophone elites in Africa.[88]

With the formation of a Rwandan Patriotic Front coalition government with the participation of Hutus a semblance of stability emerged, although the refugee camps in Zaire and Tanzania were being used by the Hutu extremists to destabilize the government and 'the tensions on the country's borders could erupt in uncontrollable violence at any moment'.[89] The Secretary-General visited the region – speaking with the President, Vice-President and Prime Minister of Rwanda – in July 1995 to undertake efforts to reduce the supply of weapons across borders, although countries neighbouring Rwanda were reluctant to accept military observers.[90] He was also shifting the mission from a military basis to one more of peacebuilding and rehabilitation in accordance with Security Council Resolution 997. It is interesting that he reported that his Special Representative was renegotiating the status and roles of UNAMIR which 'in my judgement' should be performed by the UN in light of the government's desire to reduce the size of the force.[91]

Subsequent to this, Rwanda became much firmer in its conviction that the military component of UNAMIR be withdrawn by the end of its mandate in December 1995, arguing that the force was not serving the country's real needs. Boutros-Ghali and the Security Council managed to convince the Rwandan government to accept the continued presence of a smaller force under Resolution 1029(1995), which focused on good-offices, assistance and the return of refugees. However, it was a reflection of the instability of the situation that Canada was to inform the Secretary-General that it would not participate in the renewed UNAMIR operation because the mandate was no longer realistic under the reduced force.[92]

The concentration of displaced persons was a tangible source of instability, as the Commission of Enquiry into the border camps found. Boutros-Ghali's proposal for a regional meeting to develop concrete measures to implement the repatriation agreements, and a round table meeting of Rwandan society for reconciliation, were proactive peace-building measures. Boutros-Ghali earlier had called upon the Security Council either to back an international force to police the camps or to support efforts of local countries to restore law and order.[93] The subsequent report of the Commission appeared to bear out Boutros-Ghali's alarm and that of his Special Representative regarding the instability on Rwanda's borders and the dangers of weapons circulating in the region.[94] However, in the face of multilateral caution and fatigue, and with a lessening of media interest, the Secretary-General was constrained. He did not have the necessary weight of public consciousness and opinion behind him to bring leverage to bear upon the Council. In July 1995 the outstanding assessed contributions to the UNAMIR Special Account was $64.7 million. The UNHCR in February 1996 announced that it might have to reduce drastically its humanitarian programmes for refugees in the region because of a serious shortfall in funding. The coalition government was not stable and there was no discernible effort towards national reconciliation. This necessitated substantive proactive assistance at a time when the political and financial condition of the Organization was not amenable to substantive action.

Liberia

The situation in Liberia tested the patience of the Security Council in the early 1990s at a time when numerous burdens upon the Organization were resulting in political priorities. With a lack of substantial media and therefore public attention before the Spring of 1996 and little Permanent Five interest, Liberia was not an attractive target of material resources. With an increasing reliance on regional peace efforts the UN found itself in the necessary but sometimes uncomfortable position of supporting and monitoring a local peace operation under Nigerian leadership. This is the framework within which the Secretary-General operated.

The insurrection against Samuel Doe by Charles Taylor began in December 1989 and the country was plunged into chaotic civil war. The virtual collapse of the state and refugee movements threatened the stability of the region. Peacekeeping has been the responsibility of the 12 000-strong Economic Community Observer Group (ECOMOG) force sent to Monrovia in September 1990 under the Economic Community of West African States. The main contributor was Nigeria, which strongly backed the interim government against Taylor's forces and, according to some, 'stoked up regional rivalries' with its own objectives.[95]

Peace talks and ceasefires had been on and off since 1990 and the wider international community turned its attention to Liberia in 1992. A major step was the Security Council arms embargo in November through Resolution 788, 19 November, which also requested the Secretary-General to dispatch a Special Representative to evaluate the situation. Accordingly, Boutros-Ghali sent Trever Gordon-Somers who participated in 'extensive discussions' with the parties.[96] Boutros-Ghali was also requested in June 1993 to investigate the massacre of displaced people. Under the July 1993 Geneva peace accord the transitional government was to be replaced through elections. Resolution 856 approved the Secretary-General's decision to send a technical team to gather information in preparation for a mission. On the basis of this precursor investigation the UN began to monitor the situation alongside ECOMOG with the UN Observer Mission in Liberia, established by Resolution 866 of 22 September 1993.

Subsequently, the situation deteriorated, the scheduled election did not take place, and troop contributing countries became increasingly uncomfortable. Boutros-Ghali dispatched veteran diplomat Lakhdar Brahimi in August 1994 to review the situation. Taylor was clearly doubtful of the neutrality of ECOMOG and Nigerian planes had bombed civilian areas. Reports that the US gave Nigeria military intelligence, and the US and UN support of ECOMOG, could have tainted the status of the Secretary-General. Even in difficult circumstances the Secretary-General should try to maintain some independence from Great Power involvement as far as possible, especially when force is used. In his desperation, born of an over-burdened UN and his desire to encourage regional peace operations wherever possible, the Secretary-General may have been too quick – along with the Security Council – to legitimize less than scrupulous regional efforts. This may transpire to have implications for the Office's traditional role as an innocuous and impartial third party with quasi-independence from the Council. Nevertheless, it may also be an unavoidable component of the post-Cold War Secretaryship-General. Moreover, the Secretary-General reported that the parallel operations of ECOWAS (the Economic Community of West African States) and the UN Observer Mission in Liberia 'broke fresh ground'.[97] A division of labour between the UN and regional efforts is both sensible and necessary. In this case, one must be pragmatic. Nigeria's sponsorship of the ECOWAS intervention can be seen in the context of regional politics but the international community at large was not willing or able to assist, and at least Nigeria's leadership has the objective of stability.[98] It is necessary therefore to be practical: again, few conflict situations in the post-Cold War world are of a 'black and white' nature.

The Secretary-General was requested by Resolution 985 to report if a ceasefire existed and if UNOMIL was able to carry out its mandate, and the Security Council intended to consider the future of the operation in light of this. Subsequently the Secretary-General outlined possible courses of action depending upon the behaviour of the parties, and even the possibility of a peacekeeping operation. He was able to solicit opinions by attending the ECOWAS summit of May 1995 in Nigeria which focused on Liberia, at which the factions were represented. Subsequently, under the leadership of Ghanaian mediation in August 1995 a milestone was reached with the peace accord for a council of transitional government representing all the factions, disarmament and eventual elections, signed in Nigeria. There were subsequent setbacks and violence, and the response to the appeal for aid to support the thirteenth attempt at peace was 'pathetic', according to the Under-Secretary-General for

Humanitarian Affairs.[99] Nevertheless, the trend towards disarmament and demobilization continued slowly under the observation of the Secretary-General's representative Anthony Nyakyi.[100] It is significant that the Security Council Resolution which extended the observer mission to May 1996 linked the extension to progress in the peace process. The wisdom of this was borne out by the upsurge of violence in April 1996.

El Salvador

Although the Deputy US Representative to the UN described the operation in El Salvador as 'one of the most successful in UN history'[101] there is evidence that the conclusion of the UN's main activities was partly the result of the pervading predisposition within the Security Council to withdraw as soon as possible from engagements. Boutros-Ghali reported in 1994 that the peace process had 'advanced steadily' and that after elections were completed successfully in April the former rebel FMLN was now the party of opposition.[102] The UN Observer Mission in El Salvador (ONUSAL) continued to monitor and implement the 1992 peace accords but there had been delays regarding public security, land transfer and in reintegrating ex-combatants into society. In May 1994 the timetable was revised and there appears to be some difference of opinion regarding the extent to which the mandate was fully completed when the Security Council decided to terminate the operation, except for a dozen or so observers. Most UN members were playing up the success of the operation in the midst of the popularly felt disillusionment towards the Organization. However, the Secretary-General's representative, Enrique ter Horst, stated that the mission was not quite finished in the areas of transferring land to former fighters, aid programmes for the injured, and the overhaul of the judicial system. After visiting in April 1995 Boutros-Ghali said that there was a case for extending the full mission 'before the Salvadoran peace process can be pronounced a success'.[103] However, he refrained from making the case 'in the light of the clear indications from members of the Council that the time had come to bring ONUSAL to a close'. Evidently financial and political constraints dictated a hasty withdrawal as soon as a 'success' could be judged, even though the pace of reconciliation and rehabilitation was slow. Nevertheless, the General Assembly did extend the Observer Mission until April 1996, due partly to Boutros-Ghali's appeals and those of the President. The Secretary-General, in a critically important post-Cold War role, was keeping the Security Council focused upon the issue.

Western Sahara

The UN involvement in Western Sahara has epitomized the manner in which expectations during the immediate post-Cold War 'honeymoon' gave way to an attitude of frustration, disillusionment and even retreat. Since Morocco and Polisario – the group which has struggled to achieve independence for Western Sahara from Morocco – accepted formally the need for a referendum UN efforts have centred around organizing and monitoring the modalities of the poll. Pérez de Cuéllar's efforts were still the basis of the operation, accepted by Council Resolution 691 of May 1991, and just prior to his departure he set down the contentious criteria for voter eligibility. In 1991 the UN Mission for the Referendum in Western Sahara (MINURSO) was formed on the belief that the parties – and most importantly Morocco – were ready to cooperate in a referendum over the future of the territory. The observer group's mandate was to identify and register voters, monitor the withdrawal and cantonment of forces, conduct the referendum, repatriate refugees, certify the referendum results, and supervise the outcome. However, a number of problems delayed the referendum and ultimately cast doubt on the viability of the operation.

Because of the delay – of three years – by the time the referendum was scheduled the patience and finances of the Council were flagging seriously. The original timetable scheduled a referendum for January 1992. The major issue was that of voter eligibility and identification, for the obvious reason that the complexion of the electorate can determine the outcome. Polisario wished to see the voting list based on the census of 1974, while Morocco wished to add around a

hundred thousand more whom it claimed fled the territory during colonial military operations.[104] In June 1993
Boutros-Ghali visited the region with his representative to
urge a compromise on this issue, and credit is due partly to
him that this led to a meeting between representatives of
both sides in July with the Secretary-General's representative. With the problem of voter eligibility supposedly settled,
Council Resolution 907 decided that the identification
commission of MINURSO should proceed with identification and registration on the basis of compromises made by
Boutros-Ghali. This proposed a revised timetable for the
referendum of 14 February 1995, which was delayed again.
Boutros-Ghali's personal intervention included visits to
MINURSO officials, Polisario, the Foreign Minister of
Algeria, and King Hassan in November 1994.

The February 1995 referendum date was not met. Frank
Ruddy, a senior officer responsible for preparing the voting
roles in MINURSO, spoke before a US House of
Representatives Committee and claimed that Morocco did
not want a referendum because the risks outweighed any
possible gains. Simultaneously Morocco could not afford to
appear to be rejecting the process so was wearing it down
through obstruction until the international community
became tired.[105]

The Secretary-General's visit to MINURSO in November
1994 and his ensuing report appear not to have satisfied the
Security Council. In the midst of multilateral fatigue and
severe financial constraints the $100 000 per day operation
was testing the Security Council's patience, despite the
Secretary-General's defence of the mission and his observation that it was helping to maintain the ceasefire.[106] The
Security Council pointedly dispatched its own mission to
Western Sahara in June 1995, 'to impress upon the parties
the necessity of cooperating fully with MINURSO' and to
assess progress and problems in the process of identification
in preparation for a referendum deadline.[107] In addition,
the uneasiness of the Security Council with the operation
was also indicated by its extension of MINURSO for only
one month, instead of the four recommended by Boutros-
Ghali. Thus, despite the Secretary-General's report, the
Security Council wished to investigate for itself and was

decidedly unhappy with the lack of progress. The frustration of the Council was reflected in Resolution 1033 of 19 December 1995, which requested that the Secretary-General assess options, including the possibility of withdrawing MINURSO. This injected some life into the operation and Boutros-Ghali intensified his consultations with the parties by sending a mission to the area under Chinmaya Gharekhan in early January 1996.[108] The mission concluded that there were still problems with the identification of voters and that the process could take a further year. Boutros-Ghali sought to force the pace by proposing a controversial registration system whereby voters would be identified on a simpler verification basis and the referendum be carried out as soon as possible.[109] Polisario was not happy with the idea, seeing it as a result of Morocco's persistent obstruction and the international community's desire to rid itself of the issue irrespective of Morocco's tactics.[110] If one accepts this, the Office of Secretary-General would appear to have succumbed to the atmosphere of multilateral fatigue and the dwindling interest of the international community.

In some ways Boutros-Ghali and his staff were again being made scapegoats for the lack of patience of the Security Council and the multilateral fatigue which pervades much of the UN's activities, and the apparent lack of priority given to Western Sahara. If it was made absolutely clear to Morocco by the Security Council and bilaterally by its members that continued obstruction was unacceptable, then King Hassan would realize that he could not continue just to pay lip-service to the idea of a referendum as he has for the last twenty years; perhaps this is what the Secretary-General was implying when he called upon members to 'exert efforts'.[111]

Cyprus

There are a number of dimensions to the Cypriot dispute in the 1990's, some of which represent a departure from the previous twenty-six years of UN involvement. In the immediate post-Cold War environment there was a focus in the Security Council upon addressing continuing disputes in a concerted fashion, free from the politicization of the past.

Moreover, routine peacekeeping expenditures would no longer be automatically extended without review. As the post-Cold War 'honeymoon' faded the increasing wariness of the Security Council towards a burdensome peacekeeping agenda caused many to express impatience towards the lack of progress in Cyprus, and the evident tension between peacekeeping and peacemaking. The comprehensive approach of previous UN-sponsored mediation – so often leading to disappointment – increasingly was losing credibility. Simultaneously, the apparent desire of the Turkish Cypriots to improve their economic position, the desire of Turkey to move closer to Western economic and political structures, and the possibility of future Cypriot membership of the European Union all give possibilities for leverage. Moreover the threat of a Turkish–Greek conflict contributing to southeast European instability has maintained and renewed international desire to find a settlement. However, the internationalization of the issue by the Greek Cypriots continues to fuel Turkish Cypriot entrenchment and conditions the position of the Secretary-General.

Pérez de Cuéllar's final 'set of ideas' focused on a bicommunal federal republic with shared and separate institutions. It also dealt with territorial percentages, arrangements for sensitive areas, boundaries, the distribution of federal positions, 'foreign forces', the return of displaced people, freedom of movement, and safeguards against federal power. On this basis Boutros-Ghali hosted a number of talks in 1992, in the shadow of Resolution 774, which expressed the Security Council's expectation of progress. Although a set of ideas developed and the Secretary-General was able to codify areas of consensus – in fact he apparently stated that a solution was closer than at any time since 1974 – no solution was forthcoming. Confidence and expectation were as low as ever among the UN membership – symbolized by the withdrawal or reduction of some contingents – and the Council intimated that a lack of progress in the peace process risked a collapse of the force.

In response to this stagnation Boutros-Ghali embarked upon a different approach. While the set of ideas was still seen as the basis for an overall settlement, he turned the

Secretariat's efforts towards incremental confidence-building measures (CBMs). These were first recommended by Boutros-Ghali to the Security Council in November 1992 and involved the rehabilitation of Varosha as a special area for bicommunal contact and commerce, and opening Nicosia international airport for civilian use by both sides under UN supervision. The confidence-building measures were elaborated upon in July 1993 to include cooperation on the water problems in Cyprus, education to promote intercommunal harmony, and joint cultural and sporting events. As Boutros-Ghali's report explained, '[t]heir purpose is to serve as a catalyst in the negotiations leading to a comprehensive, overall solution ...'.[112]

The Secretary-General's representatives – until April 1996 under former Canadian Prime Minister Joe Clark – sought to negotiate acceptance of these CBMs on the basis of the mutual advantage they would bring. This was demonstrated by the assessments of the UN Development Programme, the International Monetary Fund, the World Bank and the International Civil Aviation Organization. While the Turkish community would gain the most relatively, after years of a Greek Cypriot embargo and international isolation, both communities would gain and in January and February 1994 both stated acceptance in principle.

In March and April 1994 Boutros-Ghali's negotiators sought to find mutually acceptable means of implementing the package. Although both parties earlier had implied acceptance, in a fashion typical of Cyprus, the negotiations failed. The Secretary-General took the unusual step of laying blame: 'the absence of agreement was due essentially to a lack of political will on the Turkish Cypriot side.'[113] Further efforts in the Summer resulted in a similar experience: both sides implied acceptance of CBMs, but then rejected them when the Secretary-General presented them in the form of a letter.

In a response to this frustration Boutros-Ghali stated that unless the parties provided evidence of commitment to a negotiated settlement he would recommend that his mission of good offices be suspended. This is not an uncommon ploy and can encourage parties to make concessions, for neither party would wish to appear intransigent. However,

Boutros-Ghali's decision to apportion blame – particularly upon the Turkish Cypriots – risked being associated with the Greek Cypriot's campaign to internationalize the issue in their favour. This often has had the effect of hardening the Turkish Cypriot position and it was partly this that was behind the 1983 declaration of independence. Security Council Resolution 939 of 29 July requested the Secretary-General to consult with the Council, the guarantor powers – Britain, Turkey and Greece – and the leaders in Cyprus to make a 'fundamental and far-reaching reflection on ways of approaching the Cyprus problem in a manner that will yield results'.[114] Joe Clark and the Deputy Special Representative henceforth continued to confer with leaders of the two communities in Cyprus and with the Greek and Turkish governments.

Although the CBMs had the logic of mutual advantage for both communities, the benefits did not outweigh the sensitive political and physical issues which lie at the heart of the Cypriot dispute. In fact the proposed CBMs appeared incongruous in the context of the bitterness exuded daily on both sides of the UN line and by the communities' leaders.

The international climate of opinion has been reflected in the European Court of Justice decision to ban European Union countries from importing goods from Turkish 'occupied' north Cyprus, according to the Turkish Cypriot leadership 'at the instigation of the Greek Cypriot side'.[115] Similarly, the European Union has not been deterred from considering an application by Cyprus for its entry into the Union.[116] Denktash has argued consistently that such a bid for membership does not represent the whole island and is therefore illegal.

The ostracism of Turkish Cyprus and the apportioning of blame by the Secretary-General could harden the position of the north further and make the CBMs appear almost absurd. The Secretary-General himself reported excessive levels of armaments and forces in Cyprus and no progress even on modest measures to reduce confrontation along the ceasefire line. The indication by the government of Cyprus in late 1996 that it had ordered Russian ground-to-air missiles was the most inflammatory such development and indicated that years of effort on the part of the UN

Secretariat count for little against an issue of survival for these communities. As Crawshaw observed, '[t]he Turkish Cypriots are in greater need of a settlement than the Greek Cypriots. But they put security first.'[117] As long as they perceive a physical threat in a unified Cyprus and Turkey continues to sponsor *de facto* partition, this is likely to be the least risky option.

The Secretary-General has observed the importance of 'events outside the island'.[118] Leverage does exist: the Turkish customs union with the European Union and Western strategic support for Turkey's regional concerns are incentives, and Cyprus clearly wishes to join the European Union, apparently believing that membership would bring security guarantees. North Cyprus would gain economically from a settlement. The possibility of US coercion or inducements to Turkey could be the key. Yet in some ways the West needs Turkey as much as vice versa, not least as a strategic ally given Turkey's close proximity to the Middle East and its support for the West's policy on Iraq. In addition Turkey maintains that it does not have the deciding influence over the Turkish Cypriot community.

At the beginning of 1996 the US announced a 'big push' on the Cyprus dispute, in conjunction with the UN framework, feeling that there was a window of opportunity for a solution. The planned visit by US State Department envoy Richard Holbrooke – which was disrupted by a confrontation between Turkey and Greece in the Aegean Sea – reflected the importance attached by the Clinton administration to a resolution of the dispute. However, the West, and certainly the US and Britain, is not willing to put substantial pressure upon Turkey. Moreover, until Turkey has a stable government it is unlikely that effective pressure or influence can be brought to bear upon its policy. Increasingly it would appear that the *de facto* partition of the island will be long-term, possibly with the result that the Turkish north, at least, will become annexed to the 'motherland'. The US 'big push' was stalled by the Aegean confrontation and Greece felt that the US took the side of Turkey. The incident may have indicated that a 'Dayton-style' conference would not be quite so suitable in Cyprus. Denktash is most likely to fear the imposition of a solution formulated by the US, Greece and Turkey, and there is a possibility that he would be more willing to support the continuation of the consensual UN process.

Security Council Resolution 939 placed the Secretaryship-General in a pivotal position of peacemaking efforts and its status as a mediator and focus of international efforts were positive to the development of the Office's procedural authority. Moreover, the Office continued to enjoy some room for manoeuvre in the development of 'ideas', CBMs and in making public pronouncements. However, the Secretary-General has also become associated with the international pressure and the ostracism of Northern Cyprus. Whatever the rights and wrongs of the case, this may not be constructive for the Office's traditionally impartial and innocuous bases of legitimacy, either in this case or in general. In the past the Turkish side has not responded well to pressure. Indeed, a letter from a representative of the Turkish Cypriots expressed very clearly the feeling of entrenchment which had resulted from the Greek Cypriot efforts to 'bring about the total isolation of the Turkish Cypriot people and our ultimate ruination'.[119] By identifying himself with efforts to put pressure upon the Turkish north, the Secretary-General may taint his classical role of providing an impartial facilitating agent for either party to compromise when the time is right.[120]

Haiti

After many years of little or no democracy in Haiti an election in 1990 gave Bertrand Aristide a clear majority. In September a coup brought General Raoul Cedras and a military regime to power, along with a 'human rights crisis' of repression and abuse.[121] In the context of ideas of collective internationalism and democratization and under the leadership of the US, the UN felt a responsibility to restore 'freedom, democracy, just order and the potential for progress to an entire nation and state'.[122]

On 24 November 1992 General Assembly Resolution 47/20 asked the Secretary-General to assist the return of the legitimate president and democracy, in cooperation with the Organization of American States. Dante Caputo was appointed as the Secretary-General's Representative and later also as the representative of the OAS. In June the Security Council imposed sanctions and provided a coercive backdrop to the July 1993 Governors Island talks between the military leaders in Haiti and the US. Significantly, the Council was '[s]trongly supportive of the continuing leadership by the Secretary-General of the United Nations' and the OAS and furthermore clearly identified the Office in the context of Chapter VII.[123] The Governors Island agreement established procedures for the return of Aristide and democratic rule. This was formed under the auspices of the UN and OAS negotiations with the 'Friends of the Secretary-General', Canada, the US, France and Venezuela. Boutros-Ghali subsequently recommended that the sanctions be suspended as soon as there were signs of progress in facilitating the departure of the military leaders, in order to maintain momentum.[124]

The Secretary-General was overseeing preparations for the proposed UN mission when the whole process became confounded by the military authority's failure to fulfil the Governors Island agreement: Aristide was not allowed to return and there was an increase in political repression. Security Council Resolution 867, 23 September 1993, had authorized the dispatch of a UN Mission to Haiti for six months, upon the recommendation of the Secretary-General. The process of deployment was obstructed when the USS *Harlan County* was prevented from docking in October 1993, in a display which did not do much for the credibility of the UN and the US. All UN staff, including the International Civilian Mission human rights observers, were withdrawn. Caputo's negotiation process – with US envoy Lawrence – had unravelled, and wider sanctions were reimposed. The military leaders refused to attend meetings of the Secretary-General's Representative and a 'personal initiative' by Boutros-Ghali to dispatch an envoy to Haiti to try to seek agreement was rebuffed.[125]

The Clinton administration had made a commitment to assertive multilateralism and to the restoration of democracy in Haiti; it would not allow the military leaders in Haiti to remain. Thus, Council Resolution 940 of 31 July 1994 authorized 'all necessary means' to facilitate the restoration of democracy. Interestingly, the Security Council took note of the Secretary-General's support for action under Chapter VII.

Last-minute diplomacy by Jimmy Carter provided an arrangement through which Cédras could depart. UN Representative Caputo resigned as a result of this, complaining of the US muscling the UN aside, acting unilaterally and offering concessions to the military leader. The subsequent multilateral occupation of Haiti was controlled essentially by the US. Nevertheless, Boutros-Ghali did not make much of an effort to dissociate his Office from the use of force. He announced that the US had the right to intervene militarily at any time without issuing an ultimatum: 'we would have liked to handle these operations ourselves, but [with] neither the financial nor military means, one must at least have the wisdom to turn over the mandate to a group of states that are prepared.'[126] When the multinational force had finished Boutros-Ghali was in Haiti to oversee the handover to the UN mission and give symbolic effect to his takeover: the force had been a 'success story' with nearly twenty thousand weapons confiscated.[127] In a report to the Security Council the Secretary-General had recommended the switchover by the end of March 1995 after judging that the security situation had improved enough. Resolution 944 subsequently revised and extended the mandate of the UN Mission in Haiti (UNMIH), alongside the OAS, to work on the stability brought by the multinational force to professionalize certain institutions and to provide electoral assistance. With the assumption of the UN mission Boutros-Ghali appointed Brahimi as his Special Representative – and the senior foreign official in the country – reportedly resisting the US wish for an American to be appointed, which occurred with Howe in Somalia. One must consider whether Boutros-Ghali took this stand to emphasize his and the UN's independence from the US rather than trying to dissociate his Office from the use of force.

The Secretary-General participated in a number of important processes in the UN involvement in Haiti, either personally or through Caputo and then Brahimi. He was involved in mediation with the OAS Secretary-General, influencing policy through recommendations to the Security

Council both before and after the military regime reneged on the Governors Island Agreement, and he directed the UN mission which followed the multinational force. His Special Representative met with President Aristide at least every week to review the activities of the UN. The UN Electoral Assistance Team helped supervise municipal and local elections in late 1995. Finally, the justice and development branches of the Secretariat assisted with successful local, legislative and Presidential elections.[128] The two main points of contention for the Office of Secretary-General concern its association with the use of coercion and the UN's proximity to US objectives. Given the US political concerns and its history of hegemony in the area, one is left with the impression that the UN was in part an instrument or 'fig-leaf' for a US agenda. Nevertheless, it was an apparent success in the midst of a disillusioned climate, and the fact that the US needed a UN and not just an OAS 'fig-leaf' is significant.

Iraq

The implementation of the 1991 Gulf War settlement constituted a diktat of enormous proportions and continued the dominance of the activist states – particularly the US and Britain – which had trounced Iraqi forces during Desert Storm. The Secretaryship-General has been involved in the implementation of the UN's mandatory regulations with regard to weapons of mass destruction, the boundary between Iraq and Kuwait, the humanitarian agenda, sanctions, peacekeeping, and compensation. However, the room for manoeuvre for the Secretary-General has been narrow, commensurate with the sensitive political and geostrategic agenda of the activist states and the explicit and mandatory nature of the Security Council's demands under Resolutions 687, 688, and those thereafter.

The Permanent Five have not remained united underneath the surface. A cleavage emerged between Russia and France, on the one hand, who have actively sought an easing of sanctions, and Britain and the US, on the other, who have sought to maintain them. Nevertheless, the existing legal framework which underlies the sanctions regime and the presence of UN agencies in Iraq is explicit. Therefore, the position of the Secretary-General has been to organize the modalities for the implementation of its terms. The assessment of Iraq's compliance has been within the realm of the Security Council. This conforms to the thesis that, when the Security Council is in formal agreement in the post-Cold War context, the room for manoeuvre of the Secretaryship-General is narrow, in effect confined to executing the will of the Security Council. In cases where leading Permanent Council Members have a key interest and the Security Council follows their leadership, the position of the Secretary-General will be further constrained. In October 1994, for example, Iraqi military movements were interpreted by the US as threatening to regional security and therefore further reason to maintain sanctions. There was no independent input from the Secretary-General.

Nevertheless, the Secretary-General has made policy-influencing reports in the process of the Security Council's continuing review of Iraq and has coordinated the communication of information from the field. The Secretary-General's Office commands the UN Iraq–Kuwait Observation Mission which has had Permanent Member participation and was expanded by Resolution 806(1993) to include the capacity to take physical action to prevent or redress small-scale violations. The UN Special Commission, central to the involvement of the UN in Iraq, has employed unprecedented practices to impose an innovative regime of 'arms control enforcement'.[129]

Although the Secretary-General is peripheral to Council policy, the quantitative increase of the Office's activities in this case is self-evident. It is also significant that Iraqi foreign minister Tariq Aziz wrote directly to the Secretary-General when Iraq was prepared to enter into dialogue regarding the long-standing Security Council offer to allow controlled sales of oil for humanitarian reasons under Resolution 986. However, to fulfil a classical good-offices role the Secretary-General would be aided by a certain independence and room for manoeuvre from the Council. In light of the interests of the activist states and the likelihood of repercussions upon world oil prices if Iraq resumed substantial oil exports, the Secretary-General had little room for manoeuvre in the negotiations.[130] More importantly, the Office has been associated – as an instrument of the Council – with the use of coercion by the Security Council under Chapter VII through the activist states. Again, one should question if this is compatible with the Office's traditional impartial and innocuous third-party duties. In this and in other cases a recalcitrant party might be induced to employ the Secretary-General as a form of face-saving climb-down, in this case for example with regard to weapons of mass destruction and supervised oil sales. If the Secretary-General is identified too closely with the Security Council in enforcement measures this important role may be jeopardized.

GOOD OFFICES AND PREVENTIVE DIPLOMACY

In the 1990s the good offices and preventive roles of the Secretary-General have burgeoned in parallel with post-Cold War civil strife and state fragmentation and the increasing involvement of the UN in such areas. Developments in UN diplomatic and political practices have complemented these processes. The third-party activities of the Office in areas formerly considered to be the spheres of influence of Great Powers within Africa, Central America and the former Soviet Union, have been particularly important. The Secretaryship-General is experiencing more room for manoeuvre compared to the sensitivity of the Cold War which precluded the Office from many regional conflicts. Indeed Boutros-Ghali remarked in January 1996 that the Office has a distinctive role in quiet preventive diplomacy as 'an impartial figure with a global mandate'.[131] He also observed: 'preventive diplomacy is a particular responsibility of the Secretary-General. Early warning, fact-finding, confidence-building measures, personal contacts, and good offices, all are instruments of this.'[132] Within certain bounds, many UN members are supportive of this concept. Proactive initiatives are central to the Secretaryship-General's 'global mandate'. For example, the Security Council welcomed the Secretary-General's initiative in preparing, in collaboration with the government of Sierra Leone, an action plan for the demobilization and reintegration of combatants after fighting flared up there in the Autumn of 1995. Moreover, the

Secretary-General also planned to send a special envoy to Sudan to discuss with the government efforts to combat terrorism in the region. He met with Julius Nyerere regarding the escalation of violence in Burundi in September 1996, and sent a Special Envoy to the Great Lakes region of Africa in November. In highlighting the plight of refugees in Zaire as an 'all-out emergency' he hoped to nudge the Security Council towards substantive action.[133] This he conceived of as 'humanitarian diplomacy'.[134] The attempt at a leadership role by Boutros-Ghali on the eve of the March 1996 conference held in Egypt on terrorism in the Middle East was likewise interesting: he stated that the UN was waiting to implement whatever measures the conference adopted. Dozens of such examples exist, as well as many others which have not come to light.

Some believe that the Secretary-General could and should expand his remit in reporting threats to the peace to the Security Council in accordance with the increasingly wide conception of peace and security and non-military hazards.[135] It is significant that the UN and its Secretary-General are involved in domestic situations on an unprecedented scale, and that good-offices missions are publicized more than before. The number of UN interim offices around the world – for example in seven former Soviet republics – is illustrative of the quiet assistance of the UN in peaceful transition.

Preventive activities and the good offices of the Secretaryship-General have been subject to paradoxical trends. Post-Cold War attitudes towards wider conceptions of peace and security have encouraged these activities, yet multilateral fatigue from 1993 appear to have curtailed the financial and diplomatic resources necessary to do so. There is 'an undeniable disparity between the vision and the reality'.[136] Yet the constraints on finance and personnel logically should motivate UN members to encourage preventive diplomacy in the hope that some expensive disaster can be averted. However, the Secretary-General must have resources to bring to bear upon conflict situations, and good offices and preventive diplomacy can be a prelude to some form of peace operation, yet the recent political climate in the Council has not been conducive to the creation of new multifunctional operations. With the prioritization which has resulted from this climate, some areas have less attention than others and patience is often thin. This conflicts with the demands of patient diplomacy. On a practical note, the increase in these activities has necessitated the increased use of Personal and Special Representatives, appointed on the Secretary-General's initiative or at the behest of the Security Council or General Assembly.[137]

Afghanistan

In comparison to the attention of the international community and the UN in pursuance of the withdrawal of Soviet troops in the late 1980s, the UN has not committed substantial resources to Afghanistan's ensuing civil war because of the climate of multilateral fatigue and political prioritization.

The Najibullah government left behind by the Soviets was defeated in 1992, and since then *mujahidin* and other factions have vied for control, wreaking havoc and humanitarian catastrophe on the country. The combatants have allied around President Burhanuddin Rabbani, rival Gillbuddin Hekmatyar, and the Islamicist Taliban movement, and the struggle has centred upon the capital. Alliances have switched according to the military turn of events, with Rabbani and Hekmatyar joining forces against the powerful Taliban in 1996. There are ethnic and religious divisions in evidence – chiefly between the Pashtuns and non-Pashtuns – but at least one observer has suggested that regionalism and warlordism are stronger.[138] While Afghanistan has not received much multilateral political attention or humanitarian assistance, regional powers have been active in competing for influence and supporting various parties. There have been reports of Russia, Uzbekistan, Pakistan, India, Saudi Arabia and Iran being involved. Indeed, Afghanistan provides a 'mini-great game for regional powers'.[139] While the leading international powers have been reluctant to exert leverage to lessen this regional interference – and indeed may be involved covertly themselves – and the UN is contained by prioritization and fatigue, the Secretary-General and his Special Representative have been frustrated.

On 21 December 1993 General Assembly Resolution 48/208 requested the Secretary-General to send a special mission to canvass a broad spectrum of Afghan leaders regarding a UN role in assisting rapprochement and reconstruction. When serious fighting resumed in January 1994 Boutros-Ghali called for a ceasefire and engaged in consultations with Iran, Pakistan, Russia, Saudi Arabia and the USA. In February Boutros-Ghali appointed Mahmoud Mestiri to head the Special Mission, which visited the region and met all the interested parties, both inside and outside Afghanistan. The Secretary-General finally reported to the Security Council in June 1994 outlining the possibility of a new UN presence in Afghanistan, the implementation of a country-wide ceasefire, and the establishment of a transitional authority so that free and fair elections could be held. He also observed the need for greater attention to this tragedy.

A great deal rested on the possibility of creating some form of transitional authority or *loya girgha* – traditional grand assembly – Rabbani stepping down from the presidency, and the regional powers exerting influence. The Security Council outlined a step-by-step process of reconciliation, demobilization, and some form of transitional government. On a number of occasions Rabbani had agreed and was due to leave office in accordance with numerous agreements between 1992 and 1995, but had failed to do so. In order to inject some momentum into the process Boutros-Ghali met the rivals in Islamabad in early September 1994 and consulted with members of the Organization of the Islamic Conference, whose Secretary-General had also attempted to reach a settlement. Mestiri – who announced that he had won agreement among all sides about a UN presence in principle – was still urging the parties to commit themselves to a grand assembly to decide on a future government and apparently had built support for a UN transition 'mechanism', a UN-sponsored council which would replace the government in March 1995. The arrival of the Taliban upset the process, as they did not wish to participate. Mestiri continued to negotiate with all the parties and a number of neighbouring countries for a means to enable Rabbani to stand down for a transitional coalition council, although a number of the other factions are not convinced that he intended to step down at all. He was effectively toppled by the Taliban's sweeping successes in 1996 and again the negotiating process was overtaken by military events on the ground. In 1996 Mestiri shuttled throughout the country and region with the objective of facilitating a peaceful transition to a UN-proposed interim council. However any process of rehabilitation requires material support and the wariness of the international community was reflected in a UN appeal for $124 million receiving only $26.9 million.[140]

While Mestiri – with the occasional input of the Secretary-General – helped to establish a framework for a political settlement and rehabilitation, much of this rested upon a longer-term commitment to the country and the support of external parties. However, the political climate at the UN is not conducive to long-term commitments, and Afghanistan continues to attract the adverse attention of regional and international actors. The Security Council's support for the Secretary-General has thus been somewhat hollow.

Burundi

Although the Rwanda tragedy of 1994 was a starker indication of the Security Council's reluctance to become involved in a domestic catastrophe, Burundi was an earlier manifestation of the post-Somalia syndrome of multilateral fatigue, caution and political prioritization. Again, the Secretary-General was constrained by these pressures.

After the military coup of 21 October 1993 the Secretary-General sent James Jonah as his envoy to help facilitate the return of Burundi to constitutional rule and identify what the UN could do to assist. Soon after, a Security Council Presidential statement requested the Secretary-General to monitor the situation in consultation with the Organization of African Unity. It appears that the government wanted some form of peacekeeping at that stage but Jonah had to explain that the Security Council 'has shown no inclination to take on any new operations'.[141] The Security Council, under the preponderance of the US, was drawing the line at Burundi.

The Secretary-General appointed Ahmedou Ould Abdallah as Special Representative and the Security Council authorized him to dispatch a small fact-finding mission simultaneously with the launching of humanitarian assistance programmes. On 6 April 1994 the Presidents of Burundi and Rwanda were killed and ethnic violence claimed thousands of lives. A semblance of stability returned through 1994 with the assistance of Abdallah. On a shoestring he helped to persuade Hutu and Tutsi politicians to agree to power-sharing arrangements, and after the death of the President he was important in bringing politicians and the army to broadcast calls for calm. With an ethnic complexion similar to that of Rwanda – the Tutsi minority control the army – and a history of hostility Burundi contains the ingredients for a catastrophe and is therefore a prime case for substantive preventive action: senior Secretariat officer Chinmaya Gharekhan described the situation as 'a laboratory for some sort of preventive action'.[142]

However, the climate at the UN was not conducive to this logic and Boutros-Ghali was relegated to his 'bully-pulpit', urging the Security Council and OAU to take preventive action. Nevertheless, in August 1994 he embarked upon a more rigorous approach to addressing the effects of the conflict upon Burundi, Tanzania, Uganda and Zaire, by asking an envoy to tour the region with a view to strengthening the coordination of UN humanitarian efforts which are closely tied to political stability. More significantly, on 27 March the Secretary-General met the Permanent Members of the Council at his own request to discuss the deteriorating situation in Burundi.[143] The ethnic polarization of the country had intensified under the influence of extremists, foreign aid workers were being targeted, and resources needed to ameliorate suffering continued to dwindle.

Boutros-Ghali's alarm at the situation and his apparent belief that he had a responsibility to encourage 'a major initiative to prevent another tragedy' were manifested in a number of forms.[144] Most significantly, the Secretary-General made a number of proposals for a military force, authorized by the Security Council under Chapter VII, to be deployed on Burundi's border with Zaire, with a view to military intervention if necessary. Even though there was a strong case for such a pre-emptive move, the government of Burundi was most unwelcoming of any form of military intervention and the Security Council was unsupportive for other reasons. A former UK Permanent Representative to the UN commented that it was not so much Boutros-Ghali's desire to address the situation in Burundi as his high-handed method that was objectionable.[145] Yet the method worked in so far as it helped put Burundi on the Council agenda. The Secretary-General's proposal represented something of a leap forward in the development of the Office's roles. Nevertheless, Boutros-Ghali's public and private efforts could not overcome the climate of stagnation and 'preventive diplomacy' was conducted under severe constraints. In effect, this was the failure of the 'cosmopolitan Secretary-General'.

Yemen

After four years of uneasy unity fighting broke out between the traditionally socialist southern Yemen and the government forces of the north in May 1994. The Security Council called for an immediate ceasefire and requested the Secretary-General to send a fact-finding mission to assess prospects for a dialogue. However, the Secretariat was in a sensitive position. The government claimed that it was quelling a secessionist attempt and did not welcome UN intervention. Thus, the post-Cold War issue of interventionism was projected upon the Office of Secretary-General. Amidst continuing fighting the Security Council passed Resolution 931 on 29 June 1994, reiterating the call for a ceasefire. Special Representative Lakhdar Brahimi arranged a meeting in Geneva on 28 July between representatives of the parties after fighting had come to an end. In addition, the Secretary-General instructed the Department of Humanitarian Affairs to take immediate action in response to the needs of the displaced or deprived people.

Resolution 931 left the nature of the ceasefire monitors to the Secretary-General. In fact the government was reluctant to accept monitors who might lend legitimacy to the south. Moreover, the climate at the UN was not supportive of peacekeeping and the Security Council Resolution was rather vague in instructing the Secretary-General to work towards a 'mechanism' to encourage and monitor a cease-fire.[146] Both sides had accepted formally the 1 June ceasefire, but had differences over the monitors, and fighting continued. This was the focus of Brahimi's negotiations in New York and Cairo between the parties and in consultation with the Arab League and Saudi Arabia.

The vagueness of the Security Council Resolution and its lack of commitment was also a reflection of the caution which pervaded the Council at the time. While it appeared that the Secretary-General had room to manoeuvre, he and Brahimi probably knew they could not count on much support for a major UN commitment to a settlement. This is another case of prioritization and fatigue among the leading international actors: the conflict did not have major international implications and it was given to the Secretary-General without much expectation or wish for a subsequent UN commitment.

Georgia

Central Asia has been experiencing fragmentation along ethnic and national lines. The development of preventive diplomacy and the good offices of the international civil service alongside the omnipresence of Russian diplomacy is interesting. Here the Secretary-General's Office is mediating – or at least being involved – in what would traditionally have been considered a domestic context or in the sphere of influence of a Great Power.

Fighting broke out in August 1992 in the Abkhazia region of northwest Georgia and the secessionist forces eventually seized the whole area, displacing some 200 000 Georgians who formerly lived there. The Secretary-General assigned Edouard Brunner as Special Envoy and mobilized an inter-agency humanitarian effort to assist the repatriation and relief of the displaced people. On 14 May 1994 both sides signed a formal ceasefire and Brunner, in cooperation with the Russian Federation and the Organization for Security and Cooperation in Europe, was seeking a comprehensive settlement. The underlying problem was Abkhazia's demand for independent statehood and Georgia's demand to maintain its territorial integrity. Negotiations were based on the idea of Abkhazia having some autonomous rights but within the framework of a Georgian union. A central practical barrier to progress has been the tardiness of the return of Georgian refugees to the region with the assistance of the UNHCR, and reports that those who have returned home have been persecuted and even murdered by Abkhazian guerillas. Significantly, the Secretary-General singled out Abkhaz unwillingness to accept the return of refugees.[147]

On 6 July 1993 the Secretary-General recommended that 50 UN observers be deployed to discourage the escalation of the conflict within Georgia and across the whole region, even though, he acknowledged, there were risks with such a deployment. The Council gave the UN Observer Mission in Georgia (UNOMIG) an interim mandate to maintain contacts with both sides and the substantial Commonwealth of Independent States (CIS) presence, and to monitor developments relevant to a political settlement. After the parties signed a memorandum of understanding the Secretary-General sought and received authorization from the Security Council to deploy up to fifty more observers. This was increased further to 136 by Resolution 937 of 21 July 1994, which also instructed UNOMIG to monitor and verify implementation of a local agreement and observe the CIS force. There was talk of the possibility of a UN peacekeeping force – in fact Georgia had requested consideration of a force[148] – but the political climate in the Security Council was not supportive, so the Secretary-General has worked alongside the presence of the Russians, albeit under UNOMIG's monitoring. As in Tajikistan, Nagorny Karabakh (with the Organization of Security and Cooperation in Europe) and elsewhere, while the Security Council has passed Resolutions and the Secretary-General has directed field missions, the UN has acknowledged that its role is complementary or secondary to regional organizations and states, principally Russia.

Have the UN and its Secretary-General, as a result of personnel and financial constraints, legitimized Russia's regional objectives? The Secretary-General reported that the CIS forces are cooperating with UNOMIG on the basis of agreements and that the peacemaking process has the backing of the 'Friends of Georgia', France, Germany, Russia and the USA. However, there have been reports that Russia initially aided the rebels in order to bring Georgia closer into the Russian fold. One could argue that the UN's involvement is innovative anyway in an area traditionally under the Russian wing. Russia's Permanent Representative to the UN rejected the charge of 'neo-imperialist ambitions' and stated that, far from wanting to hide Russia's activities in the former Soviet republics, it would welcome greater input of the UN.[149] The decision of the Secretary-General to appoint a resident Deputy Special Envoy indicated his perseverance despite his feeling that 'both sides continue to take positions that cannot, as yet, be bridged'.[150]

A summit between Georgian President Edouard Shevardnadze, the Abkhazia leader Ardzinba, Russian Foreign Minister Andrei Kozyrev, and the Chairman of the Organization for Security and Cooperation in Europe (OSCE), was convened and chaired by Boutros-Ghali. The central issues remained the status of Abkhazia within a federal framework and the return of displaced persons, although Abkhaz leader Vladislav Ardzinba said he was not against a federal arrangement in principle, albeit on the basis on two equal entities. This was augmented by the adoption by the 'Supreme Soviet' of Abkhazia of a constitution which declared it a 'sovereign democratic state'.[151] On this basis talks were deadlocked. Boutros-Ghali undertook vigorous efforts 'in close consultation' with his Special Representative who took 'the initiative' to hold consultations with Abkhaz authorities regarding the protection of human rights, and continued to pursue contacts with the Georgian and Russian parties.[152] Although the Secretary-General described the negotiations as deadlocked, he appeared to see this process in the context of the wider cooperation between Russia and UN in the former Soviet Union.

On a procedural level the Secretary-General exercised authority through his Personal or Special Representative's good offices, in an area formally considered a sphere of influence of a Great Power. For example, responding to claims by Boutros-Ghali that Abkhaz rebels were holding up the peace process, Ardzinba wrote to the Secretary-General outlining their commitment to the process and their wish for a confederal union with Georgia. However, without the likelihood of a substantive UN commitment his activities were conditioned by the need to acknowledge a major Russian role and therefore jeopardize his impartiality with the parties. Similarly, the Secretary-General did not have a substantial degree of 'positive leverage' to bring to bear; the voluntary relief fund established by Security Council Resolution 937(1994) had received nothing in January 1995. It may be the case, as Alvaro de Soto has claimed, that the Secretary-General is not micromanaged in his mediation and that he sometimes keeps the Security Council informed 'at his discretion',[153] but this room for manoeuvre does not necessarily mean that the Office is actively backed by the Council.

Tajikistan

In 1992 the coalition governing Tajikistan broke down – some reports suggest that a Russian-backed group seized power[154] – and fighting between government and Islamic Afghan-supported rebels raged. In the autumn of 1992 the Secretary-General dispatched, in consultation with the governments of Tajikistan and Uzbekistan, a fact-finding mission and then a good-will mission to Tajikistan and four neighbouring states to assist in peacemaking efforts and to assess humanitarian needs. The UNHCR, World Food Programme and World Health Organization were poised to become involved. It is interesting that the Secretary-General stated that he 'informed' the Security Council of his intention to establish a small unit in the region, and he instructed Special Envoy Ismat Kittani to visit throughout the region in the Summer of 1993 and early 1994, again in cooperation with the OSCE and CIS. On the basis of this the President of the Council requested the Secretary-General to present recommendations regarding the role that the UN could play in assisting the implementation of the Tajik peace process.[155]

There were rounds of UN-sponsored talks in Moscow, Tehran, Islamabad, and Kazakhstan. The latter in May and June 1995 involved a discussion of a compromise plan for reconciliation, confidence-building measures, and the return of displaced persons. Progress was slow, despite

Boutros-Ghali's attempts to push the parties. The Secretary-General suspended the activities of his Envoy before the Islamabad talks until the Government and opposition parties demonstrated their commitment to political dialogue. Similarly, when it appeared that the government was reluctant to accept the confidence-building measures he suspended preparations for the third round until the parties gave evidence of commitment.

There had been optimism for this fourth round after the first meeting of the President and the leader of the rebels in Afghanistan, even though the ceasefire was frequently violated. The UN Mission of Observers in Tajikistan, set up in December 1994 and numbering about 72 in June 1995, began working alongside the CIS/Russian force of 18 000. This certainly gave confidence to the establishment of a framework for further talks in the principles for establishing peace, signed by the parties in August 1995.[156] In December 1995 the Secretary-General recommended a second six-month extension of the 72 member UN force, although progress was reported to be very slow. Nevertheless, the August agreement established acceptance of continuous inter-Tajik talks, a format favoured by Boutros-Ghali. There was initially deadlock over the location of these talks but the Secretary-General took the opportunity of the fiftieth anniversary commemorations of the Organization to speak with all the parties involved and neighbouring countries in order to successfully ease the process back on track. In January 1996 the Islamic opposition launched an assault on government troops, again plunging the process into crisis and prompting the Secretary-General's representative to undertake urgent efforts to achieve stability. A number of UN observers were taken hostage in December 1996 – and later released – and this similarly pointed to a deterioration of the situation.

The UN mediation effort must be seen in the context of international and regional power interests. Russia clearly supports the Tajik government and its force is mainly aimed at preventing supplies from Afghanistan from reaching the rebels. Many regional states – particularly Iran – also have an interest. The UN Secretariat's acquaintance with the CIS therefore jeopardizes its impartiality in the eyes of the rebels and may have wider implications for its independence. The fragmentation of power around increasingly independent warlords has increased the volatility of the situation. In an area used to the steadying influence of Russia, UN mediation is experiencing severe difficulties. Indeed, when yet another peace accord was signed in Moscow in late 1996 – establishing a 'national reconciliation commission' – it was under the guidance of Russia, under pressure to reduce its burdens in the former republics.

It is also important to consider if the Secretary-General's activities are genuinely supported by the Security Council or confounded by the differing agendas of the members toward the region. If external actors are not willing to apply leverage upon the parties in favour of a political settlement because they wish to influence the outcome in some way, then the position of the Secretary-General is undermined and out of step with the political realities at work. This challenges the idea of the Secretary-General being employed on a sincere basis by the international community or Security Council, leaving a somewhat vague role for the Office.

Guatemala

In January 1994 the military government of Guatemala and the rebel Unidad Revolucionari Nacional Guatemalteca (URNG) agreed to resume negotiations under the auspices of the Secretary-General to settle the longest conflict in Latin America. The UN had been involved since 1990 when Pérez de Cuéllar was asked to appoint an observer in talks between the government and the URNG, which is predominantly native Indian, poor, and seeks greater democracy and rights for the indigenous population.

Talks began with Jean Arnault moderating for the UN and with the input of the Group of Friends of the Guatemalan Peace Process: Colombia, Mexico, Norway, Spain, the US and Venezuela. Agreements were reached on human rights, on a timetable for a lasting settlement, and on displaced people. Once the talks were under way Boutros-Ghali sent a survey mission to assess the needs of the country. In the autumn of 1994 he announced approval of the UN Verification of Human Rights for Guatemala (MINUGUA), to uphold the human rights accord and hopefully help to restart the stalled talks. The talks stalled on the subject of indigenous rights in December 1994 and a new effort was needed to restore momentum. Boutros-Ghali called upon both sides to submit a new schedule for a final settlement and sent Undersecretary-General Marrack Goulding on a shuttle among the parties, to overcome the problem. The UN had warned that it would reassess its position if the parties did not respond positively, and in early February 1995 the URNG accepted the UN proposals in New York. According to the new schedule, from March 1995, socio-economic and agrarian agreements would be implemented, then issues of civilian power and the role of the army, followed by the reintegration of the URNG into civilian life, leading to constitutional and electoral reform. The peace accord was finally signed at the end of Boutros-Ghali's tenure in December 1996. His presence in Guatemala City for the occasion emphasized the UN mediation in the process and allowed the Secretary-General to depart from office on a positive note, at least in this case. UN mediator Jean Arnault can be singled out for maintaining momentum for the talks, pushing the parties, and helping to restart negotiations when they faltered.

The Secretary-General's Office has been a key actor in facilitating a difficult process of reconciliation and democratic transition without a great deal of resources and certainly not as much as had been available for Nicaragua and El Salvador. Although the external actors have finally exerted leverage upon their clients in this civil war – and this has been fundamental for the UN's efforts – the lack of resources at the Secretary-General's disposal put him and his mediators in a difficult position: the framework schedule was ambitious, and with a relatively small observer mission, the process was somewhat fragile. There were scant resources for 'positive leverage' or 'amelioration through assistance', activities for which the Secretary-General had sought in 1992 to better prepare his Office and the UN.[157] Some elements of Guatemalan society are opposed to the process – as indicated by the bombs which coincided with Boutros-Ghali's visit in April 1995 – and without a substantial UN presence or much world attention the process is vulnerable to disruption. Again, this is a symptom of financial constraint, political prioritization, and multilateral fatigue: good offices on a shoestring.

Korea

The North Korean nuclear issue and its relationship with South Korea have been high-profile issues, within the realm of the Security Council and particularly for the USA. In such circumstances the Office of Secretary-General can wield influence as a facilitator and face-saver, even without the traditional levers of power. It was just such a position which enabled U Thant to help to facilitate a stand-down over the Cuban Missile Crisis in 1962. In December 1993 Boutros-Ghali visited the Korean peninsula for discussions with the governments of both countries, expressing support for negotiations aimed at easing tension between the two and emphasizing concern for maintaining the Non-Proliferation Treaty, at a time when there was a growing sense of confrontation between North Korea and the international community. Boutros-Ghali's visit represented the patient approach to persuade the North to open its nuclear facilities to international inspections, a calming influence at a tense time. The Secretary-General had a meeting with Kim Il Sung and then visited China, which was seen as an indirect attempt to bring influence to bear on North Korea. There were reports that China was supportive of negotiation and was uncomfortable with US pressure or sanctions upon North Korea, and this might have enhanced the position of the Secretary-General as a channel for diplomacy.[158] In theory, with at least two members of the Security Council Permanent Five at odds, the Secretary-General is well placed to facilitate a compromise. However, North Korea apparently did not welcome Boutros-Ghali's mediation, viewing him with the UN as an instrument of the USA. One can conclude that the Secretary-General's position suffered from the coercive stance of the UN and his association with this, in addition to North Korea's perception of US hegemony at the UN. This case thus contributes to the impression that the Secretaryship-General's classical roles have been tainted through its proximity to the use of coercion and US preponderance.

East Timor

Indonesian occupation of the former Portuguese colony since 1975 has been a source of tension between the two countries and throughout the international community. The Secretary-General convened talks between the Portuguese and Indonesian foreign ministers in December 1992, but there was no progress. Portugal wanted greater rights for citizens and prisoners while Indonesia was cautious about giving any concession which might challenge its sovereignty over the island. In April 1993 Boutros-Ghali sent Representative Amos Wako to conduct an inspection tour, in particular to investigate the 1991 incident involving deaths at a demonstration. This is significant given the sensitivity of Indonesia to matters it had considered previously to be only of domestic interest. Indonesia is apparently keen to improve its international image and therefore the timing for the Secretary-General's good offices was positive. At a follow-up meeting in Rome in September 1993 under the Secretary-General's auspices, an accord was reached involving confidence-building measures on human rights, basic freedoms and outside access. However, the future political status of East Timor was not being discussed.

In May 1994 Indonesia agreed to allow a UN investigator into the territory. The following January the Foreign Ministers met in Geneva under UN auspices and reportedly agreed that the UN should host further talks on CBMs. Further to this, a UN-sponsored meeting in Austria in June, described as the first All-Inclusive Intra-East Timorese Dialogue, apparently initiated by the Secretaryship-General, produced a joint declaration. This reaffirmed the need to implement measures to promote peace, stability, justice, human rights and harmony and called for a continuation of dialogue under the Secretary-General. Subsequently in January 1996 the Secretary-General chaired the seventh biannual meeting which discussed the framework for talks and committed to continue the process in the middle of the year. It appears that the Secretary-General's Office is making progress, alongside other external actors, towards some form of settlement on an issue which has been insoluble in the past. Indonesia may be employing the UN as a means of making an honourable compromise, if not a climb-down, in at least improving conditions on the island. However, key Western and Asian states are not actively supportive of Indonesian withdrawal. They cannot prejudice economic relationships on the basis of East Timor and they see Indonesia's *de facto* annexation as a political reality. As long as this persists a substantial change in Indonesia's policy is unlikely and the Secretary-General's diplomacy will continue to be a sideshow.

Jammu and Kashmir

In the Kashmir dispute Boutros-Ghali attempted to increase the profile of his Office in an issue which has hitherto defied UN peacemaking efforts. The Secretary-General reported that he urged India and Pakistan to resume bilateral dialogue, and in Pakistan he offered publicly to be an 'honest broker to encourage a dialogue between the two protagonists'.[159] This has long been called for by Pakistan, which seeks to expose Indian practices in the disputed area to the outside world and to internationalize the issue. India, which holds firm on its sovereignty in the area and will not discuss its political future, was apparently annoyed that the Secretary-General even mentioned Kashmir in his annual report. It sees the attempts to involve the UN – such as the peace plan sent to Boutros-Ghali by the Jammu and Kashmir Liberation Front and Pakistani calls for human rights monitors and mediation by the Secretary-General – as politically motivated and has reacted coolly to the Secretary-General's overtures.

It is interesting that Boutros-Ghali apparently no longer seemed to regard any issues as 'no-go' areas and it is a symbol of progress and a widening concept of peace and security in the UN that the Secretary-General could even consider making statements about such an issue, especially in light of the secessionist sensitivities of some Permanent Members. However, there may be a price to pay. In terms of Kashmir, the Secretary-General cannot do anything unless both parties resort to mediation or external actors exert substantial influence. Although the Secretary-General's position is symbolically important, there is a danger of becoming, unintentionally, a part of Pakistan's objective of internationalizing the issue and isolating India. This could damage the credibility of the Office in the eyes of India if and when it does submit to good offices. This may demonstrate a negative consequence of the Office's post-Cold War activism.

Zaire/Congo

Zaire was another country whose internal situation had long been impenetrable to international organizations. However, with the end of the Cold War, and a wave of democratization across Africa, there were efforts from within Zaire to join this process in the years that led to the violent overthrow of the Mobutu regime. There were also powerful forces opposed to peaceful change: Mobutu, of course, but also the rebels who sought nothing less than a complete military victory. Therefore, a substantial and long-term commitment by the UN was necessary to support a process of transition and prevent a humanitarian catastrophe. However, the Secretary-General and his representatives had to negotiate with the knowledge that the UN would not support a major commitment in an unpredictable and hazardous situation and therefore could not bring a great deal of assistance. Indicative of this was the 'minimal' response to an inter-agency humanitarian appeal for $84 million in 1993.[160] Ultimately, the small possibility of peaceful transition was squandered as a result of this multilateral hesitancy.

The Secretary-General received a letter from Prime Minister Etienne Tshisekedi requesting observers to safeguard respect for human rights and to assist in the holding of elections, law and order, and humanitarian needs. In the summer of 1993 Boutros-Ghali held discussions with Zairean officials and President Mobutu in Cairo at the OAU summit. He appointed Lakhdar Brahimi to assess how the UN might assist in finding a solution to the political problems. However, in early 1994 Mobutu dismissed Tshisekedi and the situation threatened to deteriorate into civil war. Pro-democracy forces in Zaire accused the UN of moving too slowly and reportedly both Mobutu and Tshisekedi refused in May to receive Brahimi, who had been working on a power-sharing agreement. At the beginning of 1995 a group of Western governments reportedly asked Boutros-Ghali to join them in trying to prevent violence, but there was not much international interest or support. It is ironic that the new era has taken the Secretaryship-General into hitherto unknown areas, yet the climate of multilateral fatigue and financial shortages have deprived the Office of resources.

Burma/Myanmar

The government of Burma has defended and protected what it considers to be its domestic affairs from international involvement. It is interesting therefore that the government should accept the approaches of the Secretary-General at a time when it appears to be seeking to improve its reputation. Even before official contacts Boutros-Ghali met dissident Aung San Suu Kyi in 1993, a focal point of sensitivity in Burma's relationship with the outside world. In early 1994 Boutros-Ghali communicated the desire to establish contact to discuss 'various issues of concern expressed by the inter-national community', and the Burmese government agreed that a representative should meet the Secretary-General.[161] Subsequently, Assistant Secretary-General for Political Affairs, Alvaro de Soto, began a dialogue with the govern-ment.[162] Again, the Office was employed for domestic processes of transition and democratization in a manner rare before the end of the Cold War and certainly one alien to the classical model of the international civil service. However, like East Timor, the role of the Secretary-General could well be cosmetic, a diplomatic sideshow, as long as those countries which have economic and diplomatic influ-ence upon Burma do not exert substantive leverage.

Israel

Although the relationship between the Secretaryship-General and Israel may have improved somewhat, the UN is still relatively marginalized in the Arab–Israeli peace process, apart from peacekeeping and welfare roles.

Moreover, the Secretary-General's statements on the situation are often interpreted politically. Indeed, he wrote of 'the plight of the Palestinian people living under occupation' and the 'particularly grave incident' of Israel deporting over 400 Palestinians – whom Israel claimed had terrorist connections – to south Lebanon in December 1992.[163] Elsewhere the Secretary-General was even reported to have recommended taking 'all necessary steps' to bring about the return of the displaced people.[164] He sent James Jonah to the region to discuss the deportees and was active himself, communicating with PLO chairman Arafat. Later, the Secretary-General urged Israel to consider 'some kind of UN presence' in the occupied territories.[165] The Secretary-General has also been clear, on occasions, in condemning Israeli bombing of south Lebanon, suggesting that it was aimed at displacing the civilian population. After Israel's bombardment of southern Lebanon in April 1996, when approximately 100 civilians died, Boutros-Ghali's decision to make public a UN report which implied that Israeli forces might have deliberately targeted a UN camp where refugees were sheltering was a bold step which reportedly caused a furore in the US and Israel.[166] Such statements have been interpreted by Israel as bias toward the Arabs or a lack of understanding of the Israeli's special security concerns. The Office's status as a mediator is thus not enhanced by its use of the 'bully pulpit'.

The growing presence of humanitarian and security agencies in the occupied territories since the Oslo accords has signified the increased international involvement there. In September 1993 Boutros-Ghali established a high-level task force to identify projects for the UN Relief and Works Agency, the UN Development Programme and the UN Children's Fund, and the Secretary-General had top-level discussions with the PLO on UN technical assistance. In addition, Terje Larsen was appointed Special Coordinator – a position apparently founded by Boutros-Ghali – in the Occupied Territories. He has upheld the Secretary-General's approach to supporting the peace process through economic improvement, with the negotiation of the 'Larsen Plan' between Israel, the PLO and the USA.

Thus, while the Secretary-General initially met opposition to his activist stance on the Arab–Israeli process – and perhaps discovered that there is still at least one 'no-go' area for his Office – he adapted his approach to a more constructive functional role which acknowledged its political limitations.

Libya and the terrorist suspects

The Secretary-General's involvement in efforts to persuade Libya to surrender people suspected of airline terrorism has been cited as an example of the narrowing room for manoeuvre of the Office in the context of a Permanent Five – or perhaps US – directorship. When the leading Security Council members have a keen interest at stake and wish to pursue an objective through the UN – perhaps in order to gain legitimacy – and when the Security Council is operating under Chapter VII, the Secretary-General is unlikely to have any independent room for manoeuvre. The proximity of the Office to the agenda of preponderant Security Council members or alliances may also cast a shadow over the Secretaryship-General's classical third-party standing.

Security Council Resolution 731 instructed the Secretary-General to 'seek the cooperation of the Libyan Government'.[167] Resolution 748 imposed wide sanctions under Chapter VII and instructed Boutros-Ghali to continue the role undertaken by the earlier resolution. In September 1993, the Secretary-General reported that he remained 'in almost constant contact over the past seven months with the parties to the dispute and the League of Arab States'.[168] He had become involved in a possible plan to have the suspects released to the Arab League, and then to the UN Secretary-General, and then to trial somewhere. Libya apparently wanted the easing of sanctions, as did Russia, which was owed substantial amounts in debts. The USA was leading the way for additional sanctions, thus there was a split in the Council. The Secretary-General, in classical fashion, was in theory seen as the best means to resolve this. He believed he was fairly close to winning extradition in August and September 1993, and urged and received a delay in the imposition of sanctions, to encourage flexibility in the Libyan leader Gaddafi. However, this transpired to be a stalling tactic: after 'endless hours' with the Libyans

Boutros-Ghali concluded that efforts to persuade Libya to give up the suspects were a 'total failure'.[169]

The Secretary-General's role can be questioned on a number of counts. Firstly, his position was tied to a coercive Council stance and he had accepted a good-offices mission with no room for manoeuvre and therefore little independent credibility with Libya. He was not in effect given a mandate to mediate, but to deliver a message and communicate Libya's reply. Secondly, in cooperating tentatively with the Arab League's plan to give Libya a face-saving way out and have the suspects tried in a friendly country – Malta – the Secretary-General could be seen as unintentionally lending credibility to the League's dubious diplomacy which was probably aimed at protecting Libya from the West. Neither of these possibilities are constructive to the Secretaryship-General.

A POST-COLD WAR SECRETARYSHIP-GENERAL?

One should not concentrate too much upon the most dramatic cases which have set the tone of multilateral caution. The tumultuous period of experimentation and volatility is giving way to some form of stability and there are already signs of this. The challenge is to gauge the position of the Secretary-General within this. This continues to be comprised of a combination – perhaps a paradox – of opportunities and constraints. These continue to reflect the durability of the state system, alliances, and the issue of international leadership. The 'billiard ball' conception of the international system has been undermined and states are interconnected politically and economically as never before. The distinction between domestic and international peace and security is increasingly questionable. Yet such trends may suggest that sovereignty and statehood are evolving rather than being undermined. Traditional diplomacy, power balances and the political, economic and military complexion are still key tenets of international politics, particularly at the UN. In the field of peace and security the Organization remains largely a passive-reactive force. Indeed, 'the UN can perform more effectively than in the "bad old days", but ... there has been no qualitative change in its capacity'.[170]

During the Cold War the Secretaryship-General often represented a component of a Great Power formula to deal with crises which might threaten the bipolar stability, and in so doing contributed to peaceful change and conflict settlement. In the post-Cold War world the Secretary-General will continue to fulfil the institutional needs of Great Power trade-offs, but in a less predictable manner; the parameters are not clearly defined. The Secretary-General will do more quantitatively as the Organization is less constrained within former spheres of influence in Africa, Central America and the former Soviet Union. Indeed, among all the discussion surrounding the issue of a Cold War post-Cold War dichotomy in international politics and at the UN, one point that is becoming self-evident is involvement in the domestic context. This is by nature more precarious for the UN and certainly the Secretaryship-General.

The Security Council continues to be interest-based, even if it works in apparent consensus, so the Secretaryship-General's role will continue to be buffeted by competing and volatile state agendas, albeit while non-state actors and forces impinge increasingly upon the agendas. Boutros-Ghali observed that '[d]eciding when to act and when to refrain presents a profound ethical dilemma. But at present such decisions are not being made on the basis of ethics, but on the basis of pure power politics.'[171] Yet a procedural development of the Office has occurred. In sending envoys on his own initiative, talking to Security Council members and the Council informally, making normative public statements, and assuming political-military control and authority, Boutros-Ghali imposed an activist stamp upon his Office which has set the tone for the post-Cold War model. The Office may also be guiding the Organization away from its narrow, state-centric basis. The extent to which this activism – sometimes confrontationalism – is a result of the personality of Boutros-Ghali is an interesting but elusive question. Kofi Annan's early activities in Office under the theme of 'healing' the discord both within the Organization and between the UN and its sponsors certainly appeared to reflect a more conciliatory approach.[172]

One can conclude that the attitudes of governments towards the Office of Secretary-General continue to be ambivalent, and that the stature of the Office continues to fluctuate in the context of a plethora of variables.[173] It is difficult to judge if Boutros-Ghali went 'too far' in attempting to elevate the Office in its policy-influencing and command and control roles, or if he was unfortunate to have been encumbered with a series of unmanageable 'ordeals' during his tenure.[174] The US claimed that it obstructed Boutros-Ghali's reappointment because he had failed to make enough progress in reforming the UN and that he initially had committed himself to a single term of office. There was a strong element of domestic politics in the decision also. In a presidential election year the administration sought to deny the Republican camp the opportunity of associating Clinton with the Secretary-General and unpopular ideas of collective internationalism, so Clinton pre-empted this by opposing Boutros-Ghali early. However, behind these motivations there was a fundamental divergence of ideology between the cautious new thinking in the US administration and the internationalist world-view of Boutros-Ghali. He was tainted – irrespective of whether he deserved it – by the miscalculations of UN experimentation, assertive multilateralism and the overextension of the Organization in the early 1990s. While Boutros-Ghali caught the flak which resulted from this adventurism, he brought some of it upon himself. Moreover, a number of clashes had culminated in the strong opposition of Madeleine Albright on a personal level.

However Boutros-Ghali presented himself, he was all too easily the target of unilateralist and isolationist conservatives who were able to epitomize him as a psychotic internationalist. He was unable to defend himself against these unfair attacks because he failed to communicate with, or fully understand, the US political system. Most pointedly, after the US had made clear its opposition to his reappointment he campaigned globally for support and appeared to believe that the US would change its mind when he returned with some form of 'global mandate'. To believe that he could continue to work with the US under such circumstances was to fail to understand the lessons of history. Even though the behaviour of the US was high-handed in the extreme, many people believe that if Boutros-Ghali had only the interests of the UN in mind he would have withdrawn his candidacy before it came to the vote. Moreover, by attempting to pit himself and the rest of the world against the US he demonstrated himself capable of egoism and romanticism. While he realized that the Organization had been engulfed by 'the fire of realism'[175] he did not want to accept that he had been made a sacrifice of this process.

In general it is widely accepted that the major Powers will always be wary of the Office overstepping its mark, Cold War or not. In accordance with this, as a member of the British mission to the UN observed, 'at the end of the day the Secretary-General is responsible to the member states ... without the Council he has neither the money nor the men.'[176] However, he stated that 'the Secretary-General's Office is more proactive in its relationship with the Council.'[177] But in the wider attitudes and policies of the Great Powers the Secretary-General is still constrained and often manipulated.

TRENDS OF THE SECRETARYSHIP-GENERAL

There are two key trends to the Office in the 1990s. First, the narrowing of the Secretaryship-General's scope for independent action in the context of Council cohesion – or superficial cohesion – and leadership. According to Sir Anthony Parsons, 'the more the cooperation between the Great Powers, the less the room for political manoeuvre for the Secretary-General. If you regard the P5 as the Board of Directors, the Secretary-General will always be the Company Secretary. When the Board is unanimous, the Company Secretary should have clear instructions, his job being to carry them out efficiently.'[178] Similarly, Franck and Nolte also observed that in the face of a resurgent and activist Security Council, the Office can be relegated to a 'letter- carrier' function.[179] Evidence of this trend can be found in the UN activities in Iraq and in elements of the cases of Haiti, Libya and the Middle East. This is a corollary from the Cold War scenario where paralysis within the deliberative organs resulted in a certain freedom for activity on the part of the Secretaryship-General. However, a former UK Permanent Representative has suggested that such situations will clearly exist but one should not generalize from this that the Office is moving towards subservience in its relationship with the Council.[180] Indeed, the cases above illustrate this. In addition, it is clear that the consensus within the Security Council is sometimes superficial; underneath the surface there may continue to be a practice of smoothing over the cracks of indecision by bringing the Secretary-General into play.[181]

Secondly, the position of the Office has been elevated as an extension of the qualitative and quantitative expansion of the UN's activities, perhaps offering opportunities for leadership and activism, now that the Permanent Members are working cohesively.[182] Although this may appear to conflict with the first trend, the development of the Office is not an either/or situation and one should avoid simplistic models. The enhanced role is evident in the activities of the Secretaryship-General in domestic peace operations and missions of good offices, in exerting pressure upon the Security Council and influencing policy, expressing normative opinions, employing the leverage of public statements, involving the Office in the use of force, and initiating a number of preventive measures.

A further trend has arisen out of the predominance, on occasions, of the Western, and in particular American, presence in the Council. This has involved the Secretary-General in the context of the UN as an instrument of member states or alliances with respect to Iraq, Haiti and Somalia. Boutros-Ghali stated in 1996 that '[i]f one word above all is to characterize the role of the Secretary-General it is independence.'[183] Clearly the Office is not independent, either politically or financially.

One should be wary of confusing trends with short-term fluctuations in the position of the Office, and of generalizing too much from the Somalia and Bosnia cases. To the extent that it is possible to identify trends in the activities of the Secretary-General, one can conclude that there is no post-Cold War 'model' but multifaceted and sometimes paradoxical trends. 'New' and wider conceptions of international peace and security together with a decline of Cold

War spheres of influence and a burgeoning of UN activity in domestic and international conflict have increased commensurately the activities of the Secretary-General in a qualitative and quantitative sense. However, it is perhaps more the geographical areas of the Secretary-General's activities than the actual functions – such as mediation, facilitation and face-saving – which are qualitatively innovative. Good offices and preventive diplomacy in the 'domestic' context – such as Burma, the former Soviet Union, East Timor and Zaire – are illustrative of this. In multifunctional peace operations the Office is maintaining an operative function and forming a significant – if bureaucratic – component in operations where coercion is employed. In the starkest example, the Secretary-General maintained an important coordination function within an operation which had been upgraded from peacekeeping to peace-enforcement in Somalia. Yet the proximity of the Office to the use of force has adverse implications for the classical innocuous third-party functions of the Office.

The post-Cold War developments in global thinking have encouraged a greater use by the Secretary-General of the public declaratory 'pulpit', proclaiming the responsibility of the international community for issues and areas earlier ignored. However, at a time when attitudes towards peace and security are widening to embrace domestic, social and economic factors the Secretary-General is often not endowed with the resources for 'positive leverage' and post-conflict peacebuilding due to financial constraints and political caution.

A further trend concerns areas – such as domestic conflict management – where the Organization has not developed a coherent doctrine and the Secretary-General can be plunged into a precarious and volatile situation. A number of multifunctional operations, such as those of the former Yugoslavia, have demonstrated this. Just as the Office can be affected by Security Council unity or the presence of a prominent member or alliance, so is it affected by a lack of commitment or interest on the part of Council members towards items on the agenda. Angola and Western Sahara have reflected this to some extent.

Finally, the post-Cold War Secretaryship-General will

continue to perform those functions which it has always done, formally and informally, as a result of the political dynamics within the Security Council and General Assembly, and indeed within those of the wider international arena. Sometimes this will exclude the Secretary-General from a meaningful role – such as towards Iraqi military manoeuvres in October 1994 – or give it an unambiguous mandate, and sometimes there will be room for manoeuvre. The Office will occasionally be undermined when its mandate conflicts with the hidden agenda and policies of member states, or when the formal unity of the Council masks different or competing interests among its members.

In conclusion, the Office of Secretary-General under Boutros-Ghali has continued to execute the functions traditionally assigned to it. In addition, it has experienced the new opportunities and constraints which are a reflection of a volatile and possibly transient political climate. It is therefore not surprising that there is an element of paradox in the Secretaryship-General rather than a coherent model. Despite attempts by Boutros-Ghali to codify and elevate the position of the Office in an activist vein, it continues to reflect an environment which does not support a stable trend in terms either of international organization or of the Secretaryship-General.

8 Conclusions

THE INTERNATIONAL CIVIL SERVICE AND GLOBAL POLITICAL TRENDS

The trends in the post-Cold War Secretaryship-General appear to reflect the volatility – or perhaps 'turbulence'[1] – of the international community. In terms of the international civil service, some interesting conclusions present themselves.

It can be argued that the United Nations has evolved, rather unsteadily and perhaps without doctrinal support, beyond the Grotian 'international society' concept of international politics. In contrast to much of the Cold War the climate at the UN is increasingly reflective of a broader conception of peace and security. This places a new emphasis on empirical sovereignty, after years of establishing and maintaining the norms of legal sovereignty and the state-centric tenets of domestic jurisdiction and non-interference.[2] Indeed, the traditional distinction between domestic and international peace and security has been eroded and the new security agenda is increasingly recognized to embrace the wider agenda. The range of activities supported in multifunctional peace operations and through the Secretaryship-General since 1990 testifies to this.

One of the fundamental questions at issue on the fiftieth anniversary of the founding of the United Nations was whether an organization founded on international society principles and with the objective of orderly and peaceful relations between states can embrace the wider agenda of peace, human security, and non-governmental processes of global governance. What is the balance between respecting sovereignty and human needs? As this balance shifts, can the UN keep pace? What role will the Organization play in the evolution of the concept of sovereignty? Thus, are the purposes upon which the Organization was based still relevant or adequate? Further to this, how will the Organization meet its tasks with the evolving nature of leadership at the international level?

195

The range of activities supported in many peace operations – particularly peacebuilding assistance with demobilization, elections, development, and socio-economic
reform – are an indication of the new era of international
organization. These activities also indicate that the UN and
the international civil service are responding to new thinking and new needs. Developments at the Secretariat – such
as the establishment of the Departments of Humanitarian
Affairs and Peace-keeping, and the Representative of the
Secretary-General on internally displaced persons – are also
an institutional indication of progress. In terms of the
'global agenda' and the increasing interaction between
governmental and non-governmental processes of issue
management, recent and future conferences on the environment, population, nuclear non-proliferation, women,
human rights, social development and human settlements
go some way to embrace the growing global spirit.

However, despite these positive developments, the structure and ethos of the UN is increasingly being called into
question and calls for reform proliferate. The extent of
reform necessary to equip the UN to meet the demands and
complexities of the post-Cold War security agenda is
unclear. However, little discussion is questioning the prevail-
ing sovereignty doctrine of the UN or seriously suggesting
the enfranchisement of NGOs or sub-state groups. Again,
proposals regarding the reform of the Secretary-General's
Office are largely technical, aimed at improving the execution of current types of activity. Limiting an individual to a
single term of seven years would enhance the independence
of the Secretary-General from reappointment pressures and
obligations, although it could also weaken his or her position
in the last year. Appointing a deputy Secretary-General to
help conduct ceremonial and administrative tasks would
enable the Secretary-General to concentrate on his or her
burgeoning responsibilities in conflict prevention, management, and settlement.[3] Reform is still at the debate stage, and
can come only as a result of changes in attitudes and outside
pressure. The UN's ability to embrace the multifaceted and
interconnected issues of peace and security is still in question. Thus, although the Secretaryship-General and the
international civil service may try to embrace new thinking

and innovation, it is always within an organizational structure which reflects essentially conservative values.

The fundamental issue is whether the Office is more an
adjunct of the intergovernmental structure, as in the classical
mould, or part of a wider process of global governance in
peace and security which transcends – but does not oppose,
contrary to Jesse Helms' thesis – state structures. A paradox
exists. While the Secretaryship-General's immediate environment is that of an intergovernmental organization, the
Office has been at the forefront of UN activities in the
domestic context and in promoting concern for the wider
security agenda. Indeed, issues formerly considered to be
within the domestic jurisdiction of states, such as democratization and the promotion of human rights, are undoubtedly being internationalized and the Secretary-General's
Office is contributing to the momentum behind this. In one
sense the Secretaryship-General is pushing the Security
Council to commit itself to such areas of activity, which
otherwise may not have been considered within its collective
remit, or would have been outside the narrow interests of the
individual member states. Boutros-Ghali's public support of
a total ban of the production, sale and use of land-mines, and
his efforts to put numerous low-level conflicts upon the
agenda, are such examples. He has written of the overriding
responsibility of the Office and its 'global leadership' in
heightening awareness of the adverse influences of globalization and fragmentation.[4] Two eminent observers likewise
wrote of the Office's 'indispensable role in clarifying, rally-
ing, and proposing new ways forward'.[5]

Given the structural constraints within which the Office
works – most obviously that it depends upon an intergovernmental system for mandates and support – there are limits to
what the Office can do directly. Thus, the Secretaryship-
General's 'innovative' post-Cold War activities have been at
the pace of the Council; it cannot go too far ahead of the
Council without running aground. Yet in agenda-setting,
proposing institutional developments and taking proactive
steps – such as undertaking preliminary measures for good
offices – the Secretaryship-General is at the forefront of a
movement to better equip the United Nations for the peace
and security issues which are increasingly confronting the

Organization. Indeed, Boutros-Ghali argued that the concept of democratization transcends the state level and is the key to the promotion of peace and security.[6] However, tensions still exist. The Secretaryship-General is wedded to the structures of the UN and all the problems which have emerged as the Organization has struggled to meet the post-Cold War security agenda with only limited success. The intergovernmental doctrine and the bureaucratic inertia within the UN system have resulted in severe shortcomings. One can question whether the multilateral norms and structures of the UN can meet the human security demands of the future, or adapt fast enough. Of course, the Secretaryship-General is able to create some independence from the Council. However, can it represent the vanguard of processes of global governance – which embrace all manner of governmental and non- governmental, national and transnational processes – or is it inextricably constrained by the intergovernmental context? Some time ago Jordan wrote that 'the international civil service, caught between "global" responsibilities and national constraints ... can only muddle along, performing in an imperfect way according to admittedly imperfect criteria of accomplishment.'[7] The Secretaryship-General is still trapped within this paradox. If it tries to push too hard it wins the censure of the Security Council and the animosity of political commentators.

Although there is not a coherent model of global governance – indeed the subject matter defies a neat focus – a number of themes do coalesce around this area of study. It involves systems of rules involving institutional and informal, governmental and non-governmental, and domestic and transnational mechanisms. The processes and mechanisms of governance include systems at all levels of human activity as a network of control mechanisms that may transcend state boundaries in order to manage the ever increasing interdependencies and common issues. The proliferation of organizations at all levels is a manifestation of this, a response to the unprecedentedly complex nature of domestic and international life.[8] The most obvious tension is between formal government 'top-down' mechanisms and structures, such as the Security Council, and less formal non-governmental and 'bottom-up' arrangements.

The UN network would appear to be trying to reconcile these processes.

On a practical level this field of study can be applied to transnational issues and problems with the objective of improving multilateral structures and processes. The environment, refugee flows, the ethno-nationalist resurgence, human rights, population, development and democracy are some such pressures. The Secretaryship-General has been attempting to play a leadership role in managing the multilateral response to all-encompassing dimensions of security. Boutros-Ghali suggested that the 'progressive opening of the United Nations to civil society' requires the participation of individuals, the private sector, the academic community, NGOs and regional organizations, in addition to governments.[9] While it is increasingly accepted that such a variety of agencies play a role in peace and security, what is less certain is how such an enfranchisement could occur in the face of the state-centricity of the Organization and its' Charter.

Some progress has been made since the end of the Cold War, through the back door rather than major reform. NGOs have been recognized as crucial to humanitarian assistance and brought into the consultative UN fold, working closer on the ground. War crimes tribunals reflect the growing pressure to enforce humanitarian legal standards and give emphasis to the individual under international law. The UN framework is also reflecting increasingly the multilateral dynamics of collective transnational concerns in a more productive manner than during the Cold War. The statist emphasis of the Charter has not represented an insurmountable obstacle to the development of innovative responses to issues and problems unforeseen in 1945, and non-state actors have gradually been embraced on a functional basis. However, the structure and ideology of the UN remain largely static and calls for reform have not resulted in substantial institutional change. At a deeper level, normative ideas of duties beyond borders have not accompanied globalizing trends to the extent that many observers predicted.

Does this preclude the Secretaryship-General from being in the vanguard of innovation in multilateral responses to new dimensions of peace and security? Not necessarily. Rosenau believes that the Secretaryship-General has the potential to maintain the UN's relevance by promoting the Organization in new areas of activity as a vacuum emerges around sovereignty, and taking a leadership role in promoting attitudinal changes within the Secretariat.[10] This would also imply that the personality and approach of a particular incumbent is critical in guiding the organization in creative and proactive directions. According to Boutros-Ghali, the Office is 'absolutely central' to the resolution of the dialectics of globalization and fragmentation in international relations, and the disparity between demands and resources at the UN.[11]

There has always been an element of improvization to the Secretaryship-General, and it has clearly pursued activities not codified in the Charter or various rules of procedure. Indeed, one of the strengths of the Office has been its ability to respond to demands not met by the deliberative organs of the UN for constitutional and political reasons. That was often the case during the Cold War and it could continue to be so, as institutional reform is not likely to keep pace with the rate of change in the international system and the emerging security issues continue to defy the structure of the UN. However, there still remains the obvious point that the Secretaryship-General is dependent upon the predilections of the Security Council members individually and collectively. With the end of the 'Age of Ideology',[12] the post-Cold War period has seen fewer systemic political constraints on the Secretaryship-General and it has been able to pursue objectives in areas previously considered 'no-go areas'. However, the climate of multilateral fatigue and volatility has imposed severe restraints. Without political and material support the Secretaryship-General has been frustrated.

Nevertheless, the post-Cold War Secretaryship-General has developed beyond the traditional model of the international civil service which was a functional outcrop of the Grotian conception of international society, created to underpin the aspirations of international organization. The key developments which have manifested themselves in recent years are that the international civil service has become less constrained by the international and domestic dichotomy, and it is now not only responding to the system. Indeed, it is displaying a proactive kernel, taking the initiative, and influencing policy where possible.

Indeed, while a tension, perhaps a paradox, still exists, the Secretaryship-General is at the forefront of efforts to better equip an intergovernmental structure to deal with issues and problems which may sometimes defy such a structure. The UN will not be reformed radically in its structure; as Oran Young has observed, the evolution beyond the international society conception of politics may alter the content but not the character of roles played by international organizations.[13] Nevertheless, the Secretaryship-General is part of a movement which seeks to address emergent issues which may not be within the remit of 'high politics' of the Council. While the Secretaryship-General will always largely reflect the dynamics of the Security Council, it can go beyond this, albeit without the full support of the Council. The Office remains an anomaly, a political chimera.

THE SECRETARYSHIP-GENERAL, THE ACTIVIST MODEL, AND THE USE OF FORCE

The Secretaryship-General's embrace of activism and its proximity to the use of force or coercion may represent a qualitative escalation of the development of the Office. The trend has grown out of the burgeoning activity of the UN in domestic conflict, the tendency of a small number of states to employ the Organization as an instrument of narrow interests, an unprecedented level of mandatory sanctions, the increasingly interventionist agenda of multilateralism, and the freedom of expression enjoyed by Boutros-Ghali. However, while this has undoubtedly raised the profile of the Secretaryship-General and endowed the Office with a measure of authority *vis-à-vis* the Security Council, it may well have longer-term implications for the Office's traditional roles.

Boutros-Ghali proclaimed that '[n]othing is more precious to the United Nations than its reputation', and that rests upon impartiality, equity, efficiency and independence.[14]

Yet the reputation of the Organization and its Secretary-General are in danger of being jeopardized through their proximity to the use of force as an instrument of certain states or alliances. In fact, the classical, innocuous, impartial third-party role of the Secretaryship-General, which has achieved a measure of independence from the deliberative organs of the UN to some effect in the past, was jeopardized under Boutros-Ghali. This classical role does not sit comfortably with the activist trends of the UN in the post-Cold War context, especially as the political dynamics of the P5 largely determine how and when the Organization addresses issues. Moreover, Boutros-Ghali appeared to have a thirst for political activism, sometimes without much consideration for the cumulative implications for the Secretaryship-General's classical tradition. This was at the encouragement or behest of the Security Council, such as in Somalia and Haiti. It was also at the behest of political actors, such as Pakistan in its dispute over Kashmir. Finally, the activism of the Office has been a result of the initiative of the incumbent.

In one example of the latter, Boutros-Ghali called, on a number of occasions, for the deployment of a military force under UN authority in Burundi to stem the escalation of violence in that country, despite the opposition of the government of Burundi to the idea. In the context of post-Cold War attitudinal developments in peace and security at the UN and the tendency of a small number of Permanent Council members to dominate proceedings at times, there is a perceptible wariness among many states in the developing world towards interventionist trends. The last thing they want is the Secretary-General of the UN proposing an unwelcome military force. In addition, the leading members of the Council do not want their hand forced, or to be embarrassed, by the public statements of the Secretary-General. In an era where the media can exert pressure upon governments and organizations to act in cases which involve humanitarian tragedy, this is especially the case.

It would appear that the Secretaryship-General is less of a 'known quantity' as a result of post-Cold War political and attitudinal developments, and the dealignment in world politics which allows the Office to act and speak on issues which might have been considered out of bounds during the Cold War. The Office is less of a passive servant, even though the constraints reflected in political prioritization and multilateral fatigue in the Council mean that activist statements are frequently frustrated by a lack of will and resources. States and other actors may not always know what the Office will bring with it, because the Secretaryship-General now has an increasingly apparent momentum and political will of its own, and this may not always dovetail with the wishes of the other actors.

There may obviously be a tension here, both in terms of the general image of the Office and on a case-by-case basis. One must ask if the activism and increasing association of the Office with the use of force or coercion are reconcilable with the impartial and sometimes independent third-party model of the Secretaryship-General. Secondly, is the political profile of the Office a result of Boutros-Ghali's approach or an inevitable and perhaps necessary reflection of multilateralism in the post-Cold War context? As one experienced practitioner in the UN's Department of Political Affairs commented, the Secretary-General's Office must embrace the direction that the UN is taking and the demands that exist, even if proximity to power and narrow Council interests might taint its bureaucratic image.[15] Thus, the international civil service must evolve to maintain relevance and centrality, and this may indeed result in a systemic shift, perhaps even a radical departure, in the development of the international civil service. One might suggest that the activism and increasing politicization of the Office, its readiness to be associated with Council cliques, with the political dynamics of regional organizations, and with force or coercion, are a natural extension of the activities and demands of the post-Cold War UN.

Lack of patience and intermittent multilateral fatigue have resulted in a lack of stamina within the Security Council to some of the issues it engages. Subsequently, the Secretary-General has attempted to wield declaratory leverage to mobilize and push the Council into certain courses of action. Again, this may not be particularly graceful for those who idealize the Drummond model, but it is necessary when the UN is in financial crisis and the Council is increasingly wary of committing itself. The activism of the Secretaryship-General and the tension that exists between this model and the administrative servant – while not welcome to the bureaucratic purist – are commensurate with the post-Cold War condition of the UN. However, this must be balanced against the need to maintain impartiality, independence and restraint. This is a major challenge.

The Secretaryship-General should be seen to serve the international community and the Organization, rather than narrow interests within the Security Council. It should also be seen to be impartial to local parties in conflict situations. An element of the 'Peking Formula' is necessary for the facilitative and face-saving functions of the Office; it must remain a route of negotiation which is seen to have some independence from the Council. However, independence is difficult when the Organization is clearly dependent upon certain Security Council members, and impartiality is increasingly ambiguous in the context of domestic conflict where the UN Charter does not easily allow a judgement of aggression or culpability.

The trends of the Secretaryship-General represent something of a paradox. The Office still reflects the use of the UN as an instrument of certain states or transient alliances within the Security Council. The continued lack of definition to the role and responsibility of the UN in relation to post-Cold War peace and security issues, coupled with worries regarding the cost and practicalities of multifunctional peace operations, has been reflected in the volatility of members' support for the UN and an atmosphere of multilateral fatigue. The absence of firm leadership at the UN and in international politics in general has contributed to this. Thus, while the level of the Secretaryship-General's activity has burgeoned and it has performed tasks and encouraged discussion at the forefront of innovative UN practices, material shortages and political constraints condition the Office. Moreover, the inherent sensitivity of the intergovernmental structure towards political developments in the international civil service is in evidence. The Secretaryship-General continues to be regarded with ambivalence by most of the actors in contact with it, and it continues to reflect paradoxical trends. It has the potential to help guide the

UN's attempts to adapt to the complexities of the post-Cold War world, but it will also reflect that difficult and painful process.

Notes

INTRODUCTION

1. G. Langrod, *The International Civil Service. Its Origins, its Nature, its Evolution*, (New York: Oceana Publications, 1963) p.24.
2. A.A. Evans, 'The International Secretariat of the Future', *Public Administration*, vol.43, Spring 1945.
3. E.F. Ranshofen-Wertheimer, *The International Secretariat: A Great Experiment in International Administration*, (Washington: Carnegie Endowment, 1945) p.435.
4. F. Fukuyama, *The End of History and the Last Man*, (London: Hamish Hamilton, 1992); S.P. Huntington, 'The Clash of Civilizations?', *Foreign Affairs*, vol.72, no.3, 1993.
5. The Secretary-General's Cyril Foster Lecture, Oxford University, 15 January 1996.
6. J. Helms, 'Saving the UN', *Foreign Affairs*, vol.75, no.5, 1996, p.3.
7. Brian Urquhart and Erskine Childers, *A World in Need of Leadership: Tomorrow's United Nations. A Fresh Appraisal*, (Uppsala, Sweden: Dag Hammarskjöld Foundation, 1996) p.7.

CHAPTER 1 THE INTERNATIONAL CIVIL SERVICE

1. G. Langrod, *The International Civil Service. Its Origins, its Nature, its Evolution*, (New York: Oceana Publications, 1963) p.294.
2. I.L. Claude Jr., *Swords Into Plowshares. The Problems and Progress of International Organization*, 4th edn, (New York: Random House, 1984) p.viii and p.5.
3. Ibid., p.191.
4. G. Langrod, op.cit., p.46. F.R. Scott concurs, 'The World's Work', *International Conciliation*, January 1954, p.298; and L.C. Green, 'The Status of the International Civil Service', *Current Legal Problems*, vol.7, 1954, p.192.
5. G. Langrod, op.cit., pp.24–5.
6. S. Mailick, Introduction, in S. Mailick ed., 'A Symposium: Towards an International Civil Service', *Public Administrative Review*, vol.30, no.3, 1970, p.207.
7. J.W. Macy Jr, 'Towards an International Civil Service' in S. Mailick ed., op.cit., p.259.
8. R.W. Cox and H.K. Jacobson, *Anatomy of Influence. Decision Making in International Organization*, (London: Yale University Press, 1974) pp.6–7.
9. Ibid., p.4.

10. From 'The World Today', March 1924, cited by N.L. Hill, 'The Personnel of International Administration', *American Political Science Review*, vol.23, no.4, 1929, p.981.
11. F.P. Walters, *A History of the League of Nations*, (London: Oxford University Press, 1960) p.76.
12. T. Lie, *In the Cause of Peace: Seven Years with the United Nations*, (New York: Macmillan, 1954) p.41.
13. D. Owen, 'Reflections of an International Civil Servant', in S. Mailick ed., op.cit., p.208.
14. Cited by G. Langrod, op.cit., p.51.
15. M. Weber, 'Bureaucracy', in J.A. Litterer, *Organizations: Structure and Behavior*, (New York: John Wiley, 1969).
16. Cited by I.L. Claude, op.cit., p.210. See also O. Schachter, 'Some Reflections on International Officialdom', in J.E. Fawcett and R. Higgins eds, *International Organization*, Royal Institute for International Affairs, (London: Oxford University Press, 1974) p.60.
17. E.F. Ranshofen-Wertheimer, *The International Secretariat: A Great Experiment in International Administration*, (Washington: Carnegie Endowment, 1945) p.390; G. Langrod, op.cit., p.134.
18. R.S. Jordan, 'Truly International Bureaucracies: Real or Imagined?' in L.S. Finkelstein, ed., *Politics in the United Nations System*, (Durham, NC: Duke University Press, 1988) p.43. He poses a key question relating to the contextual restraints of international organization: 'Institutionally, can we speak of globalism?'

CHAPTER 2 THE OFFICE OF SECRETARY-GENERAL

1. J. Pérez de Cuéllar, 'The Role of the UN Secretary General', Cyril Foster Lecture, Oxford, 13 May 1986, in A. Roberts and B. Kingsbury eds, *United Nations, Divided World. The UN's Roles in International Relations*, (Oxford: Clarendon Press, 1993) p.125.
2. S.M. Schwebel, *The Secretary-General of the United Nations: His Political Powers and Practice*, (New York: Greenwood Press, 1952) p.vii.
3. R.W. Cox, 'The Executive Head: An Essay on Leadership in International Organization', *International Organization*, vol.23, no.2, 1969, p.206.
4. J. Knight, 'On the Influence of the Secretary-General: Can We Know What It Is?', *International Organization*, vol.24, 1970, pp. 594 and 597.
5. For example S. Marks, *The Illusion of Peace. International Relations in Europe 1918–1933*, (London: Macmillan, 1976).
6. A.W. Rovine, *The First Fifty Years. The Secretary-General in World Politics 1920–1970*, (Leyden: A.W. Sijthoff, 1970) p.17.
7. G.A. Johnston, *International Social Progress. The Work of the International Labour Organization of the League of Nations*, (London, George Allen & Unwin: 1924).

8. C.H. Alexandrowicz, 'The Secretary-General of the United Nations', *The International and Comparative Law Quarterly*, vol.11, part 4, October 1962, pp.1110 and 1111. For S.M. Schwebel '[t]he success of that [ILO] leadership may be said to be the positive lesson for the future of international administration, as the League experience is in some ways a negative lesson of the past', *The Secretary-General of the United Nations*, pp.11 and 13.

9. J. Barros, *Betrayal From Within. Joseph Avenol, Secretary-General of the League of Nations, 1933–1940*, (New Haven: Free Press, 1969) p.vii.

10. E.F. Ranshofen-Wertheimer, 'The Position of the Executive and Administrative Heads of the United Nations International Organizations', *The American Journal of International Law*, vol.39, no.2, 1945, p.324.

11. J. Barros, *Office without Power. Secretary-General Sir Eric Drummond, 1919–1933*, (New York: Oxford University Press, 1979) p.385.

12. Ibid., pp.78–9 and chapter 7.

13. E.F. Ranshofen-Wertheimer, *The International Secretariat: a Great Experiment in International Administration*, (Washington: Carnegie Endowment, 1945) p.38.

14. E.J. Phelan, *Yes and Albert Thomas*, (London: Cresset Press, 1936) p.ix.

15. See L. Goodrich, E. Hambro, and A.P. Simons, *The Charter of the United Nations. Commentary and Documents*, (New York: Columbia University Press, 1969) pp.572–609.

16. G. Langrod, *The International Civil Service. Its Origins, its Nature, its Evolution*, (New York: Oceana Publications Inc., 1963) p.202.

17. L. Gordenker, *The UN Secretary-General and the Maintenance of Peace*, (New York: Columbia University Press, 1969) p.21.

18. S.M. Schwebel, *The Secretary-General of the United Nations*, p.36.

19. Report of the United Nations Preparatory Commission, UN document PC/20, December 1945.

20. Pérez de Cuéllar referred to the Secretary General's 'independent responsibilities of "a principal organ"', in 'The Role of the Secretary General', p.63.

21. B. Urquhart, *A Life in Peace and War*, (New York: Harper & Row, 1987) pp.227–8.

22. For example B. Urquhart, 'Selecting the World's CEO. Remembering the Secretaries-General', *Foreign Affairs*, vol.74, no.3, 1995; B. Urquhart and E. Childers, *A World in Need of Leadership: Tomorrow's United Nations. A Fresh Appraisal*, (Uppsala: Dag Hammarskjöld Foundation, 1996) p.33.

23. Referring to Article 98 – 'such other functions as are entrusted to him' – L. Goodrich, E. Hambro and A.P. Simons wrote that: '[t]hese words, inclusive in purpose, do not exclude functions of a secretarial nature, but they do go beyond these and provide the basis for the Secretary-General's being entrusted with responsibilities involving the exercise of considerable discretion and political judgment.' Op.cit., p.585.

24. L.L. Fabian, 'The International Administration of Peace-keeping

Operations', in R.S. Jordan ed., *International Administration: Its Evolution and Contemporary Applications*, (London: Oxford University Press, 1971) p.127.

25. E.J. Phelan, op.cit., p.124.
26. Pérez de Cuéllar, op.cit., p.65.
27. D. Hammarskjöld, 'The International Civil Servant in Law and in Fact', Oxford Lecture, 30 May 1961, in W. Foote ed., *The Servant of Peace. A Selection of the Speeches and Statements of Dag Hammarskjöld*, (London: Bodley Head, 1962) p.335.
28. Report of the Preparatory Commission, paragraph 16.
29. See S.M. Schwebel, 'The Origins and Development of Article 99 of the Charter', *The British Yearbook of International Law*, vol.28, 1951, generally and pp.372–6.
30. D. Hammarskjöld, 'The International Civil Servant in Law and in Fact', in W. Foote ed., op.cit., p.335.
31. Annual Report on the Work of the Organization, September 1982.
32. B. Boutros-Ghali, 'An Agenda for Peace: One Year Later', *Orbis: A Journal of World Affairs*, vol.37, no.3, Summer 1993, p.324.
33. T.E. Boudreau, *Sheathing the Sword. The U.N. Secretary-General and the Prevention of International Conflict*, (New York: Greenwood Press, 1991) p.11, and chapter 1.
34. D. Hammarskjöld, 'The International Civil Servant in Law and in Fact', in W.Foote ed., op.cit., pp.337–8.
35. I.L. Claude, *Swords into Plowshares*, 4th edn, (New York: Random House, 1984) p.211.

CHAPTER 3 THE FRAMEWORK AND FUNCTIONS OF THE OFFICE

1. For example L.L. Fabian, 'The International Administration of Peace-keeping', in R.S. Jordan, *International Administration. Its Evolution and Contemporary Applications*, (London: Oxford University Press, 1971): '[t]he politico-military apparatus is simply one part of those sections of the Secretariat into which political affairs have been progressively concentrated as the political responsibilities of Secretaries-General have expanded over the years.' p.155.
2. See T.E. Boudreau, *Sheathing the Sword. The U.N. Secretary-General and the Prevention of International Conflict*, (New York: Greenwood Press, 1991) p.75, and B.G. Ramcharan, 'The Good Offices of the United Nations Secretary-General in the Field of Human Rights', *American Journal of International Law*, vol.76, 1982.
3. L. Gordenker, *The UN Secretary-General and the Maintenance of Peace*, p.xiii.
4. A.L. George, 'Case Studies and Theory Development: the Method of Structured, Focussed Comparison', in P.G. Lauren ed., *Diplomacy. New Approaches in History, Theory, and Policy*, (New York: Free Press, 1979) p.44.

5. J. Van Maanen, 'Reclaiming Qualitative Methods for Organizational Research', in J. Van Maanen ed., *Qualitative Methodology*, (Beverly Hills: Sage Publications, 1983) p.9.
6. R.S. Lazarus, *Personality and Adjustment*, (New Jersey: Prentice Hall, 1963) pp.27–8.
7. E.F. Ranshofen-Wertheimer, *The International Secretariat. A Great Experiment in International Administration*, (Washington: Carnegie Endowment for International Peace, 1945) p.435. A.W. Rovine, 'A More Powerful Secretary-General?', Symposium, *American Journal of International Law*, vol.85, 1991.
8. J. Barros, *Betrayal from Within. Joseph Avenol, Secretary-General of the League of Nations, 1933–1940*, (New Haven: Free Press, 1969) pp.264–5.
9. See Hammarskjöld's essays in W. Foote ed., *The Servant of Peace. A Selection of the Speeches and Statements of Dag Hammarskjöld*, (London: Bodley Head, 1962). Boutros-Ghali's support of Third World development issues was underlined during his visit in April 1996 to the UNCTAD conference in South Africa and the meeting in Nairobi to spearhead a multi-billion dollar, 10-year initiative for Africa, in which he was closely involved.
10. J.Z. Rubin, 'International Mediation in Context', in J. Bercovitch and J.Z. Rubin eds, *Mediation in International Relations*, (New York: St. Martin's Press, 1992) pp.19–20.
11. J.O.C. Jonah, 'The United Nations and International Conflict: the Military Talks at Kilometre Marker-101', in J. Bercovitch and J.Z. Rubin eds, op.cit., p.177. V. Pechota presented the traditional ideal, that a Secretary-General's 'presence provides a guarantee that the settlement process will take place on a basis of international legality and within the framework of the legitimate interests of the international community.' *The Quiet Approach. A Study of the Good Offices Exercised by the United Nations Secretary-General in the Cause of Peace*, (New York: UNITAR, 1972) p.80.
12. V. Pechota op.cit., p.79.
13. As B. Urquhart wrote, '[f]or over 40 years the Security Council largely operated under Chapter VI ... relying increasingly on the Secretary-General's good offices and using processes of mediation, conciliation and peace- keeping...', 'The Role of the United Nations in the Iraq–Kuwait conflict in 1990', *SIPRI Yearbook 1991: World Armaments and Disarmaments*, Stockholm, p.621; T.M. Franck, 'The Good Offices Function of the UN Secretary-General', in A. Roberts and B. Kingsbury eds, *United Nations, Divided World. The UN's Roles in International Relations*, (Oxford: Clarendon Press, 1993); L. Gordenker, 'The Secretary-General' in J. Barros, *The UN. Past, Present and Future*, (New York: Free Press, 1972) p.115; K. Skjelsbaek, 'The UN Secretary-General and the Mediation of International Disputes', *Journal of Peace Research*, vol.28, no.1, 1991; H. Caminos and R. Lavalle, 'New Departures in the Exercise of Inherent Powers by the UN and OAS Secretaries-General: the Central American Situation', *American Journal of International Law*,

vol.83, no.3, April 1989; I.J. Rikhye, 'Critical Elements in Determining the Suitability of Conflict Settlement Efforts by the United Nations Secretary-General', in L. Kriesberg and S.J. Thorson eds, *Timing the De-escalation of International Conflicts*, (New York: Syracuse University, 1991); B.G. Ramcharan, 'The Good Offices of the United Nations Secretary-General in the Field of Human Rights', *American Journal of International Law*, vol.76, no.1, 1982; E. Jenson, 'The Secretary-General's Use of Good Offices and the Question of Bahrain', *Millennium: Journal of International Studies*, vol.14, no.3, Winter 1985; A.W. Rovine op.cit.; M.W. Zacher, 'The Secretary-General and the United Nations Function of Peaceful Settlement', *International Organization*, vol.20, 1966; H.H. Lentner, 'The Diplomacy of the United Nations Secretary-General', *Western Political Quarterly*, vol.18, no.3, 1965; L. Gordenker, *The UN Secretary-General and the Maintenance of International Peace and Security*, (New York: Columbia University Press, 1967) pp.159–203.

14. J. Bercovitch, 'The Structure and Diversity of Mediation in International Relations', in J. Bercovitch and J.Z. Rubin, op.cit.

15. See J. Bercovitch and J.Z. Rubin eds, op.cit., including L. Susskind and E. Babbit, 'Overcoming the Obstacles to Effective Mediation of International Disputes'.

16. Pérez de Cuéllar spoke of the ethical diplomacy of the United Nations, in contrast to 'traditional diplomacy', which 'was often limited to a stable balance of power: whether the balance conformed to justice was a lesser concern'. op.cit., p.68.

17. Chapter VIII (The Secretariat) Section 2, paragraph 16.

18. A.W. Rovine, op.cit., p.453–5.

19. L.L. Fabian, op.cit.

20. R.S. Jordan, 'Prologue: The Legacy which Dag Hammarskjöld Inherited and his Imprint on it', in R.S. Jordan ed., *Dag Hammarskjöld Revisited*, (Durham, NC: Carolina Academic Press, 1983) p.8.

21. B. Boutros-Ghali, *An Agenda for Peace. Preventive Diplomacy, Peacemaking and Peace-keeping*, (New York: United Nations, 1992) paragraph 20.

22. R.W. Cox emphasised this. See 'The Executive Head: An Essay on Leadership in International Organization', *International Organization*, vol.23, no.2, 1969, p.230.

23. E.F. Ranshofen-Wertheimer, *The International Secretariat: A Great Experiment in International Administration*, (Washington: Carnegie Endowment, 1945) p.435.

24. 'Boutros-Ghali Angrily Condemns All Sides for Not Saving Rwanda', *New York Times*, 26 May 1994, p.1.

25. For Rovine, '[a] positive expression of policy by the Secretary-General … can usually be taken as a statement of predominant sentiment among the community of nations, and one that generates an aura of righteousness and legitimacy.' Op.cit., p.445.

CHAPTER 4 THE DEVELOPMENT OF THE OFFICE, 1945–82

1. B. Urquhart, *A Life in Peace and War*, (New York: Harper & Row, 1987) chapter 8; J. Barros, *Trygve Lie and the Cold War*, (North Illinois: Illinois University Press, 1989); S.M. Schwebel, *The Secretary-General of the UN*, (New York: Greenwood Press, 1952) p.181.
2. T. Lie, *In the Cause of Peace. Seven Years with the United Nations*, (New York: Macmillan, 1954) pp.15–17.
3. Cited by S.M. Schwebel, *The Secretary-General of the UN*, (New York: Greenwood Press, 1952) p.90.
4. He also employed this tactic concerning the powers of the Security Council and the Trieste Statute, 1947, the enforcement of the Palestine partition in 1948, regarding the question of representation – especially Chinese – at the UN, 1950, and concerning the competence of the Council to deal with the Korean invasion, 1950. See S.M. Schwebel, op.cit., pp.92–103.
5. S.M. Schwebel, op.cit., p.86.
6. T. Lie, op.cit., chapter 15.
7. Ibid., p.277.
8. A.W. Rovine, *The First Fifty Years. The Secretary-General in World Politics 1920–1970*, (Leyden: A.W. Sijthoff, 1970) pp.232–4; S.M. Schwebel, op.cit., p.156.
9. T. Lie, op.cit., pp.323 and 328.
10. Ibid., chapter 18; A. Rovine, op.cit., pp.237–49.
11. B. Urquhart, 'International Peace and Security: Thoughts on the Twentieth Anniversary of Dag Hammarskjöld's Death', *Foreign Affairs*, 60, 1981–82, p.1. Also B. Urquhart, *Hammarskjöld*, (London: Bodley Head, 1972) pp.23 and 32.
12. D. Hammarskjöld, 'Address before the Students' Association', Copenhagen, Denmark, 2 May 1959, in W. Foote ed., *The Servant of Peace. A Selection of the Speeches and Statements of Dag Hammarskjöld*, (London: Bodley Head, 1962) p.211.
13. D. Hammarskjöld, 'Address at the University of California, UN Convocation', Berkeley, 25 June 1955, in W. Foote ed., op.cit., p.3.
14. General Assembly Resolution 906(9), 10 December 1954, paragraph 4.
15. Security Council Resolution 113, 4 April 1956, paragraph 3.
16. For J.P. Lash '[a] resolution "giving it to Dag" might get by the Soviet Union where a more specific directive might not ... And if the mission failed, the blame would be on Hammarskjöld rather than on them.' *Dag Hammarskjöld*, (London: Cassell, 1962) p.68.
17. B. Urquhart, *Hammarskjöld*, p.165. The US feared the prospect of British and French aggression and the danger of Egypt running into the protective arms of the Soviet Union.
18. Cited by W. Foote ed., op.cit., p.124.
19. General Assembly Resolution 998, 4 November 1956.
20. General Assembly Resolution 1000(1956), ES-1. According to Indar

Jit Rikhye, Hammarskjöld 'concerned himself with every detail and supervised every discussion in deciding their [UNEF and ONUC] organization and operations'. 'Hammarskjöld and Peacekeeping', in R.S. Jordan ed., *Dag Hammarskjöld Revisited*, p.78.

21. B. Urquhart, *A Life in Peace and War*, p.133.
22. Ibid., p.159, and personal correspondence, 11 March 1994.
23. Security Council Resolution 128, 11 June 1958, paragraph 2.
24. Cited by B. Urquhart, *Hammarskjöld*, p.265.
25. A. James, 'The Role of the Secretary-General of the United Nations in International Relations', *International Relations*, vol.1, no.2, October 1959, p.627.
26. D. Hammarskjöld, 'Introduction to the Annual Report', 31 August 1960, in W. Foote ed., op.cit.,
27. See L.M. Gordenker, *The United Nations Secretary-General and the Maintenance of Peace*, (New York: Columbia University Press, 1967) pp.215–22.
28. Statement on reappointment, General Assembly 26 September 1957, in W. Foote ed., op.cit., p.150.
29. D. Hammarskjöld, 'The International Civil Servant in Law and in Fact', in W. Foote ed., op.cit., p.335.
30. A. James, 'The Secretary General: A Comparative Analysis', in A. Jennings and G.R. Berridge, *Diplomacy at the UN*, (London: Macmillan, 1985) p.39.
31. Interview with Sir Brian Urquhart, former Under Secretary-General for Special Political Affairs, New York, 25 May 1994.
32. Security Council Resolution 143, 14 July 1960, paragraph 2. B. Urquhart recalled that '[t]o put it briefly, the U.N. operation was to fill a vacuum that would probably otherwise be filled by the conflicting forces and influences of East and West, and by a variety of racial, economic, ideological, political, and tribal conflicts as well.' *Hammarskjöld*, p.402.
33. The Resolution again called upon Belgium to withdraw, this time specifically from Katanga, under 'speedy modalities determined by the Secretary General'. Security Council Resolution 146, 9 August 1960, paragraph 2.
34. Security Council Resolution 181, 21 February 1961, paragraph 1. However, the Secretary-General was not named; for B. Urquhart, 'once again the Council had passed the buck to him'. *Hammarskjöld*, p.509.
35. B. Urquhart, *Hammarskjöld*, p.596.
36. L.M. Goodrich 'Hammarskjöld, the UN, and the Office of Secretary General', *International Organization*, vol.28, no.1, 1974, p.482.
37. E. Stein, 'Mr. Hammarskjöld, the Charter Law and the Future Role of the United Nations Secretary General', *American Journal of International Law*, vol.56, no.1, 1962, p.31. Also H.F. Armstrong, 'UN on Trial', *Foreign Affairs*, vol.39, no.3, April 1961, pp.388–415.
38. For example H.H. Lentner, 'The Political Responsibility and Accountability of the United Nations Secretary General', *Journal of Politics*, vol.27, no.4, September 1965.

39. B. Urquhart, *A Life in Peace and War*, p.189.
40. For example see W.D. Jackson, 'The Political Role of the Secretary-General under U Thant and Kurt Waldheim: development or decline?', *World Affairs*, vol.140, no.3, Winter 1978.
41. S.D. Bailey, *The Procedure of the UN Security Council*, (New York: Oxford University Press, 1988) pp.75–6.
42. J. Barros, *Office Without Power. Secretary-General Sir Eric Drummond, 1919–1933*, (New York: Oxford University Press, 1979) pp.399 and 402.
43. U Thant, press conference 6 July 1966, cited by L. Gordenker, 'U Thant and the Office of U.N. Secretary-General', *International Journal*, vol.22, no.1, Winter 1966-67, p.3. For Urquhart, 'U Thant's moral sense overrode his political sense and caused him to do what he believed right, even if it was politically disadvantageous to him. His stewardship had none of the flair or high personal style of Hammarskjöld, but his undertakings were just as courageous.' *A Life in Peace and War*, p.190.
44. Allegations, revealed by the World Jewish Congress and journalists, identified Waldheim as an intelligence officer with German army units involved in war crimes in Yugoslavia and Greece, including the execution of British commandos, attacks on civilians, and the deportation of Jews to concentration camps. A thorough and interesting study is S.M. Finger and A.A. Saltzman (with G. Schwab, adviser), *Bending with the Winds. Kurt Waldheim and the United Nations*, (New York: Praeger, 1990) pp.1 and 5. Their verdict: '[w]e have seen no conclusive evidence to date that Waldheim ordered or personally committed a war crime, but he was definitely a bureaucratic accessory. Whatever qualms he may have had about the Nazi crimes in the Balkans, he did nothing to stop or impede them. Indeed, he was part of the deadly machine. The intelligence reports he processed included information used by Nazi military authorities in identifying targets for destruction and war crimes' pp.9–10. In his first book of memoirs Waldheim describes his 'disaffection' with Nazism and being called-up with his brother: 'our only alternative was a court-martial', *The Challenge of Peace*, (London: Weidenfeld & Nicolson, 1980) pp.23–4. He claims he was wounded on the Russian front late in 1941 and left the army to resume his law studies in early 1942, p.24. Was Waldheim being controlled or blackmailed while at the UN? S. Hazzard gives a summary of the main conspiracy theories, *The Countenance of Truth. The United Nations and the Waldheim Case*, (New York: Viking, 1990) pp.59–65.
45. K. Waldheim, *The Challenge of Peace*, p.5.
46. Ibid., p.208.
47. S.M. Finger and A.A. Saltzman, op.cit., p.86.
48. K. Waldheim, *In the Eye of the Storm*, (London: Weidenfield & Nicolson) 1980, p.140.
49. K. Waldheim, 'Dag Hammarskjöld and the Office of United Nations Secretary-General' in R.S. Jordan, op.cit., p.15.
50. K. Waldheim, *In the Eye of the Storm*, p.111.

51. S.M. Finger and A.A. Saltzman, op.cit., p.33.
52. In *R.N. The Memoirs of Richard Nixon*, (Sidgwick and Jackson, 1978) he did not present the UN as having had significance during his tenure, apart from following the 1973 war, pp.937–41.
53. H. Kissinger, *Years of Upheaval*, (London: Weidenfeld & Nicolson and Michael Joseph, 1982). He regarded Waldheim as 'a great gossip', p.455, who 'could be useful' for distributing information, p.805. Although it is often suggested that Kissinger was 'won over' to the importance of the UN by the role it played in separating the warring parties after the Yom Kippur war of 1973, he patently manipulated the Security Council by juggling various interests and pressures, pp.471–4 and pp.480, 486, 502.
54. Ibid., p.472. Waldheim 'would give what he was told wide distribution to those – mostly among the non-aligned – more willing to rely on information from a third party than from us', p.805.
55. B. Urquhart, *A Life in Peace and War*, p.240; A. James noted that '[w]hat is not yet public knowledge, however, is the origin of the idea ... that a United Nations Force should once again stand between Israel and Egypt. It might be that Waldheim had once again been at work behind the scenes'. 'Kurt Waldheim: Diplomat's Diplomat', *The Yearbook of World Affairs*, vol.37, 1983, p.89.
56. Resolution 340, 25 October 1973.
57. Interview with Sir Brian Urquhart, New York, 25 May 1994.
58. H. Kissinger, op.cit., p.601; R. Nixon, op.cit., pp.937–41.
59. H. Kissinger, op.cit., p.788, and see pp.790–1. Anthony Parsons wrote that Kissinger's 'tactics were to eliminate the Soviet Union and the troublesome UN from the negotiations and the deal bilaterally with the parties'. *From the Cold War to the Hot Peace. UN Interventions, 1947–1995*, (London: Penguin Books, 1995) p.26.
60. B. Urquhart, *A Life in Peace and War*, p.266.
61. *New York Times*, 17 July 1974, p.12.
62. M. Necatigil, *The Cyprus Question and the Turkish Position in International Law*, (Oxford: Oxford University Press, 1989) p.80.
63. K. Waldheim, *In the Eye of the Storm*, p.83. He was reported to have requested an increase in numbers from 2300 to 5000, *New York Times*, 23 July 1974, p.18.
64. K. Waldheim, *In the Eye of the Storm*, p.85. A Resolution was eventually adopted which expanded UNFICYP's mandate, *New York Times*, 2 August 1974.
65. According to A. James, 'he effectively turned UNFICYP from a law and order force, spread throughout the island, into a barrier force – one which interposed itself along and watched over the demarcation line between the two formerly warring sides', op.cit., p.91.
66. Security Council Resolution 367, 12 March 1975. 'Thus I was faced for six years with the most thankless and frustrating task of my term of office.' K. Waldheim, *In the Eye of the Storm*.
67. *New York Times*, 15 March 1978.
68. B. Urquhart, op.cit., p.287.
69. Security Council Resolution 425, 19 March 1978, paragraph 3.

70. B. Skogmo, *UNIFIL. International Peacekeeping in Lebanon, 1978–1988*, (Boulder, Colo.: Lynne Rienner, 1989) p.12.
71. J. Mackinlay, op.cit., p.44. Waldheim recalled that '[o]nce again we proved how fast we could move given the necessary backing and authority', and that the consent necessary to redeploy troops from the UN Disengagement Observer Force came quickly because of the 'personal relations I had always been at such pains to build up with heads of state and government'. *In the Eye of the Storm*, p.190.

CHAPTER 5 JAVIER PÉREZ DE CUÉLLAR

1. Sir Brian Urquhart, interview, 25 May 1994, New York. Pérez de Cuéllar recalled that this transition divided his two terms almost exactly, 'Reflecting on the Past and Contemplating the Future', *Global Governance*, vol.1, no.2, 1995, p.159.
2. Interview, New York, 25 May 1994.
3. See J. Pérez de Cuéllar, 'The Role of the UN Secretary-General', in A. Roberts and B. Kingsbury eds, *United Nations, Divided World: the UN's Roles in International Relations*, (Oxford: Clarendon Press, 1993).
4. J. Pérez de Cuéllar, 'Report of the Secretary-General on the work of the Organization', September 1982. He later conceded that this was something of an overstatement, 'Reflecting on the Past and Contemplating the Future', p.161.
5. One must be cautious of judging the UN's performance: it is a subjective pursuit and there are no historical parallels against which to compare the Organization. See A. Roberts and B. Kingsbury, 'The UN's Roles in International Society since 1945', in their edited volume, op.cit., pp.14–17.
6. F. Halliday, *The Makings of the Second Cold War*, (London: Verso, 1986).
7. J. Pérez de Cuéllar, 'Reflecting on the Past and Contemplating the Future', p.153.
8. S.D. Krasner, *Structural Conflict. The Third World against Global Liberalism*, (California: University of California Press, 1985) p.65.
9. General Assembly Resolution 37/233, 20 December 1982.
10. T.M. Franck, 'Soviet Initiatives: US Responses – New Opportunities for Reviving the United Nations System', *American Journal of International Law*, vol.83, no.3, July 1989, pp. 532–3.
11. S.D. Krasner, op.cit., p.300.
12. E.B. Haas, 'Regime Decay: Conflict Management and International Organizations, 1945–1981', *International Organization*, vol.37, no.2, Spring 1983.
13. J.J. Kirkpatrick in L.M. Fasulo ed., *Representing America: Experiences of US Diplomats at the UN*, (New York: Praeger, 1984) p.284.
14. M. Thatcher, *The Downing Street Years*, (London: HarperCollins, 1993) chapter 6.

15. W.C. Sherman, Deputy Representative to the Security Council 1981–83, in L.M. Fasulo ed., op.cit., p.299.
16. J.J. Kirkpatrick, 'The Superpowers; is there a moral difference?', *The World Today*, May 1984, p.185.
17. See T.M. Franck, op.cit., 'Soviet Initiatives: US Responses – New Opportunities for Reviving the United Nations system', pp.536–7.
18. L. Freedman, 'The War of the Falkland Islands', *Foreign Affairs*, vol.61, no.1 Fall 1982, p.196.
19. A. Parsons, 'The Falklands Crisis in the United Nations, 31 March–14 June 1982', *International Affairs*, vol. 59, no.2, Spring 1983, p.172.
20. I.L. Claude Jr, 'UN Efforts at Settlement of the Falkland Islands Crisis', in A.R. Coll and A.C. Arend eds, *The Falklands War. Lessons for strategy, diplomacy, and international law*, (London, George Allen & Unwin, 1983) p.119.
21. Interview with a former senior Secretariat officer and member of Pérez de Cuéllar's Falklands Islands crisis team. Despite initial worries about Pérez de Cuéllar's background, his 'quality of gaining confidence shone through'. New York, June 1994.
22. *The Times*, 17 April 1982, p.4; A. Parsons, op.cit., p.172.
23. *The Times*, 1 May 1982, p.1.
24. A. Parsons, op.cit., p.173, and a personal correspondence, 12 August 1995.
25. Ibid., p.174.
26. M. Thatcher, op.cit., p.173.
27. Security Council Resolution 505, 26 May 1982, paragraph 4.
28. Correspondence to the author, 12 August 1995.
29. I.L. Claude, op.cit., p.122.
30. Ibid., p.222. The *Sunday Times* Insight Team even claimed that '[i]t has to be said that the British never appeared anything except suspicious of the UN negotiations.' *The Falklands War*, (London: Sphere Books, 1982) p.172. However, Anthony Parsons later claimed that the negotiations were in good faith, in a personal correspondence, 12 August 1995.
31. R. Thakur, 'A Dispute of Many Colours: France, New Zealand, and the "Rainbow Warrior" Affair', *The World Today*, vol.42, no.12, December 1986, p.210. See also M. Pugh, 'Legal Aspects of the Rainbow Warrior Affair', *International and Comparative Law Quarterly*, vol.36, July 1987, p.656.
32. *New York Times*, 8 July 1986, p.1; *Financial Times*, 8 July 1986, p.3.
33. R. Thakur, op.cit., p.211.
34. General Assembly Resolution 36/34, 62nd Plenary Meeting, 18 November 1981.
35. T.M. Franck and G. Nolte, 'The Good Offices Function of the UN Secretary-General', in A. Roberts and B. Kingsbury, op.cit., p.149; and J. Pérez de Cuéllar, 'Reflecting on the Past and Contemplating the Future', p.153.
36. S.S. Harrison, 'Inside the Afghan Talks', *Foreign Policy*, no.72, Fall 1988, p.32. For an interesting analysis of the Secretaryship-

General's 'surrogates in the field' see D.J. Puchala, 'The Secretary-General and his Special Representatives', in B. Rivlin and L. Gordenker, eds, *The Challenging Role of the Secretary-General. Making 'The Most Impossible Job in the World' Possible*, (Westport, Connecticut: Praeger, 1993).

37. S.S. Harrison, op.cit., p.32.
38. *New York Times*, 25 January 1983, p.10.
39. B.R. Rubin, 'Afghanistan. The Next Round', *Orbis*, vol.33, no.1, 1989, p.57.
40. J. Pérez de Cuéllar, 'Reflecting on the Past and Contemplating the Future', p.153.
41. General Assembly Resolution 44/15, 1 November 1989, paragraph 10.
42. The first prominent example was the celebrated case of Hammarskjöld assisting in the release of US pilots from China following the Korean War, giving rise to the 'Peking formula', whereby the Secretaryship-General cultivates some measure of autonomy. Waldheim was involved in the successful release of French hostages from Polisario and less successful attempts to secure the release of American hostages in Iran. Pérez de Cuéllar also attempted to secure the release of Western hostages in Iraq and Kuwait in 1990–91. In conflict situations the Secretary-General has also been involved in encouraging and facilitating the exchange of prisoners and hostages, for example in Cyprus and during the Iran–Iraq war.
43. *Los Angeles Times*, 8 December 1991, p.1; *New York Times*, 6 December 1991, p.1.
44. J. McCarthy and J. Morrell, *Some Other Rainbow*, (London: Corgi Books, 1994) p.467.
45. Y.H. Zoubir, 'The Western Sahara Conflict: Regional and International Dimensions', *Journal of Modern African Studies*, vol.28, no.2, 1990, p.232.
46. General Assembly Resolution 3458 A(XXX) 10 December 1975.
47. Y.H. Zoubir, op.cit., p.242.
48. Security Council Resolution 621, 20 September 1988.
49. Security Council Resolution 691, 6 May 1991.
50. Security Council Resolution 510, 15 June 1982; the same every six months afterwards.
51. R.R. Denktash, *The Cyprus Triangle*, (London: K.Rustem & Brothers, 1988) p.117.
52. L.H. Bruce, 'Cyprus: A Last Chance', *Foreign Policy*, no.58, Spring 1985, p.115.
53. R.R. Denktash, op.cit., p.142.
54. *New York Times*, 3 March 1985, p.8.
55. P. Oberling, *Negotiating for Survival. The Turkish Cypriot Quest for a Solution to the Cyprus Problem*, (Princeton: Aldington Press, 1991) pp.31 and 39.
56. A. James, 'The UN force in Cyprus', *International Affairs*, vol.64, no.3, 1989, p.499.

57. Security Council Resolution 435, 29 September 1978 established the UN Transition Assistance Group.
58. Security Council Resolution 532, 31 May 1983.
59. M. Thatcher, op.cit., p.157.
60. Security Council Resolution 602, 25 November 1987.
61. See V. Tome, 'Maintaining Credibility as a Partial Mediator: United States Mediation in Southern Africa, 1981–1988', *Negotiation Journal*, July 1992.
62. C.A. Crocker, *High Noon in Southern Africa. Making Peace in a Rough Neighborhood*, (New York: W.W. Norton, 1992) pp.336–7.
63. For example see G.R. Berridge, 'Diplomacy and the Angolan/Namibian accords', *International Affairs*, vol.65, no.3, 1989, p.465.
64. J.E. Spence, 'A Deal for Southern Africa?', *The World Today*, vol.45, May 1989, p.80. For C.W. Freeman Jr, the US was the 'indispensable mediator of peace', 'The Angola/Namibian Accords', *Foreign Affairs*, vol.68, no.3, Summer 1989, p.126.
65. P. Robbins, 'Iraq in the Gulf War: Objectives, Strategies and Problems,' in H.W. Maull and O. Pick, *The Gulf War. Regional and International Dimensions*, (London: Pinter, 1989) p.46.
66. Security Council Resolution 479, 28 September 1980, paragraphs 1 and 4. Resolution 514, 12 July 1982 used stronger language but on largely the same terms. In theory the Council could and should have taken mandatory action under Chapter VII of the UN Charter.
67. H. Hubel, 'The Soviet Union and the Iran–Iraq War', in H.W. Maull and O. Pick, op.cit., p.140.
68. See D. Segal and E. Karsh, 'Lessons of the Iran–Iraq War', *Orbis*, Summer 1989; D. Segal, 'The Iran–Iraq War: A Military Analysis', *Foreign Affairs*, vol.66, no.5,1988.
69. *New York Times*, 1 April 1985, p.9; *New York Times*, 8 April 1985, p.9.
70. T.E. Boudreau, op.cit., p.92. On the basis of one of Pérez de Cuéllar's reports Council Resolution 612, 9 May 1988, condemned the continued use of chemical weapons.
71. J. Pérez de Cuéllar, 'Reflecting on the Past and Contemplating the Future', p.163; C.R. Hume, 'Pérez de Cuéllar and the Iran–Iraq War', *Negotiation Journal*, April 1992, p.178.
72. C.R. Hume, op.cit.
73. Security Council Resolution 598, 20 July 1987. Pérez de Cuéllar wrote of dramatic and profound change in 1987, 'Reflecting on the Past and Contemplating the Future', p.161.
74. *Los Angeles Times*, 16 September 1987, p.23; C.R. Hume, op.cit., pp.180–1. According to one report, Secretary of State George Shultz said the Security Council wanted the two sides to 'sit down with the Secretary-General.' *Chicago Tribune*, 22 July 1987, p.6.
75. F. Halliday, 'Iran–Iraq: the Uncertainties of Peace', *The World Today*, vol.44, no.10, 1988.
76. *Newsday*, 19 July 1988, p.5.
77. Interview with a former aide of Pérez de Cuéllar, June 1994, New York. Apparently Pérez de Cuéllar felt that his involvement in the

Iran–Iraq and Central American conflicts were his two greatest achievements.

78. For example P. Kornbluh, 'The Covert War', in T.W. Walker ed., *Reagan Versus the Sandinistas. The Undeclared War on Nicaragua*, (Boulder, Colorado: Westview Press, 1987) p.21.

79. Cited in H.W. Briggs et.al., 'Appraisals of the ICJ's decision: Nicaragua v. United States', *American Journal of International Law*, vol.81, no.1, 1987, p.79.

80. *New York Times*, 21 August 1991, p.7.

81. Ibid.

82. J.G. Sullivan, 'How Peace Came to El Salvador', *Orbis: A Journal of World Affairs*, vol.38, no.1, 1994, p.93.

83. T.L. Karl, 'El Salvador's Negotiated Revolution', *Foreign Affairs*, vol.71, no.2, 1992, p.159. For *The Times*, 2 January 1992, 'El Salvador pact crowns UN leader's 10-year reign'.

84. J.G. Sullivan suggested that '[i]t is uncertain whether any amount of outside pressure could have brought the parties to the table considerably before they were ready for final agreement'. op.cit., p.97.

85. T.M. Franck, 'The Good Offices Function of the UN Secretary-General', p.152. See also H. Caminos and R. Lavalle, 'New Departures in the Exercise of Inherent Powers by the UN and OAS Secretaries-General: the Central American Situation', *American Journal of International Law*, vol.83, no.2, April 1989, p.395.

86. P. Wehr and J.P. Lederach, 'Mediating Conflict in Central America', *Journal of Peace Research*, vol.28, no.1, 1991, pp.90–98.

87. *Los Angeles Times*, 3 November 1989, p.1; *Los Angeles Times*, 9 November 1989, p.17.

88. Security Council Resolution 637, 7 November 1989. This built upon the results of the International Support and Verification Commission, representing the UN and OAS Secretaries-General.

89. Security Council Resolution 653, 20 April 1990.

90. A. Gemayel, 'The Price and the Promise', *Foreign Affairs*, vol.63, no.4, Spring 1985, p.760.

91. B. Skogmo, *UNIFIL. International Peacekeeping in Lebanon, 1978–1988*, (London: Lynne Rienner, 1989) p.214.

92. Security Council Resolution 508, 5 June 1982.

93. *New York Times*, 21 September 1982, p.16.

94. *New York Times*, 8 February 1984, p.9.

95. J. Pérez de Cuéllar, *Report on the Work of the Organization*, September 1982.

96. Security Council Resolution 512, 19 June 1982.

97. H. Sirriyeh, *Lebanon: Dimensions of Conflict*, (Adelphi Papers 243, International Institute for Strategic Studies, Autumn 1989) p.52.

98. B. Skogmo, op.cit., chapters 7 and 8.

99. S.J. Solarz, 'Cambodia and the International Community', *Foreign Affairs*, vol.69, no.2, Summer 1990, p.99.

100. T.M. Franck and G. Nolte, op.cit., p.151.

101. *New York Times*, 2 February 1985, p.3.

102. Security Council Resolution 688, 20 September 1990, paragraph 10.

103. H. Annabi, 'The United Nations Plan for Cambodia', in B. Kirnan ed., *Genocide and Democracy in Cambodia*, (New Haven: Yale University Southeast Asia Studies, 1993) p.286.
104. *New York Times*, 24 October 1991, p.1.
105. B. Boutros-Ghali, *An Agenda for Peace*, (New York: United Nations, 1992) paragraphs 55–9.
106. Security Council Resolution 745, 28 February 1992.
107. J. Pérez de Cuéllar has 'no doubt' that the US would have acted unilaterally if necessary, 'Reflecting on the Past and Contemplating the Future', p.164.
108. *New York Times*, 27 August 1990, p.10.
109. *Washington Post*, 2 September 1990, p.21; interview with a former senior member of the Executive Office of the Secretary-General, New York, June 1994.
110. Security Council Resolution 674, 29 October 1990, paragraph 12.
111. Interview with a senior member of the Executive Office of the Secretary-General under Pérez de Cuéllar, New York, June 1994.
112. *Sunday Times*, 13 January 1991.
113. *New York Times*, 10 January 1991, p.1.
114. Interview with a senior member of the Executive Office of the Secretary-General under Pérez de Cuéllar, New York, June 1994.
115. S. Greffenius and J. Gill, 'Pure Coercion vs. Carrot and Stick Offers in Crisis Bargaining', *Journal of Peace Research*, vol.29, no.1, 1992.
116. Ibid., p.178.
117. E. Newman, 'The Realpolitik and the CNN Factor of Humanitarian Intervention', in D. Bourantonis and J. Wiener eds, *The United Nations in the New World Order. The World Organization at Fifty*, (London: Macmillan, 1995) pp.196–7.
118. J. Pérez de Cuéllar, *Report on the Work of the Organization*, September 1982.
119. *A Description of the Functions and Organization of the Office for Research and the Collection of Information*, ST/SGB/Organization Section: ORCI, 3 October 1988, p.1.
120. Interview with a founder of ORCI, New York, June 1994.
121. Interviews with former ORCI officials, New York, May and June 1994. Also J. Pérez de Cuéllar, 'Reflecting on the Past and Contemplating the Future', p.153.
122. Interview with a founder of ORCI, New York, June 1994.
123. Interviews with former ORCI officials, New York, May and June 1994.
124. This account derives from an interview with a former senior member of the Executive Office of the Secretary-General, New York, June 1994.
125. Interview, May 1994, New York.
126. Interview with a former close colleague of Pérez de Cuéllar, New York, June 1994.
127. Interview, ibid.
128. J. Pérez de Cuéllar, 'Reflecting on the Past and Contemplating the Future', p.163.

129. Interview, former colleague of Pérez de Cuéllar, New York, June 1994.

CHAPTER 6 BOUTROS BOUTROS-GHALI

1. Interviews, Department of Political Affairs and the Executive Office of the Secretary-General, UN, May–June 1994.
2. Ibid.
3. L. Gordenker, 'The UN Secretary-Generalship: Limits, Potentials, and Leadership', in B. Rivlin and L. Gordenker eds, *The Challenging Role of the UN Secretary-General. Making the 'Most Impossible Job in the World' Possible*, (Westport, Connecticut: Praeger, 1993) p.275.
4. The Secretary-General's Cyril Foster Lecture, Oxford University, 15 January 1996.
5. A former Assistant Secretary-General, Giandomenico Picco, wrote that 'Boutros-Ghali's unwillingness to take the moral high ground on issues like the war crimes in the former Yugoslavia, his inability to pursue a role complementary to that of the Security Council rather than competing with it and his unwillingness to use the secretariat staff and instead humiliating its officials have brought about the practical annihilation of the role of the secretary-general.' *Japan Times*, 10 November 1996, p.19.
6. S. Meisler, 'Dateline UN: A New Hammarskjöld?', *Foreign Policy*, no.98, March 1995, pp.101–2.
7. J. Gedmin, 'The secretary-generalissimo', *American Spectator*, November 1993.
8. K.N. Waltz, 'The New World Order', *Millennium*, vol.22, no.2, 1993; A. Parsons, 'The United Nations in the Post-Cold War Era', *International Relations*, vol.xi, no.3, 1992.
9. B. Boutros-Ghali, *An Agenda for Peace. Preventive Diplomacy, Peacemaking and Peace-keeping*, (New York: United Nations, 1992) paragraph 6.
10. Security Council Summit Meeting, New York, 31 January 1992, p.1.
11. J.S. Nye Jr, *Bound to Lead. The Changing Nature of American Power*, (New York: Basic Books, 1990).
12. J.S. Nye Jr, 'What New World Order?' *Foreign Affairs*, vol.71, no.2, 1992, p.84.
13. President Bush, Security Council Summit Meeting, p.33.
14. *Guardian*, 20 February 1995, p.9.
15. *Washington Post*, 7 February 1996, p.16.
16. The Secretary-General's Cyril Foster Lecture, Oxford University, 15 January 1996. Yet Boutros-Ghali's presentation of the idea was not politically wise. In an interview with *Liberation*, 12 January 1995, he was quoted as saying: 'If I could levy $1 on each airline ticket sold in the world, if I could issue certain stamps, I would have an income of my own.'
17. Congressional Press Releases, 22 January 1996.

18. J.R. Gerlach, 'A UN Army for the New World Order?', *Orbis. A Journal of World Affairs*, vol.37, no.2, Spring 1993; J.G. Ruggie, 'No, the World Doesn't Need a United Nations Army', *International Herald Tribune*, 26 September 1992; J.J. Kirkpatrick, 'Refusing to Subordinate U.S. Policy to United Nations isn't Isolationism', *Sacramento Bee*, 12 January 1995.

19. *Boston Globe*, 3 April, 1995, p.1.

20. T.P. Sheehy, 'No More Somalias: Reconsidering Clinton's Doctrine of Military Humanitarianism', *Heritage Foundation Reports*, (Backgrounder no.968, 20 December 1993); H. Kissinger, 'Recipe for Chaos', *Washington Post*, 8 September 1993, p.19.

21. Unofficial US document made available at the United Nations, May 1994.

22. B. Boutros-Ghali, 'Peacemaking and Peace-keeping for the Next Century', Transcript of a speech delivered 2 March 1995, City News Publishing Company Inc.

23. T.G. Weiss, 'The United Nations and Civil Wars', *Washington Quarterly*, vol.17, no.4, Autumn 1994.

24. UN Press Release SG/SM/6133/Rev.1, 17 December 1996.

25. Declaration of the Security Council Summit 31 January 1992, p.93.

26. A member of the UK Mission to the UN stated that 'preventive deployments, on a case by case basis, can be useful.' Interview, New York, May 1994.

27. Article 43 calls upon UN members to agree to make available to the Security Council armed forces to contribute to the maintenance of international peace and security.

28. For summaries and analyses of *An Agenda for Peace*, see D. Cox, op.cit.; T.G. Weiss, 'New Challenges for UN Military Operations: Implementing an Agenda for Peace', *Washington Quarterly*, Winter 1993; A.J.R. Groom and P. Taylor, 'Beyond the Agenda for Peace', *Peace and the Sciences*, December 1993.

29. Interview, member of the UK Mission to the UN, New York, May 1994.

30. D. Cox, op.cit., p.13.

31. Secretariat Interoffice Memorandum, 19 March 1993.

32. Note by the President of the Security Council, S/25696, 30 April 1993.

33. L.S. Finkelstein, 'The Coordinative Function of the UN Secretary-General', in B. Rivlin and L. Gordenker eds, op.cit.

34. A. James, 'UN Peace-keeping: Recent Developments and Current Problems', *Paradigms*, vol.8, no.2, Winter 1994.

35. Report of the Secretary-General to the Security Council, S/1994/777, 30 June 1994, paragraph 2. Paragraph 5 continues that 'The Secretariat will maintain a comprehensive database of these details for proper planning...'.

36. B. Boutros-Ghali, 'An Agenda for Peace: One Year Later', p.327.

37. Interview, New York, May 1994.

38. B. Boutros-Ghali, 'Supplement to An Agenda for Peace', para. 41.

39. Ibid., paragraph 43.

40. Interview, New York, 25 May 1994. See also his 'The United Nations and International Security After the Cold War', in A. Roberts and B. Kingsbury eds, op.cit., p.93.
41. Interview with a former UK Permanent Representative to the UN, London, February 1996.
42. For example, France produced an *aide memoire* in response to the supplement to *An Agenda for Peace*, proposing 'conflict moderation' forces authorized by the Security Council, a rapid reaction capacity, improvements in training, and early operation planning units within the Department of Political Affairs; UN Document A/50/869, S/1996/71, 30 January 1996.

CHAPTER 7 THE POST-COLD WAR SECRETARYSHIP-GENERAL

1. B. Boutros-Ghali, 'Report on the Work of the Organization', September 1993, paragraph 6.
2. UN Document S/1995/906, A/50/765, 17 November 1995.
3. UN News Summary, London, NS/21/95, 18 October 1995.
4. UN Document S/1995/827, 27 September 1995.
5. B. Boutros-Ghali, 'Agenda for Peace: One Year Later', p.328.
6. For example B.D. Berkowitz, 'Rules of Engagement for UN Peace-keeping Forces in Bosnia', *Orbis*, vol.38, no.4, Fall 1994.
7. For domestic peacekeeping and its hazards, see A. James, 'Internal Peace-keeping. A Dead End for the UN?', *Security Dialogue*, vol.24, no.4, 1993; J.R. Rudolph, Jr, 'Intervention in Communal Conflicts', *Orbis*, vol.39, no.2, Spring 1995; T.G. Weiss, 'The United Nations and Civil Wars', *Washington Quarterly*, vol.17, no.4, 1994; D. Rieff, 'The Illusions of Peacekeeping', *World Policy Journal*, vol.xi, no.3, 1994.
8. Interview with a former UK Permanent Representative to the UN, February 1996, and interviews with members of the Department of Political Affairs, June 1994.
9. UN Document S/1994/1122, 30 September 1994, paragraph 5.
10. R. Higgins, 'The new United Nations and former Yugoslavia', *International Affairs*, vol.69, no.3, July 1993.
11. J. Hoey wrote that 'Bosnia has become the theater of war in which the rivalries among the world powers are being played out ... The people pulling the strings are in Washington, Bonn, London, Paris and Moscow.' 'Policy Without Principle. The US "Great Game" in Bosnia', *The Nation*, vol.260, no.4, January 1995, p.133.
12. *Agence France Presse*, 10 December 1992.
13. B. Boutros-Ghali, *Building Peace and Development*, paragraph 705.
14. *New York Times*, 3 August 1992, p.1; *New York Times*, 23 July 1992, p.3.
15. UN News Summary, London, NS/16/94, 12 May 1994, and D. Owen, *Balkan Odyssey*, (London: Victor Gollancz, 1995) p.278.

16. T.G. Weiss wrote that the UN is 'a convenient forum for governments to appear to be doing something without really doing anything substantial to thwart aggression, genocide, and forced movement of peoples'. 'UN Responses in the Former Yugoslavia: Moral and Operational Choices', *Ethics and International Affairs*, vol.8, 1994, p.20.

17. M.N. Barnett, 'The United Nations and Global Security: the Norm is Mightier than the Sword', *Ethics and International Affairs*, vol.9, 1995; R.K.Betts, 'The Delusion of Impartial Intervention', *Foreign Affairs*, vol.73, no.6, 1994.

18. R. Higgins, op.cit., p.468.

19. F. Ajami, 'The Mark of Bosnia. Boutros-Ghali's Reign of Indifference', *Foreign Affairs*, vol.75, no.3, 1996; D. Rieff, 'The Institution that Saw No Evil', *New Republic*, 12 February 1996.

20. UN News Summary, London, NS/13/95, 2 June 1995.

21. Ibid.

22. Interviews, Department of Political Affairs, New York, May–June 1994.

23. *Washington Post*, 4 August 1993.

24. UN News Summary, London, NS/31/93, 5 August 1993. The Secretary-General later informed the Council in a letter that he would not hesitate to initiate the use of close air support if UNPRO-FOR personnel were attacked, UN News Summary, London, NS/3/94, 3 February 1994.

25. UN News Summary, London, NS/4/94, 10 February 1994.

26. Letter from the Secretary-General to the President of the Security Council, S/1995/470, 9 June 1995.

27. Interview, New York, June 1994. He concluded that the use of force therefore should be leased out. See also G. Picco, 'The UN and the Use of Force. Leave the Secretary-General Out of It', *Foreign Affairs*, vol.73, no.5, 1994, p.15.

28. Interview, Department of Political Affairs, UN, New York, June 1994.

29. Interview, London, February 1996.

30. Security Council Resolution 751, 24 April 1992, paragraphs 2 and 7.

31. B. Boutros-Ghali, 'Report on the Work of the Organization', September 1992, paragraphs 158 and 148.

32. B. Boutros-Ghali, 'Report on the Work of the Organization', September 1993, paragraph 428.

33. Ibid., paragraph 430; R. Thakur, 'From Peacekeeping to Peace Enforcement: the UN Operation in Somalia', *Journal of Modern African Studies*, vol.32, no.3, 1994, p.394.

34. J.R. Bolton, 'Wrong Turn in Somalia', *Foreign Affairs*, vol.73, no.1, 1994, pp.58–9.

35. Security Council 794, 3 December 1992, paragraphs 6 and 7, on the basis of the 'recommendation of the Secretary-General'.

36. President Bush's Address to the Nation, Department of State Dispatch, 7 December 1992.

37. B. Boutros-Ghali, 'Report on the Work of the Organization', September 1992, paragraphs 147 and 148.
38. J.R. Bolton, op.cit., p.60.
39. C.A. Crocker, 'The Lessons of Somalia. Not Everything Went Wrong', *Foreign Affairs*, vol.74, no.3, 1995, p.4.
40. *Independent*, 30 June 1993, p.10; a good account is 'A Humanitarian Gesture Turns Deadly', *Washington Post*, 10 October 1993, p.A1.
41. Letter from the Secretary-General to the President of the Security Council, S/24868, 30 November 1992.
42. B. Boutros-Ghali, 'Report on the Work of the Organization', September 1993, paragraph 433.
43. Cited by J.W. Bolton, op.cit., p.62.
44. Security Council Resolution 837, 6 June 1993, paragraph 5.
45. T.G. Weiss, D.P. Forsythe, R.A. Coate, *The United Nations and Changing World Politics*, (Boulder: Westview Press, 1994) p.80.
46. Boutros-Ghali was also reported to have 'instructed' the UN operation to apprehend the killers of four journalists in Mogadishu, UN News Summary, London, NS/28/93, 15 July 1993.
47. J.L. Hirsch and R.B. Oakley, *Somalia and Operation Restore Hope: Reflections on Peacemaking and Peacekeeping*, (Washington: United States Institute of Peace, 1995) p.102.
48. *Financial Times*, 6 January 1993, p.4.
49. J.L. Hirsch and R.B. Oakley, op.cit., pp.104–5.
50. Ibid, pp.126–7; *New York Times*, 1 October 1993, p.1.
51. *Los Angeles Times*, 23 October 1993, p.1.
52. Informal consultations of the Security Council, 19 March 1993.
53. The Secretary-General's Cyril Foster Lecture, Oxford University, 15 January 1996.
54. W. Clarke (former Deputy Chief of Mission, US Embassy in Somalia) and J. Herbst, 'Somalia and the Future of Humanitarian Intervention', *Foreign Affairs*, vol.75, no.2, 1996, p.73.
55. *Washington Post*, 10 October 1993, p.A1.
56. J.L. Hirsch and R.B. Oakley, op.cit., p.129.
57. *New York Times*, 16 October 1993, p.1.
58. W. Clarke and J. Herbst, op.cit., p.75.
59. UN Document S/1995/451, 31 May 1995. Earlier he had promised: 'I shall not hesitate to revert to the Security Council with recommendations for the continuation of some United Nations presence in Somalia beyond March 1995 if that is justified.' S/1994/1166, 14 October 1994, paragraph 23.
60. Ibid.
61. UN Document S/1995/231, 28 March 1995, paragraph 65.
62. C.A. Crocker, 'Can This Outrageous Spectacle be Stopped?', *Washington Post*, 13 October 1993, p.21.
63. M.J. Anstee, 'Angola: The Forgotten Tragedy. A Test Case for UN Peacekeeping', *International Relations*, vol.xi, no.6, 1993. Also C. Pycroft, 'Angola – The Forgotten Tragedy', *Journal of Southern African Studies*, vol.20, no.2, 1994.
64. *Guardian*, editorial, 19 February 1996.

65. B. Boutros-Ghali, 'Building Peace and Development', paragraph 447.
66. C. Pycroft, op.cit., p.253; Victoria Brittain wrote that 'Every round of negotiations with the UN has given him [Savimbi] another lease of respectability.' *Guardian*, 12 August 1995.
67. *Independent*, 28 November 1994, p.10.
68. UN Document S/1995/350, 3 May 1995, paragraph 22.
69. UN Document S/1995/230, 28 March 1995.
70. UN Document S/1995/1012, 7 December 1995.
71. UN Document S/1996/75, 31 January 1996.
72. Ibid.
73. J. Wurst, 'Mozambique. Peace and More', *World Policy Journal*, vol.11, no.3, 1994, p.80.
74. A. Parsons, *From Cold War to Hot Peace. UN Interventions 1947–1995*, (London: Penguin Books, 1995) p.152. See also C. Alden, 'The UN and the Resolution of Conflict in Mozambique', *Journal of Modern African Studies*, vol.33, no.1, 1995.
75. UN Document S/1994/1449, 23 December 1994.
76. Ibid., paragraph 35.
77. Interview, Department of Political Affairs, June 1994.
78. M. Plant, 'Rwanda – looking beyond the slaughter', *The World Today*, vol.50, no.8–9, 1994, p.151.
79. *New York Times*, 10 June 1994, p.A8.
80. UN Document S/1994/470, 20 April 1994.
81. *Newsday*, 29 May 1994, p.39.
82. *New York Times*, 29 December 1994.
83. *New York Times*, 26 May 1994, p.1.
84. A phrase used, among others, by J.N. Rosenau, *The United Nations in a Turbulent World*, International Peace Academy Occasional Paper, (London: Lynne Rienner Publishers, 1992) pp.74–6.
85. The Secretary-General's Cyril Foster Lecture, Oxford University, 15 January 1996.
86. 'Supplement to An Agenda for Peace: Position Paper of the Secretary-General on the Occasion of the Fiftieth Anniversary of the United Nations', A/50/60 S/1995/1, 3 January 1995, paragraph 43.
87. UN News Summary, London, NS/23/94, 5 August 1994.
88. See Gwynne Dyer in the *San Diego Union-Tribune*, 31 July 1994, p.G5.
89. UN Document S/1995/678, 8 August 1995, paragraph 41.
90. Ibid.
91. UN Document S/1995/457, 4 June 1995, paragraph 53.
92. Letter from the Permanent Representative of Canada to the Secretary-General, S/1996/35, 17 January 1996.
93. *Independent*, 7 January 1995, p.12.
94. UN Document S/1996/82, 2 February 1996.
95. S.P. Riley, 'Intervention in Liberia: too little, too partisan', *The World Today*, March 1993, p.42.
96. B. Boutros-Ghali, 'Report on the Work of the Organization', September 1993, paragraph 371.
97. UN Document S/1995/473, 10 June 1995, paragraph 46.

98. A. Adeleke, 'The Politics and Diplomacy of Peacekeeping in West Africa: the Ecowas Operation in Liberia', *Journal of Modern African Studies*, vol.33, no.4, 1995, p.586.

99. *Inter Press Service*, 25 and 26 October 1995. Boutros-Ghali chaired a donor conference in New York to raise the estimated $150 million required.

100. UN Document S/1996/47, 23 January 1996.

101. *United Press International*, 28 April 1995.

102. B. Boutros-Ghali, 'Building Peace and Development', paragraph 506. The election was reported to have taken place in an atmosphere of 'freedom, competitiveness, security', *UN Chronicle*, vol.31, no.3, September 1994, p.48.

103. UN Document S/1995/220, 24 March 1995, paragraph 68; Alvaro de Soto elaborated upon this, describing how post-conflict peacebuilding is hampered by complacency and financial pressures and concerns about over-extension, 'Implementation of Comprehensive Peace Agreements: Staying the Course in El Salvador', *Global Governance*, vol.1, no.2, 1995. He also outlines how the Secretary-General kept the Security Council focused on El Salvador, and the use of the 'Friends of the Secretary-General', pp.198–90.

104. *Guardian*, 15 July 1993, p.13.

105. Statement of Frank Ruddy before the House Appropriations Committee, *Federal News Service*, 25 January 1995.

106. Spokesman for the Secretary-General in the *New York Times*, 16 March 1995, p.24.

107. UN Document S/1995/498, 21 June 1995, paragraph 3.

108. UN Document S/1996/43, 19 January 1996.

109. UN News Summary, London, NS/25/95, 1 December 1995.

110. S.C. Saxena, *Western Sahara: No Alternative to Armed Struggle* (Delhi: Kalinga, 1995).

111. UN Document S/1996/43, 19 January 1996, paragraph 35.

112. B. Boutros-Ghali, 'Report on the Work of the Organization', September 1993, paragraph 392.

113. Ibid., paragraph 496.

114. Security Council Resolution 939, 29 July 1994, paragraph 3.

115. Letter from the Permanent Representative of Turkey to the United Nations Addressed to the Secretary-General, S/1994/953, 9 August 1994; *Times*, 6 July 1994, p.12.

116. *Guardian*, 25 June 1994, p.14.

117. N. Crawshaw, 'Cyprus: a crisis of confidence', *The World Today*, vol.50, no.4, April 1994, p.72.

118. UN Document S/1994/1407, 12 December 1994, paragraph 32.

119. UN Document A/48/981, S/1994/953, 9 August 1994.

120. This is supported by a personal correspondence by Rauf R. Denktash, President of the Turkish Republic of Northern Cyprus, to the author, 6 May 1996.

121. UN Document S/1995/46, 17 January 1995.

122. B. Boutros-Ghali, 'Report on the Work of the Organization', 1993, paragraph 324.

123. Security Council Resolution 841, 16 June 1993.
124. Security Council Resolution 861, 27 August 1993.
125. UN Document S/1994/1012, 26 August 1994, paragraph 12.
126. *Agence France Presse*, 2 September 1994; UN Document S/1994/828, 15 July 1994, paragraph 25.
127. UN Document S/1995/305, 13 April 1995.
128. UN Document S/1995/922, 6 November 1995, paragraph 3.
129. R. Ekeus, 'Iraq: The Future of Arms Control', *Security Dialogue*, vol.25, no.1, 1994. See also A.J.R. Groom, Paul Taylor and Edward Newman, 'Burdensome Victory: the UN and Iraq', in D. Bourantonis and A.M.L. Evriviades, eds, *A United Nations for the Twenty-First Century: Peace, Security, and Development*, Netherlands, Kluwer Law International, 1996.
130. Interview with a former UK Permanent Representative to the UN, London, February 1996.
131. The Secretary-General's Cyril Foster Lecture, Oxford University, 15 January 1996.
132. B. Boutros-Ghali, 'An Agenda for Peace: One Year Later', *Orbis. A Journal of World Affairs*, vol.37, no.3, Summer 1993, p.324.
133. UN Press Release SG/SM/6107, 12 November 1996.
134. B. Boutros-Ghali, 'Friedman Award Address', *Columbia Journal of Transnational Law*, vol.33, no.2, 1995, p.254.
135. Interview, former member of the Executive Office of the Secretary-General, New York, June 1994.
136. B. Boutros-Ghali, 'Report on the Work on the Organization', September 1993, paragraph 25.
137. See D.J. Puchala, 'The Secretary-General and His Special Representatives', in B. Rivlin and L. Gordenker eds, op.cit.
138. B.R. Rubin, 'Afghanistan in 1993. Abandoned but Surviving', *Asian Survey*, vol.34, no.2, February 1994.
139. Z. Khalilzad, 'Afghanistan in 1995. Civil War and Mini-Great Game', *Asian Survey*, vol.36, no.2, February 1996, and *Agence France Presse*, 10 January 1996.
140. UN News Summary, London, NS/1/96, 7 February 1996.
141. *Time*, 15 November 1993, p.66; *Guardian*, 29 October 1993, p.14.
142. UN News Summary, London, NS/24/94, 17 August 1994.
143. UN News Summary, London, NS/10/95, 5 April 1995.
144. Letter from the Secretary-General to the President of the Council, S/1996/36, 17 January 1996.
145. Interview, London, February 1996.
146. Security Council Resolution 931, 29 June 1994, paragraph 4.
147. UN Document S/1994/1160, 14 October 1994, paragraph 28.
148. UN News Summary, London, NS/1/94, 20 January 1994. Later, the Secretary-General reported to the Council that conditions were not right for the deployment of a peacekeeping force, UN News Summary, London, NS/16/94, 12 May 1994.
149. S. Lavrov, 'The Russian View of Peacekeeping: International Activity for Peace', *Brown Journal of World Affairs*, vol.3, no.1, Winter/Spring 1996, p.32.

150. UN Document S/1995/657, 7 August 1995, paragraph 52.
151. UN Document S/1995/10, 6 January 1995.
152. UN Document S/1996/5, 2 January 1996.
153. Letter in *Foreign Affairs*, vol.74, no.1, 1995, p.186.
154. *Agence France Presse*, 17 September 1994.
155. Statement by the President of the Security Council, S/PRST/1994/65, 8 November 1994.
156. UN Document S/1995/1024, 8 December 1995.
157. B. Boutros-Ghali, *An Agenda for Peace*, paragraph 40; the Secretary-General complained of the constraints in his 'Supplement to An Agenda for Peace', A/50/60, S/1995/1, 3 January 1995.
158. *Washington Post*, 28 December 1993, p.9.
159. Reuters, 8 September 1994.
160. B. Boutros-Ghali, *Building Peace and Development*, paragraph 627.
161. Ibid., paragraph 602.
162. UN News Summaries, London, NS/5/95, 23 February 1995 and NS/20/95, 12 October 1995.
163. 'Report on the Work of the Organization', September 1993, paragraph 377.
164. *Atlanta Journal and Constitution*, 26 January 1993, p.3.
165. *New York Times*, 28 February 1994, p.8.
166. See Anthony Parsons' article in the *Independent*, 11 May 1996.
167. Security Council Resolution 731, 21 January 1992, paragraph 4.
168. B. Boutros-Ghali, 'Report on the Work of the Organization', September 1993, paragraph 376.
169. *Washington Post*, 2 November 1993, p.13.
170. A. Parsons, 'The UN and the National Interests of States', in A. Roberts and B. Kingsbury eds, op.cit., p.119.
171. The Secretary-General's Cyril Foster Lecture, Oxford University, 15 January 1996.
172. The Secretary-General's address to the UN staff, Press Release SG/SM/6140, 9 January 1997.
173. B. Urquhart, 'Selecting the World's CEO. Remembering the Secretaries-General', p.21. This is reflected in T.M. Franck and G. Nolte, 'The Good Offices Function of the United Nations Secretary-General', in A. Roberts and B. Kingsbury eds, op.cit., p.149; B. Rivlin wrote that '[i]t would be a mistake to assume that there has been a linear expansion upward of the role of the Secretary-General. A more accurate depiction would be one of ups and downs. What largely determines the fluctuations is the overall state of the United Nations, which is a function of the changing international political climate.' 'The UN Secretary-Generalship at Fifty', *Paradigms*, vol.8, no.2, Winter 1994, p.51.
174. B. Rivlin, 'Boutros-Ghali's Ordeal: Leading the United Nations in an Age of Uncertainty', in D. Bourantonis and M. Evriviades, *A United Nations for the Twenty-First Century. Peace, Security and Development*, (The Hague: Kluwer Law International, 1996).
175. UN Press Release SG/SM/6053, 16 September 1996.
176. Interview, New York, May 1994.

177. Ibid.
178. Personal correspondence to the author, 12 August 1995.
179. T.M. Franck and G. Nolte, op.cit., p.163.
180. Interview, London, February 1996.
181. Interview with a member of the Executive Office of the Secretary-General, New York, June 1994.
182. B. Rivlin, 'The Changing International Political Climate and the Secretary-General', in B. Rivlin and L. Gordenker eds, op.cit.: '[t]he changed international political climate has greatly increased the demands for the services of the Secretary-General as mediator, conciliator, peacekeeper, peacemaker, election supervisor, dispenser of emergency humanitarian assistance, and implementer of unprecedented Security Council decisions.' p.17. Also J.S. Sutterlin, 'United Nations Decisionmaking: Future for the Security Council and the Secretary-General', in T.G. Weiss ed., *Collective Security in a Changing World*, (London: Lynne Rienner Publishers, 1993) pp.132 and 137.
183. The Secretary-General's Cyril Foster Lecture, Oxford University, 15 January 1996.

CHAPTER 8 CONCLUSIONS

1. See J.N. Rosenau, *The United Nations in a Turbulent World*, International Peace Academy Occasional Paper (London: Lynne Rienner Publishers, 1992).
2. See, for example, M. Barnett, 'The New United Nations Politics of Peace: From Juridical Sovereignty to Empirical Sovereignty', *Global Governance*, vol.1, no.1, 1995.
3. See J. Pérez de Cuéllar, 'Reflecting on the Past and Contemplating the future', *Global Governance*, vol.1, no.2, 1995; B. Urquhart, 'Selecting the World's CEO. Remembering the Secretaries-General', *Foreign Affairs*, vol.74, no.3, 1995; D. Hannay, 'Anyone for the Roller-Coaster?', *The World Today*, February 1996.
4. B. Boutros-Ghali, 'Global Leadership After the Cold War', *Foreign Affairs*, vol.75, no.2, 1996, pp.88–93.
5. B. Urquhart and E. Childers, *A World in Need of Leadership. Tomorrow's United Nations. A Fresh Appraisal*, (Uppsala: Dag Hammarskjöld Foundation, 1996) p.10.
6. B. Boutros-Ghali, 'Democracy: A Newly Recognised Imperative', *Global Governance*, vol.1, no.1, 1995.
7. R.S. Jordan, 'Truly International Bureaucracies: Real or Imagined?', in L.S. Finkelstein ed., *Politics in the United Nations System*, (Durham, NC: Duke University Press, 1988) p.41.
8. J.N. Rosenau, 'Governance in the Twenty-first Century', *Global Governance*, vol.1, no.1, 1995. *Our Global Neighbourhood*, the Report of the Commission on Global Governance, (Oxford: Oxford University Press, 1995); M. Simai, *The Future of Global Governance:*

Managing Risk and Change in the International System, (Washington: US Institute of Peace Press, 1994); O. Young, *International Governance: Protecting the Environment in a Stateless Society*, (Ithaca: Cornell University Press, 1994).

9. B. Boutros-Ghali, *Confronting New Challenges*, Annual Report on the Work of the Organization, 1995, paragraphs 25–7.

10. J.N. Rosenau, *The United Nations in a Turbulent World*, p.42. However, he concedes that '[o]n the East River the sovereignty principle predominates', and that attitudinal changes take time, p.70.

11. The Secretary-General's Cyril Foster Lecture, Oxford University, 15 January 1996.

12. According to D.J. Puchala, 'World Images, World Orders, and Cold Wars: Mythhistory and the United Nations', *International Social Science Journal*, vol.47, no.2, 1995.

13. O.R. Young, 'Systems and society in world affairs: Implications for international organizations', *International Social Science Journal*, vol.47, no.2, 1995. In the same issue Leon Gordenker is more optimistic, 'UN at 50: Institutional development'.

14. The Secretary-General's Cyril Foster Lecture, Oxford University, 15 January 1996.

15. Interview, New York, June 1994.

Index

Life as a

Playwri

Also available from Methuen Drama

Simon Stephens: A Working Diary
How to Write About Theatre
Fifty Playwrights on Their Craft